ELECTION DAY

Election Day

How We Vote and What It Means for Democracy

Emilee Booth Chapman

PRINCETON UNIVERSITY PRESS

PRINCETON AND OXFORD

Published by Princeton University Press
41 William Street, Princeton, New Jersey 08540
99 Banbury Road, Oxford OX2 6JX

press.princeton.edu

All Rights Reserved

ISBN 9780691239095
ISBN (e-book) 9780691239071

British Library Cataloging-in-Publication Data is available

Editorial: Rob Tempio & Chloe Coy
Production Editorial: Ali Parrington
Jacket Design: Karl Spurzem
Production: Lauren Reese
Publicity: Kate Hensley & Charlotte Coyne

Jacket credit: "I Voted" sticker © flysnowfly / Shutterstock

This book has been composed in Adobe Text and Gotham

10 9 8 7 6 5 4 3 2 1

For my mom, who took me with her when she voted, who taught me to love books, and told me I could write one too, if I wanted.

And for my dad, who taught me to do and to love political theory before I knew there was any such thing.

CONTENTS

As I write this at the start of 2022, it is surprisingly hard to predict what the state of voting law and its political and electoral impact will be by the time you read this. This is not just because of the potential for new far-reaching federal laws. In 2022, we will see how controversial changes to voting laws in Texas and Georgia—which received so much attention when they passed in 2021—play out on the ground in a federal election. State-level elections in 2022 will also affect the prospects of Donald Trump's "Stop the Steal" campaign to seize political control of the election apparatus in key states. And whatever happens in election law, the focus of public debates about voting and election reform will no doubt shift many times over the upcoming year, as it always does.

With all of this on the horizon, it might seem like a strange choice to send this book to press now. Why not wait? There are three answers to this question. The first is simply that this book is not exclusively about or for the United States. I argue that popular voting[1] plays a similar role in established democracies around the world. Though examples from the United States loom large in this book (because I am a US citizen, educated and living in the United States), its guidance is relevant almost everywhere there are democratic elections.

The second is that, even if we focus primarily on the US, things are always changing. The past decade has seen several landmark moments for voting in the United States. The 2013 Supreme Court decision in *Shelby County v. Holder* marked a seismic shift in US voting rights law and paved the way for contemporary battles over state-level election administration. Other Court

---

1. By popular voting, I mean voting in which all (or nearly all) adult citizens of a jurisdiction are eligible to participate. The practice of popular voting includes elections as well as referenda and votes on other ballot measures. I use the term popular voting to distinguish this practice from voting within legislatures or private organizations. Voting is a ubiquitous decision-making procedure, but it does not always serve the same purposes or realize the same values.

cases, like *Gill v. Whitford* (2018)[2] and *Rucho v. Common Cause* (2019),[3] which challenged the practice of partisan gerrymandering, garnered attention for the transformative potential they failed to realize. Donald Trump's victory in 2016, of course, brought renewed attention to the Electoral College, to political polling and media coverage of election campaigns, and to turnout disparities. 2016 also upended many assumptions about the nature of parties and partisanship and their role in electoral agenda-setting. 2018 saw record-breaking numbers of women running for and winning office in the United States, and a remarkable surge in turnout among young adults. The pandemic conditions in 2020 brought massively increased availability and uptake of mail-in and early voting opportunities. And, of course, in 2020 and 2021, we have seen the systematic efforts of one party—led by Donald Trump—to discredit the election results, and we saw insurrection at the Capitol as the 2020 presidential election results were being certified. There is no reason to think that things will settle down anytime soon. And this rapid pace of change and resulting uncertainty gives us all the more reason to take time now to reflect on how we vote and why it matters.

The third answer is that, while this book certainly speaks to contemporary issues and debates, they are not its main motivation. This book has been ten years in the making, conceived and almost entirely written prior to November 2020. The thing that initially gave birth to this book was not the rise of populism. Nor was it even the demise of the preclearance coverage regime or the subsequent explosion in strict voter ID laws and polling place closures. What drove me to write this book was as much a problem in democratic *theory* as a problem in democracy. Whenever I told family, friends, or friendly strangers that I study the ethics of democracy, I was usually met with some remark about voting (most often: "how can we get young people to care about voting?"). But voting was conspicuously absent from the democratic theory that I was reading as a young academic. What discussions of voting I did find were largely skeptical of "folk" attitudes toward voting and saw a need for theory to correct the overemphasis on voting in popular discourse. This dismissive treatment of popular voting in academic democratic theory struck me as both odd and troubling. Political theorists had done a great job of demonstrating what voting can't do but had left us without an adequate theory of what it *can* and *should* do. That is the problem to which this book responds.

2. Gill v. Whitford, 585 U.S. ___ (2018).
3. Rucho v. Common Cause, 588 U.S. ___ (2019).

I believe it is *because* much of this book was written in a different electoral context, that the ideas I develop here offer important resources for responding to our current moment. Scholarship that primarily responds to specific, recent events runs the risk of overfitting its models to the particulars of these events or to the salient narratives that emerge about them. The arguments in this book, on the other hand, have been developed over a decade that has seen many dramatic changes in the electoral context and the focus of public debate. These arguments, therefore, point to a set of concerns as well as a set of recommendations that have not received enough attention in recent public conversations about voting and elections.

Elections are not just information-gathering exercises. They also structure the discursive environment of democratic communities, facilitate mobilization and organization, and socialize citizens into their role as equal political agents. Occasions for popular voting make the abstract notion of democracy concrete and manifest for citizens. They enable us to see how the collective activity of democracy is constructed from the contributions of individual citizens. As I argue in the book, when we highlight these functions of popular voting, it becomes clear that the democratic value of elections depends on how citizens perceive and experience electoral moments.

Here is one example of how this holistic, big-picture understanding of popular voting's role in modern democracies can help us respond to the problems of the moment: it can help us diagnose and address the narratives of widespread voter fraud that have altered the meaning of recent elections for many American citizens. Even if these narratives do not prevent the peaceful transfer of power, they nevertheless undermine a crucial democratic purpose of popular voting. Discussions of this problem commonly focus on the mechanical properties of elections as a procedure for fairly selecting representatives and peacefully settling political conflict. But, as I demonstrate in this book, popular voting also plays an important role in mediating citizens' relationship to democracy. Voting shapes citizens' attitudes toward and interactions with democracy, and how we see our place within it. Even if efforts to delegitimize the results of a particular election fail in the moment, they may still do lasting damage to our most important tool for political socialization.

The arguments in this book also suggest that our response to this problem must go beyond assessing the truth of these delegitimizing narratives and criticizing the individuals and organizations who help to circulate them. We must also examine how individuals' experiences of elections, as shaped by our regime of election administration, make certain narratives about an election seem plausible or resonant. Increased variety in the methods of voting likely makes it easier for false narratives about an election to gain traction, particularly when voting methods become politicized and polarized and when the act of voting is less visible to our fellow citizens. It is natural to treat unfamiliar things with suspicion and to underrate their value. The complexity, opacity, and variety of electoral administration across US states also makes it difficult to provide voters with clear and accurate counter-narratives that can displace the false narratives.

None of this diminishes the blame owed to elites who knowingly circulate these falsehoods, nor should it stop us from interrogating how our media and information environments have contributed to their popularity. But these are not the only responses available to us. We can also aim to give citizens an experience of elections that is more resistant to the false narratives of opportunistic elites. And we should not see this as a secondary goal of election administration. As I argue in this book, how citizens perceive and experience occasions for popular voting affects voting's democratic value as much as the existence of objectively fair rules.

The 2020 US federal election cycle gave us yet another reason to direct more attention to the experience of voting. For the first time since the institution of a uniform Election Day in the mid-19th century, well over half of voters cast a ballot *before* Election Day, and most of these were mail-in ballots. The widespread adoption of mail-in voting in 2020 was partly due to expanded access to and interest in these options because of the COVID-19 pandemic. But it was also an acceleration of an existing trend. In the 2016 and 2018 federal elections, nearly 40 percent of votes were cast before Election Day. The character of Election Day has changed dramatically over the past decade, and it is clearer now than it has ever been that we must grapple with what this change means for democracy.

Finally, the past several years have seen heated battles over a new wave of voter suppression efforts in some US states. Though democratic theory has supplied plenty of accounts of the value of political equality and opportunities for political participation, existing theories do not offer an adequate explanation for why these new voter suppression efforts are so worrisome. Opportunities to vote in the United States are more widely accessible and more equitably distributed than opportunities to engage in other forms of participation. Democratic theorists often lament the special attention that voting receives in popular discourse about democracy. A healthy democracy depends on a wide array of participatory practices of which voting is only one. Citizens also influence public life through protest, petition, campaigning, and adding their voice to public deliberation. But if voting should be seen as just one among many ways for citizens to participate, this raises a serious question for contemporary debates about voter suppression. Why should we devote so much attention to resisting efforts to constrict the electorate instead of redirecting that attention to political arenas with more severe political inequalities?

The account of popular voting that I offer in this book supplies an answer to this question. Unlike other participatory practices, popular voting is partly constituted by mass participation, and in fact, by an ambition toward universal participation. This core and distinctive feature of the practice of popular voting is integral to the functions it serves and the values it realizes in modern democracies. Efforts to shrink the electorate, then, even if they only make a difference at the margins, strike at the very heart of what makes voting a unique and valuable democratic practice.

At the same time, the account of voting that I offer reveals significant limitations in existing discourse about voter suppression. This discourse tends to focus exclusively on the costs of voting and on opportunities to vote. But realizing the value of popular voting, I argue, requires more than opportunities to vote. It requires actual turnout. We thus need to expand our discussion of election administration beyond creating opportunities to vote. We must also think about how we create positive motivations to vote. Voting will never be completely costless, so citizens will only do it if they perceive some positive reason to. Election administration, then, should be expected not only to make voting easy, but also to make it appealing. Voting systems can do this directly—by creating an enjoyable and meaningful voting experience—or indirectly—by fostering an environment that incentivizes and facilitates widespread mobilization efforts.

As these examples demonstrate, the questions, ideas, and principles in this book offer much needed critical leverage on salient contemporary issues even though—or perhaps because—they were initially conceived in a different political environment. I do not want to leave readers with the impression, though, that my thinking has remained entirely unchanged as the events of the last decade have unfolded. So before concluding this preface, I want to note a few ways that the book has evolved in response to some of the trends I described above. I also want to flag some questions that remain for future scholarship.

I believe the broad principles for evaluating and reforming voting systems offered in this book have largely held up even amidst what seem like seismic changes to the way we vote in the United States. I have, however, updated my beliefs about how these principles can apply to contemporary electoral reform debates. First, though I remain skeptical of convenience voting methods, the extent of their uptake in 2020 (which was only an acceleration of an existing trend), has made clear that useful guidance on this subject cannot be exclusively negative. Thus, chapter 5's discussion of when and where we vote not only highlights the most serious concerns about the demise of Election Day; it also introduces ideas for how we can best mitigate those concerns. In-person Election Day voting is no longer the norm in the United States. So, it should no longer be the baseline against which we evaluate other voting regimes, either. Beyond defending a traditional Election Day, the principles of this book can also help us compare and improve the alternatives.

Second, and relatedly, 2020 introduced a new concern about convenience voting that I had not previously given enough attention to: the potential for polarization of voting methods. Prior to 2020, the use of convenience voting was not particularly polarized. In states that offered optional early in-person or absentee voting, there was no pronounced or consistent pattern in partisan affiliation among those who took advantage of these options. In 2020, however, the use of non-traditional voting methods, especially of mail-in voting, became polarized, with Democrats opting to vote by mail at much higher rates than Republicans. Though this difference may diminish in subsequent elections, it nevertheless represents a very serious risk that can undermine the value of voting as a shared and integrative experience. As we saw in 2020, polarization of voting method also creates new openings for targeted delegitimation of opponents' votes. Policy-makers and election administrators must take this problem seriously.

Third, I have become less convinced of the value of local control of elections. The earliest drafts of this book contained a full-throated defense of local control over electoral administration. Local control, I thought, contributes to citizens' trust in elections (since trust in local and state governments is much higher than trust in the federal government), allows for a voting experience that is better adapted to and integrated with diverse neighborhood conditions, and enables citizens to better appreciate the connections between the abstract idea of democracy and our immediate, daily lives. The past several years have made the pathologies of local control increasingly salient, however. And especially in a highly polarized environment, variations in election administration across jurisdictions can undermine the sense in which voting is a shared activity. It can also erode the legitimacy of the electoral system taken as a whole. The final version of chapter 5 thus contains a more nuanced account of the relative virtues of local versus centralized control of elections and imagines a larger role for federal election administration.

Of course, no book can do everything, and there remain plenty of important issues that I have not been able to address in this one. I will mention one here that I believe is particularly in need of more attention from democratic theorists. The aftermath of the 2020 election cycle—including the January 6 insurrection, but also Donald Trump's "Stop the Steal" campaign and the associated activities of several Republican state governments—have demonstrated that the peaceful transfer of power cannot be taken for granted, even in long-established democratic regimes. This minimalist achievement is an important part of voting's democratic value, as I observe in this book. But I give less attention to it than to other of popular voting's less appreciated purposes. Though I have not been able to provide it here, I have become convinced that we need a fuller account of how and under what conditions popular voting works to secure the peaceful transition of power. We also need a fuller account of how the optimal conditions for this function can be made to fit with or should be traded off against the optimal conditions for voting's other key purposes that I have focused on in this book.

This book focuses on what happens on and before Election Day. Future work must expand and build on this account to consider what happens after Election Day. How does the energy of popular voting moments dissipate? How do we transition from extraordinary, disruptive moments of mass participation back to normal inter-election politics? And how does the process of counting votes, auditing election procedures, certifying results, and transitioning governments affect citizens' experience of voting and its democratic purposes? These are crucial questions that the events of the past few years invite us to think more deeply about. I believe and fervently hope that the insight into popular voting's purposes contained in this book can guide us in reflecting on and responding to these concerns of the moment and the new ones that will undoubtedly arise as we continue the unceasing and necessary task of improving our democracies.

Emilee Chapman
January 12, 2022

ELECTION DAY

Introduction

In the spring of 2014, the Indian government administered what was then the largest election in history. Over the course of five weeks, from April 7 to May 12, over 550 million Indians cast a vote for members of the Lok Sabha, the Indian parliament.[1] The election required over 900,000 polling places and an estimated 11 million personnel.[2] Administering the election cost the Indian electoral commission the equivalent of about 580 million US dollars.[3] The scale of this civic exercise was spectacular, but also, for the world's largest democracy, a matter of course. In 2019, India conducted an even bigger election; over 600 million people voted in the 2019 Lok Sabha elections.[4] The time and resources devoted to making the polls accessible to each of the approximately 900 million members of India's eligible electorate provide just one striking example of the massive effort democratic communities routinely undertake to administer elections. No other public effort to encourage citizen participation approaches the scale and expense of elections.[5]

Of course, to focus only on dramatic events like these would present a misleading picture of voting in today's democracies. With a few notable exceptions, turnout has been declining across the United States and Western

1. "Statewise Turnout for General Election—2014."
2. Vyawahare, "A Primer on India's Parliamentary Elections."
3. Sivakumar, "Polls to Cost Country Rs 3,500 Crore This Year."
4. Jain, "Lok Sabha Elections: At 67.1%, 2019 Turnout's a Record, Election Commission Says."
5. For comparison, France spent 12 to 15 million euros on its 2019 "Great Debate," which has been described as "the world's biggest 'deliberative democracy' exercise to date" (Landemore, "Can Macron Quiet the 'Yellow Vests'").

Europe for more than half a century. This is true even as political parties offer voters more direct influence over electoral agendas and platforms and even as many governments work to make voting more convenient. And, in the United States in recent years, electoral administration has become a site of bitter political conflict which reaches to the very heart of voting's democratic purpose. Consequently, narratives of a crisis in electoral democracy abound in both academic and popular discourse.

This dual reality of voting in contemporary democracies demands the attention of democratic theorists. If we are at a crossroads for electoral democracy, how should we move forward? Should we view this as an opportunity to recover the value of popular voting and reinvigorate elections as spectacular moments of mass participation? Or should we instead see this crisis as an opportunity to rid ourselves of a defunct practice and to rethink democracy from the ground up?

A number of academics and journalists have recently argued for the latter approach. The past few years have seen an explosion of interest in sortition or "lottocracy"—an approach to choosing representatives that uses random selection rather than election. Many defenders of lottocracy argue that the contemporary crisis of electoral democracy is merely the inevitable failure of a defunct and elitist paradigm of democracy. Some claim that popular elections betray the ideal of political equality because they reflect "a commitment to the idea that some are better able to rule than others."[6] Others argue that electoral democracy invariably creates a distinction between a "ruler" class and the bulk of "ordinary" citizens.[7] Different accounts of lottocracy vary in their prescriptions.[8] But many assert that the current crisis in electoral democracy calls for a paradigm shift that would displace voting from the center of thinking about democracy.[9]

While lottocrats critique popular voting for being too elitist, epistocrats argue that it is not elitist enough. At the extreme, defenders of epistocracy— that is, rule by the wise or knowing—question the value of electoral democracy

6. Guerrero, "Against Elections," 169.

7. E.g., Landemore, *Open Democracy*, 4–5. Landemore describes the defining characteristic of this distinction as the "enclosure of power."

8. Most contemporary proponents of lottocracy argue for using sortition alongside elections, to constitute a second legislative chamber (typically to replace "upper" parliamentary houses), or to create "citizens' assemblies" charged with various advisory, oversight, or agenda-setting functions. But some view these institutional reforms as transitional steps toward more extensive lottocracy. See Gastil and Wright, *Legislature by Lot* for a varied collection of lottocratic visions.

9. E.g., Landemore, *Open Democracy*, xvii; Van Reybrouck, *Against Elections*.

altogether.[10] But more moderate versions hold that low turnout and wide-spread disengagement may be desirable if they lead to power being exercised by a more educated or knowledgeable segment of the populace.[11]

Neither the lottocratic nor the epistocratic take on voting represents a dominant position among democratic theorists or among citizens of contemporary democracies. But those of us who believe that electoral democracy is worth saving require a clear account of what, exactly, the purposes of voting are, and what preserving or recovering voting's value will require of us. It is not enough to fall back on a familiar democratic creed. To adequately respond to voting's increasingly numerous and vocal critics, and to assess competing proposals for electoral reform, we must have a clear-eyed explanation of what voting is for, one that is sensitive to voting's limitations and specific about its functions within complex and multi-faceted democratic systems. That is what this book provides.

This book examines the purposes of popular voting in modern democracies with two aims in mind. The first is to defend the centrality of voting in popular conceptions of democratic citizenship as well as the spectacle of elections. Even among the large body of political theorists who reject the radical critiques of voting I have just described, it is still commonplace to lament the social norms and discursive tropes that seem to treat voting as the alpha and omega of democracy.[12] Some theorists go further to criticize particular aspects of popular treatment of voting, including the widespread idea of a duty to vote,[13] the emphasis on high turnout,[14] and the spectacle and expense of elections.[15]

These criticisms are misguided. Skeptics of voting's centrality rightly observe that voting is just one among many essential components of a complex modern democracy. A thriving democracy also requires practices of deliberation, consultation, negotiation, petition, contestation and even resistance.[16] But we do not need to believe that voting is more important than other democratic practices to justify its singular treatment. We need

---

10. Brennan, *Against Democracy*.

11. E.g., Caplan, *The Myth of the Rational Voter*, 198.

12. Shiffrin, "Speaking Amongst Ourselves," 147; Chalmers, *Reforming Democracies*.

13. Brennan, *The Ethics of Voting*; Lomasky and Brennan, "Is There a Duty to Vote"; Lever, "Liberalism, Democracy and the Ethics of Voting," 226.

14. Lever, "Compulsory Voting: A Critical Perspective"; Brennan, "Medicine Worse Than the Disease?"; Saunders, "Increasing Turnout: A Compelling Case?"

15. Chalmers, *Reforming Democracies*, 138.

16. Cf. Warren, "A Problem-Based Approach to Democratic Theory"; Mansbridge, "What Is Political Science For?"

only believe that voting is *different* from these other practices, that it serves a unique set of purposes. Popular voting combines an ambition toward universal participation, a concrete and transparent application of equality, and a rhythm of decisive, consequential, participatory moments to create a singular experience of democratic citizenship. In this book, I show that some of these features of popular voting practices that have drawn the most criticism are actually essential to voting's purposes. They instantiate—that is, they create real instances of—unique and important aspects of democratic values, and they contribute to vital democratic functions.

The second aim of the book is to guide efforts to improve elections and voting so that they better realize the values they are meant to serve. Voting reforms of one kind or another are a constant subject of debate in modern democracies, but interest in and conflict over voting reforms has reached a fever pitch in the United States over the past few years. Many state governments, Republican and Democratic alike, have made substantial changes to their electoral administration in recent years, but they have taken divergent reform paths. Voting administration has become a salient and contentious issue in national politics as well. Congressional Democrats have declared federal voting reform a top priority and introduced sweeping reform proposals that touch on everything from campaign finance and redistricting to same-day voter registration and mail-in voting. States' scramble to accommodate a high-turnout presidential election in the midst of the COVID-19 pandemic and Republican leaders' insistent claims of fraud in the 2020 election have further increased the bitterness and the urgency of US electoral reform debates.

Enthusiasm for electoral reform, propelled by the faith that electoral democracy can and should be made to work better, is widespread. But this alone does not help us assess competing reform agendas or the rationales behind them. Effective reform efforts should be grounded in a clear account of the purposes voting is meant to serve. This book provides just such an account.

Treatises on electoral reform are in no short supply, but the guidance I offer in this book differs from others. I do not aim to provide a detailed blueprint or agenda for electoral reform. Rather, I offer some guiding principles for would-be reformers. At times I illustrate how these principles might bear on some live issues, such as the principles for drawing electoral districts or the move toward "convenience voting." But the account of voting's distinctive value that I offer in this book is intended to be portable across contexts. It can inform a range of controversies about how we vote, and different insights from the book will have more relevance or resonance to different political systems at different times. The principles I offer for evaluating and improving voting practices therefore will continue to be relevant even after we have moved on from the debates of the moment. They can also be applied beyond the North American and European polities which receive disproportionate attention in this book.

The guidance for improving elections that I offer in this book differs from typical electoral reform tracts in two additional ways. First, its relevance is not limited to formal electoral institutions, but also bears on the social norms and customs maintained by the actions of parties, campaigns, interest groups, businesses, churches, and other social institutions, and, of course, individual citizens. Second, the guiding principles for reform that I offer in this book are derived from a systemic and holistic account of voting's purposes in modern democracy.

In the remaining pages of this introduction, I will say a bit more about the practical and theoretical problems that motivate this book, provide a sketch of the argument, and then offer readers some guidance for navigating the book.

The Practical Problem—Reforming in the Dark

Calls for political reform—especially the reform of voting institutions—are a constant feature of modern democracy. Finding ways not only to live side-by-side, but also to build and maintain a flourishing civilization in societies characterized by troubled histories and deep disagreements is hard work. And it is made even harder by our commitment to treating one another as equals in the task. This work of democracy is inevitably frustrating and messy, fraught with false starts, mixed successes, and disappointed hopes. Our institutions inevitably fall short of the ideals that justify them. But those ideals of democracy retain their allure. We can't help but hope that we can do right by them if we revisit our political institutions and reshape them with enough thoughtfulness and virtue. However endless the task of democratic reform may be, this constant push to improve democratic processes—and the perpetual tinkering it prompts—is undoubtedly necessary to keep the frustrating, messy, and yes, essential, project of democracy chugging along.

Voting and elections tend to occupy most of our attention in these reform efforts. But without a clear account of the relationship between voting and democracy—of the particular purposes that voting is meant to serve—these reform efforts can end up being counter-productive. Some readers will no doubt call to mind reforms like strict voter ID laws that increase the material costs of voting, making it more difficult for some citizens to exercise their right to vote. Voter ID requirements enjoy widespread support among US citizens in part because they appeal to an important political principle: election integrity. For many people, it can be hard to understand why critics make such a big deal about voter ID requirements. We already require a photo ID to access many social goods, after all. Why shouldn't we treat voting like we treat driving a car or boarding an airplane? Furthermore, voter ID requirements are commonplace in other countries, and not particularly controversial. And while there is emerging evidence that the strictest photo ID laws may deter some participation, the absolute size of the turnout effect appears quite small.[17]

By adopting a more holistic perspective on the value of voting, this book offers new insight into the debate over ID requirements and other contentious issues in electoral reform. Whether or not they ultimately depress turnout among targeted groups, ID requirements in the United States, especially strict photo ID requirements, impose a significant burden on some citizens. And these burdens fall disproportionately on those who are already the most socially and politically marginalized. This book shows why this differential burden is especially objectionable in the context of voting: because, as I will argue, voting is meant to be a floor on political participation—a uniquely easy and egalitarian way for citizens to access political influence. The decentralized character of US election administration exacerbates the burden imposed by voter ID laws. Variations in voter ID requirements from state to state, along with frequent changes to the status of existing voter ID laws can leave citizens unsure about whether and how they can meet the requirements to vote.[18] And citizens can face additional discrimination as they attempt to navigate these requirements.[19] Voter ID requirements in the United States—and to some extent even the public debate around them— have also created an atmosphere of suspicion that clouds the experience of voting as a shared, collective undertaking. Voter ID laws in the United States

---

17. Grimmer and Yoder, "Durable Differential Deterrent Effects"; Fraga and Miller, "Who Does Voter ID Keep from Voting." There is a great deal of debate about the size and distribution of voter ID's turnout effects, which are hard to measure for a variety of reasons (see, e.g., Grimmer et al., "Obstacles to Estimating Voter ID"). There is also some evidence counter-mobilization might offset some of the otherwise damping effect on turnout of voter ID laws (Valentino and Neuner, "Why the Sky Didn't Fall").

18. Jones, "Many Americans Unaware."

19. White, Nathan, and Faller, "What Do I Need to Vote?"

have also been enforced in arbitrary and discriminatory ways.[20] In the particular context of US elections, then, voter ID laws negatively affect many citizens' experience of voting in ways that might not apply elsewhere.[21] For the most affected groups of citizens, voter ID laws create yet another layer of bureaucratic complexity and potential discrimination in an exercise that should instead give them a feel for their own power.

Introducing additional barriers to voting is not the only way that reforms can go awry, though, and this book highlights how some reforms that are more popular among political progressives can also be counter-productive. One example of this is the shift toward "convenience voting" reforms like early voting and mail-in voting, which aim to make voting easier. Like voter ID laws, convenience voting policies enjoy widespread popular support in part because they appeal to a core political value: making the opportunity to vote more widely accessible.[22] But, contrary to popular belief, most convenience voting reforms do little to increase actual turnout, especially among those citizens who are least likely to vote.[23] At the same time, as I will argue in chapter 5, the widespread use of convenience voting radically changes citizens' experience of voting in ways that could undermine popular voting's distinctive democratic functions.

By offering a clearer and more complete understanding of which purposes voting serves in a democracy and how it performs those purposes, this book better enables us to assess the trade-offs that arise with any election laws. This is not all it does, though. It also invites a more creative and productive conversation about election reform. When we better understand the purposes of voting and keep them squarely in sight, we can look for reforms that minimize or offset the costs of changes we deem essential. We can also imagine new ways of producing or instantiating values that may suffer with a particular reform. The discussion of convenience voting in chapter 5 provides an example of what this kind of conversation can look like.

A third variety of misguided reform simply demands too much of voting. This manifests most clearly in electoral excess—the idea that more voting is better voting. Voters, especially in the United States, often face

20. Cobb, Greiner, and Quinn, "Can Voter ID Laws Be Administered in a Race-Neutral Manner?"

21. Voter ID laws are less objectionable where they are paired with the free provision of a standard (national) voting ID for all registered voters (as, for example, in Mexico), and other efforts to reduce barriers to turnout (such as automatic voter registration).

22. Of course, they are also popular because people just like convenience for themselves.

23. See chapter 5 for an overview of this research and discussion of its significance.

an overwhelming number of electoral decisions. For example, in November 2020, registered voters in Palo Alto, California (like myself) were charged with filling 16 elected offices and considering 12 statewide and 3 local ballot measures. The "more voting is better voting" principle has also fueled a recent explosion of direct democracy around the world.[24]

Many scholars have observed that increases in the number of elections probably have diminishing democratic value, as citizens are more likely to abstain from some decisions and have to work harder to locate reliable information about their choices.[25] But an examination of voting's distinctive role in modern democracies provides two more reasons to be skeptical of the idea that more voting is better voting. First, like all decision-procedures, voting has distinctive benefits and drawbacks, and for some aspects of democratic decision-making, popular voting is not the most appropriate procedure. Second, I argue that one of the core features that helps to constitute the value of voting is that elections (or other occasions for popular voting) are uncommon and special events. They create distinctive and disruptive political moments that capture the attention of the mass public. If popular voting becomes too frequent or common, then it no longer has this momentousness. Instead, it fades into the background of our lives. When this happens, voting loses some of its distinctive democratic value.

These examples of reform enthusiasm gone awry illustrate the need for a clear account of how voting contributes to democracy in contemporary societies, and what that means for the nitty-gritty details about how, when, and where we vote. Academic political theory has not adequately met this need. To be sure, there is no shortage of remarks about voting and elections within contemporary democratic theory, but these remarks are not typically grounded in a full account of what popular voting is, and what it is for. Only when we examine practices of popular voting holistically and seek to understand the purposes they serve within a broader democratic system can we adequately evaluate them against alternatives or work to make them better.

Voting at the Margins of Democratic Theory

Normative democratic theory has many purposes. One of those purposes is to provide guidance to citizens about how they should act in pursuit of democratic ideals. Political theory ideally supplies the standards that citizens

---

24. Kaufmann and Mathews, "Critical Shift."
25. See, e.g., Cain, *Democracy More or Less*, 70–78.

and political leaders use to assess how well political institutions are functioning, and the criteria for justifying and comparing potential reforms.

When it comes to voting, contemporary democratic theory has not fulfilled this purpose as well as it might. There is a substantial disconnect between the way that democratic theorists think and talk about voting and the way that most citizens think and talk about voting. This disconnect amounts to more than the expected difference in precision and sophistication between popular and academic discourse. Voting occupies a central place in the popular democratic imagination. But contemporary democratic theory tends to de-emphasize voting. Recent democratic theory has yielded rich accounts of the value of democratic deliberation and of the best approaches to fostering meaningful deliberation, but similar treatments of popular voting are rare.

Some democratic theorists will argue that the gap between academic and popular views of voting exists because the popular or "folk" treatment of voting is fundamentally unsound.[26] More commonly, though, scholars choose to de-emphasize voting as a corrective to what they see as an overemphasis on voting in earlier democratic theories, and a tendency of citizens to overlook other essential aspects of democracy.[27] If popular views of democracy are too centered on voting, this could have negative consequences for democracy in practice. Some argue that the fetishization of voting distracts citizens from more effective modes of pursuing their political goals.[28] Others argue that too much emphasis on voting distorts popular views of democratic citizenship, casting citizens as consumers or spectators whose primary job is to listen to and judge the claims of political elites, while neglecting many other valuable roles and activities of democratic citizens.[29]

Democratic theorists are not wrong to be concerned about the public's tendency to lay all of their hopes for democracy at the feet of voting. But correcting this tendency requires articulating what voting *can* do, as well as what it can't. First, and foremost, this is because without an adequate account of voting's democratic purposes, we are likely to reach the wrong conclusions about the ethics of voting and electoral reform. As I have suggested, a sustained examination of voting in contemporary democracies reveals that some of the features that have received the most criticism from

26. E.g., Brennan, *The Ethics of Voting.*

27. Shiffrin, "Speaking Amongst Ourselves," 147.

28. See, e.g., Chalmers, *Reforming Democracies,* 66–67; Lever, "Compulsory Voting: A Critical Perspective."

29. Cohen, "Money, Politics, and Political Equality," 299.

political theorists are actually essential features of a practice of popular voting that realizes unique and important facets of democracy's value. And at the extreme, the failure to provide a positive account of what voting does contribute to democracy has opened the door to the radical critiques of popular voting that I described at the start of this introduction.

Moreover, as I will argue in this book, by neglecting to examine the modern practice of popular voting, democratic theorists have missed many opportunities to offer much-needed insight into live debates about how democratic principles should be applied to electoral institutions. It is true that popular voting is one among many essential elements of democratic practice. But that truth alone is incomplete and inadequate to resolve many weighty conflicts about how we should vote. This book reveals that attention to the distinctive functions of popular voting in modern democracy provides important insight for leaders designing and administering elections, and for citizens discharging their civic duties.

Normative democratic theorists—at least those of us who hope to contribute to the maintenance and improvement of democratic regimes—should be worried when large gaps emerge between popular and academic discourse around democracy. At the very least this is true because effective communication depends on directly addressing people's existing beliefs. Democratic theorists who hope to influence popular understandings of democracy must be attentive to how the ideals they articulate will be received given the views that citizens already bring to the table. And if we only casually acknowledge what so many people regard as the centerpiece of democratic practice, there is a risk that the normative guidance of democratic theory will seem too unfamiliar to be relevant.

There is yet another reason for theorists to devote more attention to a practice that occupies such a central role in popular conceptions of democracy. This is that democratic theory ought to be, well, democratic. Most justifications for democracy give us reasons to take seriously the shared understandings of democracy that sustain its practice in existing communities. Democratic theorists who hope to provide citizens and political leaders with guidance on how to promote democratic values should begin by locating the value in our existing institutions and practices.

The word "democracy" denotes a political ideal. But it also denotes a kind of political regime or activity that embodies that ideal. This means that practical reasoning about how to contribute to democracy must always tack back and forth between contemplation of democratic principles and the requirements of the practices that embody those principles. To make matters even more complicated, the ideal of democracy itself embeds a notion of shared activity. The ideal of democracy only applies in situations where a group of people acts together. And the quintessential embodiment of the ideal of democracy—a self-governing political community—involves a group of people finding ways to act together in spite of deep and serious disagreements that even touch on the nature of democracy itself. The fact that the democratic practice of popular voting has secured such widespread acceptance and is celebrated and perpetuated by citizens who in other respects disagree so deeply and seriously should give pause to anyone inclined to denigrate its democratic credentials.

The goal of doing *democratic* democratic theory motivates the starting point of this book. Rather than beginning—as theory often does—with the definition of democracy or an elaboration of democratic principles, this book begins with a description of voting practices as they exist in contemporary democratic societies. In chapter 6, I dive deeper into questions about the definition of democracy and democratic principles. In doing so, I explain and justify the method of democratic democratic theory I employ here, which is a form of what political theorists call "constructive interpretation." Readers who want to better understand the relationship between the descriptive and normative claims in this book may wish to skip ahead.

I have saved the discussion of this methodology for the end of the book, though, because I want this book to be interesting and accessible to readers who are not well versed in academic debates about democratic theory. This book is for anyone who wants to better appreciate the value of popular voting, and to have an account of its democratic purposes that can help us navigate ethical and policy debates about voting. Despite its fancy name, the method of constructive interpretation, at least as I employ it here, is not an exotic invention of the ivory tower. It is a common feature of public discourse in democratic societies, where, in determining what we ought to do, we often appeal to the shared values implicit or explicit in the things we already do together. Readers who are comfortable with this sort of argument, then, can get right to the main contributions of this book, without having to wade through the kind of conceptual debates that academics like me live for. Of course, some readers who don't live for such discussions and are not yet familiar with the relevant jargon of democratic theory may also want to know more about the concept of democracy and its value that informs the arguments of this book. I believe these readers will find the more abstract philosophical account of this book's methodology that I offer in chapter 6 easier to follow once they have seen it in action.

The Value of Voting

The approach I take in this book differs from other scholarship on voting and from other treatises on electoral reform in a few key ways. I provide an account of the distinctive value of *popular* voting that is grounded in a *holistic* view of the practice and a *systemic* perspective on democracy. Let me now explain each of these ideas.

This book is about popular voting. I argue that the value and purposes of popular voting in elections or on ballot measures are different than those of voting in, for example, legislatures and juries. There are, of course, some overlapping features and values common to any use of voting procedures. All of the familiar uses of voting in democratic governance apply an aggregative interpretation of equality. The values of popular voting, and its distinctive role within democracy, though, are created by the conjunction of aggregative equality with other key features that form part of the practice of *popular* voting, in particular.

Relatedly, I adopt a holistic perspective on the practice of popular voting. This means considering how formal voting procedures and administrative policies interact with the many informal aspects of the practice. The social norms, discursive tropes, and popular attitudes that have developed in relation to popular voting are no less a part of the practice of popular voting than its formal elements. I will argue that the interaction of formal voting procedures with social norms and expectations creates much of the value of voting. Consequently, efforts to improve the way we vote must be attentive to how reforms to electoral institutions or administration affect attitudes and norms related to voting.

Finally, the account of popular voting's value I offer here comes from adopting a systemic perspective on democracy. My starting point is a view that democracy is a rich and multi-faceted political ideal. No single institution or practice should be expected to realize the full value of democracy. Instead, democracy's value is best realized in democratic systems. Within democratic systems, different practices may evince different aspects of democratic values.[30] Some practices may also perform functions that help to support the value of other institutions or practices. I do not argue that popular voting realizes democratic values better than other participatory practices. Rather, I argue that popular voting instantiates or exemplifies

---

30. See Warren, "A Problem-Based Approach to Democratic Theory."

aspects of democratic values that other practices do not, and it also performs essential functions that support a healthy democratic system.

The core thesis of the book is that voting should not be evaluated simply as one possible mode of democratic participation. The practice of popular voting is constituted by a set of features that work together to create voting's unique value. This book focuses on three core features of popular voting. The first is an expectation of approximately universal participation. Declining voter turnout rates around the world have rightly prompted much handwringing about the state of democratic citizenship. Yet despite these declining turnout rates, we still treat high voter turnout as a standard for evaluating elections. Public discourse around elections reflects a social ambition toward universal participation as well as an expectation that citizens will, in fact, show up at the polls, en masse. And when they do not, we take that as a sign that something is going wrong.

The second core feature of contemporary voting practices is the application of aggregative equality. Voting involves a decision-procedure that treats individual contributions equally and symmetrically. This is the feature that most scholarly accounts of voting have emphasized, since it is common to voting procedures in many different political contexts. But aggregative equality also takes on special significance in the context of popular voting. I will argue that the counting of votes according to a predefined, transparent, and replicable voting rule exhibits unique virtues when combined with mass participation and the spectacle of elections.

The third core feature of popular voting that I emphasize in this book is what I call, for lack of a better word, voting's momentousness. I use the word momentous in two senses. First, the practice of popular voting centers around temporally defined, decisive participatory moments. These are moments when the relationship between citizens' acts of participation and important public decisions are rendered as transparent as possible. These moments also recur predictably and periodically, creating a rhythm to public life that aids in the formation of political identities and projects. Second, voting is momentous in the colloquial sense of marking a significant, memorable occasion. Partly because they are temporally well defined, occasions for popular voting create moments that can command widespread attention. These moments interrupt the ordinary, delegated, and diffuse business of government with a spectacle of mass participation. They serve as an unavoidable reminder and public reaffirmation that democracy is something we must all do together.

This constellation of features realizes aspects of democratic values that may be suppressed or underemphasized in other democratic practices.

Popular voting renders the equality of citizens concrete, formal, and transparent. And because each vote is counted, it also means that the constitution of political power rests on the dignity and equal worth of each individual contribution. Even as it depends on individual contributions, though, voting also makes salient the fact that modern democracy is a mass collective phenomenon. Voting is irreducibly something we do together. It serves as a reminder that our political agency depends on joining together with others. The practice of popular voting, then, especially when it conforms to the ideal of approximately universal participation, provides an occasion for the community to express its commitment to democracy's core values of political equality and popular sovereignty, and for citizens to affirm and participate in this expression.

Occasions for popular voting also perform valuable functions in large, modern democracies that help to support and maintain other aspects of a healthy democratic practice. The ritual of mass participation on formally equal terms serves as a periodic reminder of democratic norms, made all the more effective because citizens do not merely observe the message, but participate in expressing it. The practice of popular voting, when characterized by the expectation of universal participation, also plays an important role in the socialization of citizens into their role as political agents by establishing a floor for political engagement and clearly defining an age of political maturity. And not least, of course, as other scholars have argued, the practice of popular voting disciplines public officials to attend to the concerns of citizens from all sectors of society.

This account of the distinctive value of voting within modern democracies has important implications for the standards that we use to evaluate and improve electoral institutions and practices. This book draws out several principles that are often underappreciated in both theoretical and practical discussion of electoral reform. I have already alluded to these in this introduction. First, voting best serves its role in democracy when it is characterized not only by meaningful access or opportunity to vote, but by actual high turnout. Second, understanding the value of voting and how we can improve it requires adopting a systemic perspective on democracy. We cannot adequately assess the relationship between voting and democratic values in isolation from complementary political practices. Third, any effort to evaluate or reform practices of popular voting should place heavy emphasis on how citizens *experience* the act of voting and the public occasion of elections. Much of the value of popular voting comes from what it communicates to citizens, and how they see themselves and their actions fitting within the broader project of democracy. Evaluating electoral institutions and practices, then, requires careful attention to how electoral rules—including and especially administrative decisions about how citizens cast their votes—affect how citizens interpret the act of voting. In later chapters of the book, I draw out the implications of these evaluative insights for specific issues within election systems, including the role of political parties in electoral agenda-setting and the value of simultaneous, in-person vote-casting.

By directing attention to the distinctive role of voting in modern democracy, this book charts a course between minimalist democratic theories that reduce democracy to elections and radical democratic theory that minimizes the value of voting as an act of participation or practice of citizenship. This book takes on board a clear-eyed assessment of voting's limitations. Even with the most well-designed institutions, voting's value cannot be fully realized unless it is also embedded within a broader democratic system that enables the formation and aggregation of meaningful political preferences. But, as I will show, voting need not be able to bear all of the normative weight of democracy on its own to be worthy of its prominence in our civic life.

A Note on Scope

Readers will no doubt detect a disproportionate focus on examples and public debates from the United States. This focus, of course, reflects the concerns about voting that are most salient to me. As a citizen and resident of the United States, I have greater familiarity with and a personal stake in the character of US democracy. Additionally, because of the breadth and bitterness of electoral reform debates in US politics at the time I am writing this, I expect many readers of this book will be interested in its application to the US context.

But this book is not just about voting the United States. The account of voting's democratic value that I provide here is common to most, if not all, established democracies. This includes not only so-called "Western" democracies of North America, Europe, and the English-speaking world, but also many polities in East and South Asia, Latin America, and Africa. If there is an exception among established democracies, it is Switzerland, where elections and referenda have been conducted by mail for decades, where occasions to vote are more frequent, and where turnout exhibits a different pattern than is typical in places where voting is a more infrequent occurrence.[31] Switzerland

31. See Dermont, "Taking Turns at the Ballot Box."

perhaps aside, though, popular voting plays a similar role across today's large democracies. Of course, there is variation in the extent to which the norms or institutions of any given society reflect different aspects of this account. But there is no prototypical electoral system on which this account is based. It is compiled from research on democracy around the world.

Indeed, despite this book's bias toward anecdotes and applications from the United States, many polities exhibit the core features of popular voting much better than the United States. Turnout rates in the United States are below average.[32] Our redistricting practices regularly contravene aggregative equality. The increasing and unregulated length of campaigns combined with widespread use of early voting dilutes the impact of electoral moments. Some of the clearest normative guidance from this book—such as the case for compulsory voting, an Election Day holiday, and limits on both the campaign and voting periods—constitutes an ambitious reform agenda in the United States, but a justification of existing institutions in other countries. It is important, then, to note that even though I hope that this book provides a constructive intervention into US debates about voting reform, the principles and recommendations I offer are not intended exclusively for the United States, and many will be more immediately feasible in other contexts.

Plan of the Book

Chapter 1 characterizes the practice of popular voting and lays out the account of the value(s) of this practice that is at the heart of this book. Drawing on survey research, public discourse, histories of suffrage movements, administrative practices, and empirical scholarship, I demonstrate the depth of citizens' attachment to the practice of voting and I identify the three core normative features of popular voting as a democratic practice. In this chapter I provide an overview of the aspects of democracy's value that voting most uniquely instantiates. I also argue that popular voting performs essential functions that support a healthy democratic culture. The argument of this chapter is not that voting is the only or even the most important participatory practice in democratic societies, but rather that it plays an essential role—especially in large communities—and is not interchangeable with other forms of participation. Moreover, the value of voting's distinct role in modern democracy is partly constituted by its special salience in citizens' beliefs about democracy.

32. "Civic Engagement."

Chapter 2 outlines important limitations of voting's ability to realize democratic values. I argue that these limitations do not undermine the value of voting, but they do reveal how voting's value is dependent on its fit within a broader democratic system. This chapter focuses on two potential challenges to the value of voting procedures. The first is the "inputs" problem: the value of elections and electoral outcomes is derived from the value of individual citizens' political agency. The preferences that voters express with their votes, then, should reflect what we think is valuable about their individual agency. Voting's value may therefore be attenuated if voters' judgments fall too far short of standards of rationality or authenticity, reflecting the influence of cognitive biases, elite manipulation, or poor information. The second potential challenge to the value of voting procedures is the "outputs" problem, also known as the social choice problem. Even if individual votes do bear the value of individual agency, it is not always possible to aggregate them in a way that preserves and transfers that value to the electoral outcome. Any account of voting's role in modern democracy must be sensitive to these potential challenges. However, I argue that in responding to these challenges, democratic theorists have sometimes been overzealous in distancing the ideal of democracy from the central practice of popular voting. A systemic approach to evaluating democratic practices shows how popular voting can occupy a prominent and central role in our civic life while avoiding the "realist" critiques to which theories of electoral democracy are often vulnerable.

Chapter 3 builds on the insights from the first two chapters to elaborate on the normative guidance that my account of voting's value can offer citizens and political leaders who hope to make voting practices better conform to their animating purposes. The chapter discusses evaluative standards related to three key aspects of popular voting: the goal of universal turnout, the choice of voting rules that instantiate aggregative equality, and the importance of attending to how citizens experience voting moments. This chapter also compares the character of popular voting in elections versus referenda and considers the kinds of questions best suited to a popular vote.

Chapter 4 introduces another element in the practice of popular voting: party politics. Political parties and party systems have played a major role in the development and maintenance of contemporary practices of popular voting. Party politics also plays a major role in voting's integration into the broader system of democratic governance. This chapter examines the role of political parties in the practice of voting and the principles that we should use to evaluate different forms of party politics. The chapter begins where chapter 3 leaves off, with the observation that the value of popular voting depends on the democratic character of prior agenda-setting processes. But we cannot apply the same evaluative standards that we use to assess voting procedures when we assess agenda-setting processes. In particular, democratic agenda-setting processes must exhibit a non-aggregative form of political equality. After briefly identifying some core principles of democratic agenda-setting, I defend the party system paradigm as the appropriate starting point for conceptualizing democratic agenda-setting processes. Finally, I consider some candidate models for healthy party politics, and argue that an ideal of "parties-as-mobilizers" provides the best standard for evaluating party politics and for guiding efforts to improve party systems, party organizations, and practices of partisanship.

The distinctive value of popular voting in democracy revolves around citizens' shared experience of Election Day. In chapter 5 I discuss the importance of some of the nitty-gritty details of electoral administration that shape the environment in which citizens cast their votes and that consequently affect how citizens perceive the significance of voting. This chapter makes a case for simultaneous, in-person vote casting and for an Election Day holiday. The chapter also discusses the pros and cons of decentralized electoral administration and the visibility of parties on Election Day.

Chapter 6 takes a step back to respond to potential concerns about the book's methodology. The defense of voting that I offer in this book begins with the—perhaps historically contingent—role that voting has actually come to play in our democratic practices. This starting point might prompt a radical criticism. Why should we care what values voting happens to serve in existing democracies? Why not instead focus our energy and attention on designing participatory practices for an *ideal* democracy? In this chapter, I provide a rejoinder to this line of criticism that is inspired by the realist[33] tradition in political theory. But more importantly, I argue that there are

---

33. The term "realist" has multiple uses within political theory, and I engage with a couple of them in this book, so it is worth briefly disambiguating these two uses of the term. The first kind of realism I discuss first appears in chapter 2 in a discussion of what has come to be called "democratic realism." Democratic realists cast doubt on the value of citizens' political judgments and expressed preferences. They argue that realistic assessments of citizen competence and political behavior undermines many traditional theories of democracy. I am largely critical of the normative claims offered by democratic realists, though I argue that their concerns should be taken seriously. The second kind of realism I discuss in this book appears in chapter 6. There I draw on the tradition of political realism, which I argue is best understood as attentiveness to a particular set of risks in politics, especially those associated with the concentration of political power. This form of realism I tentatively embrace.

reasons internal to democracy for valuing existing practices and that those reasons play an important role in practical reasoning about the ethics of democracy. As part of this argument, I sketch an account of democracy as shared agency dependent upon a structure of shared plans.

Because this book serves two aims—to defend voting's centrality in modern democracies and to guide efforts to improve voting practices—readers who are more interested in one or the other of these two purposes may wish to skip some sections of the book. In particular, readers who are unmoved by skepticism about the primacy of voting and elections and who are primarily interested in practical questions of electoral reform may wish to skip chapters 2 and 6. These chapters delve into scholarship on voting and democracy that can at times be rather technical. I have endeavored to render the discussion of this work in layman's terms where I am able, because I believe it does help us understand how we should—and should not—evaluate voting institutions and practices. But I have also tried to write the book in such a way that readers who wish to skip some of these more technical discussions can still make sense of the book's core arguments and practical guidance.

As human societies change in the coming decades, the way we vote will change, too. It is important that we have a clear understanding of the values voting serves in modern democracies to guide these changes and understand their implications for our civic life. More than a blueprint for the future of voting, though, this book stands as a celebration of what we have achieved with the modern practice of voting. Most importantly, this book extends an invitation to scholars, policy makers, political leaders, and all citizens to reflect on how the unique value of voting can be preserved and strengthened for a new era of democracy.

1

The Distinctive Value of Elections

In April of 1910, a parade of 50 vehicles delivered to Congress more than 404,000 signatures on a petition to pass a federal women's suffrage amendment.[1] This petition, delivered more than 60 years after the Seneca Falls Convention, followed decades of sustained legal battles, lobbying efforts, prior petitions, and marches for women's suffrage across the United States. Yet, another seven years passed before Alice Paul, Lucy Burns, Rose Winslow, and the other "Silent Sentinels" began their hunger strike and endured force-feeding, beatings, and torture, after being arrested with hundreds of other suffragists for picketing the White House. After that, three more years went by before Tennessee became the 36th state to ratify the 19th amendment, granting women a constitutional right to vote. In the meantime, suffragists marched and marched and marched.

Nearly half a century after the passage of the 19th amendment, 600 men and women, marching to demand voting rights for African Americans, were met with teargas and severe beatings on the Edmund Pettus bridge outside of Selma, Alabama. Two weeks later, voting rights activists again began to march from Selma; after four days of walking, 25,000 people arrived in Montgomery to demand the right to vote for all citizens.[2] The Selma to Montgomery March was one dramatic part of a long, arduous—and ongoing—push for African American voting rights in the United States. In the early years of this struggle, thousands of volunteers, many of them

1. Cooney, Jr., *Winning the Vote*.
2. "Selma to Montgomery March."

students, risked violent retaliation to register new voters in the American South.[3]

Voting occupies a central place in the democratic imagination, the focal point of democratic hopes. Movements for suffrage expansion in the United States and around the world are full of heroic moments of activists enduring bodily harm in the fight for voting rights. And these movements succeeded because of the decades of dogged persistence from activists who devoted their lives to pursuing the franchise that many of them would not live to exercise. Voting has become recognized as a central pillar of democratic citizenship; so much so that the struggle for democracy and equal citizenship is often equated with the expansion of voting rights and opportunities.

Voting's special prominence in how we conceptualize democracy is perhaps even more pronounced when we take a global perspective. Images of voters in new democracies proudly and joyfully displaying ink-stained fingers have become almost cliché in celebrations of democracy's expansion. World leaders call for free and fair elections as the surest sign of democratization. Global watchdog groups like Freedom House construct indicators of democracy that focus heavily on voting and elections.[4] The Universal Declaration of Human Rights declares the will of the people "expressed in periodic and genuine elections" as "the basis of the authority of government."[5]

In countries where democracy already has a firm foothold, the centrality of voting to democratic thought and practice reveals itself in more mundane ways in the attitudes of citizens, the resources devoted to the administration of elections, the rhetorical tropes of mobilization campaigns, and the news coverage of voter turnout.

The special prominence of voting in popular conceptions of democracy represents something of a puzzle for normative democratic theorists. No serious scholars of democracy believe that voting is all that is required to realize democracy in practice. Democratic governance depends on a wide range of other, less romanticized forms of citizen engagement. Democracy requires some citizens to stand for office and more to staff campaigns. It requires some citizens to report on the activities of government and the major public issues

3. McAdam, *Freedom Summer.*

4. Of Freedom House's 10 "political rights" indicators, for example, 7 explicitly mention voting or elections (Freedom House, "Methodology 2019."). Similarly, within the Global State of Democracy Indices, 14 of 21 indicators of "representative government" and 5 of 7 indicators of "participatory engagement" explicitly mention voting or elections ("About | The Global State of Democracy Indices").

5. "Universal Declaration of Human Rights."

of the time. Democracy requires some citizens to demand publicly that officials give an account of how they use their public power. And it requires some citizens to bring legal claims against government agencies that fail to uphold the terms of their mandate. These are only a few of the minimal requirements for a representative democracy to work. Even the democratic value of voting itself depends on the quality of agenda-setting processes and the ability of citizens to form their political opinions freely. Political theorists who examine the core values of democracy have shown how these values are realized in a wide range of participatory practices and institutions.

If citizens can contribute to democratic governance in many different ways, and if democracy depends on many different institutions and practices, why should voting occupy such a central role in how we conceive of the rights and duties of democratic citizenship? At best, it might seem that voting is simply overemphasized in our public life—that it should be treated as just one among a number of ways for citizens to contribute to democratic governance. But worse, many democratic theorists have suggested that the institution of popular voting is not even a particularly good way of contributing to the values we think democracy is supposed to realize.[6] Viewed in this light, the special attention that voting receives in democratic thought and practice might look like a mere superstition.

In this chapter, I defend the special prominence of voting in contemporary democracies. The practice of popular voting, I argue, plays a distinctively valuable role in modern democratic systems. Voting is one among many forms of democratic participation, but its value cannot be understood simply in terms of the general value of participation. The practice of popular voting instantiates democratic values in a unique and important way, and it also performs functions that support a healthy democratic system, especially within very large polities. The practice of popular voting in contemporary democracies is constituted not only by formal equality and widespread opportunities for participation; it is also constituted by a standard of approximately universal participation and by the creation of participatory moments able to command widespread attention. The singular prominence of voting in popular conceptions of democracy, especially in our models of citizen participation, contributes to the ability of popular voting to perform its special role in realizing democratic values. Appreciating this special place of voting in democracy does not depend, then, on thinking it is the only, or even the most important, act of democratic citizenship.

---

6. E.g. Landemore, *Open Democracy*; Olsen, *Participatory Pluralism*.

In the first two sections of this chapter, I characterize the practice of popular voting in contemporary democracies, drawing out three key features: the standard of universal participation, the creation of discrete, attention-grabbing moments of participation, and the application of aggregative equality. The first section provides an overview of empirical work on citizens' attitudes toward voting, on political behavior, and on administrative practices, to make the case that an operative standard of universal participation plays an important role in shaping the way we vote. The second section elaborates the other two, less controversial, key features of the practice. In the second half of the chapter, I explain how this constellation of features enables the practice of popular voting to contribute to the realization of democratic values. The third section argues that voting *instantiates* core democratic values in a unique and meaningful way, while the fourth section argues that the practice of popular voting also performs a functional role that contributes to a healthy democratic practice by creating favorable conditions for mobilization, facilitating the socialization of citizens, and disciplining public officials.

The account of voting that I offer in this chapter is a partially idealized one. The characterization of the key features of popular voting is drawn from empirical description of the practice of voting, but it also abstracts from the contradictions and distortions that characterize any system or instance of popular voting. This account is meant to illuminate the purposes of voting in a way that can provide concrete normative guidance for evaluating and reforming our actual practices. It offers a view of which aspects of how we vote—and how we think about voting—contribute to voting's role in democracy, and which might undermine or diminish that role. My goal in providing this account is not only to vindicate the special prominence of voting in our view of democratic citizenship, but also to show how voting practices can be improved to better realize the values they are meant to serve. The subsequent chapters build on this account of popular voting's purposes to identify principles for assessing and reforming voting systems.

"Voting is *Sui Generis*": the Standard of Universal Turnout

Perhaps the most significant feature that sets popular voting apart from other participatory practices is an expectation of approximately universal participation. I use the term expectation here in two senses. The first is prescriptive—"expectation" can refer to a standard or benchmark to

which we will hold each other accountable. The second is descriptive—
"expectation" can indicate what we believe will actually or likely occur. When
it comes to voting, the expectation of universal participation operates in
both senses. Universal turnout serves as a salient normative standard in the
practice of voting. This standard shapes the practical deliberations of citizens and officials, especially when they expect to be held accountable to
public norms. And while no one believes that truly universal turnout will
be achieved, the descriptive expectation that turnout might approach universality is essential for maintaining the salience of that standard. Universal
turnout is more than a mere aspiration or desire. It plays a more normatively
demanding role in how we think and talk about voting—especially in public
deliberation. As I will argue in the second half of this chapter, the expectation of universal turnout—in both the prescriptive and the descriptive
sense—is an indispensable feature of the practice of popular voting that
contributes to both its inherent and functional value. Voting more completely fulfills its role in a democracy to the extent that turnout approaches
100 percent and to the extent that participants in the practice—citizens,
public officials, and political agents—*believe* that just about all citizens will
vote and behave accordingly.

Of the three features of popular voting that I will emphasize in this chapter, the expectation of universal turnout is the most tenuous and vulnerable
part of the practice. Turnout rates in many established democracies have
been declining for decades. Consequently, the claim that this expectation of
universal turnout is a core, distinguishing feature of the practice of popular
voting will likely be among the most controversial claims in this book, at
least among academic scholars of democracy. An alternative reading of the
practice of popular voting might emphasize the importance of rights and
real opportunities to vote but suggest that the number of citizens who actually cast a ballot is not of primary importance to understanding the role of
popular voting in contemporary democracies.

My goal in this section is to show that actual voter turnout, not just
opportunities to vote, does play a crucial role in how citizens understand the
point of popular voting. I draw on empirical research on political attitudes
and behavior to show that citizens think about voting differently from other
forms of political participation. Whereas many forms of political participation are seen as discretionary or perhaps part of a "division of civic labor,"[7]

---

7. I take this phrase from Jason Brennan's critique of the "folk" theory of the duty to vote
(Brennan, *The Ethics of Voting*, 43).

voting is not. Even more important than individual beliefs about voting, though, is the set of public norms that these beliefs reflect and reinforce. The expectation of universal participation shapes the practice of popular voting by establishing communal norms to which citizens, public officials, and political actors expect to be held accountable, and to which they can appeal to justify their actions or critique those of others. The account I provide in this chapter of how the standard of universal participation shapes the practice of popular voting and how it contributes to the realization of democratic values suggests that we should view low and declining turnout as troubling phenomena that threaten to erode a valuable democratic practice. We have strong reasons to seek measures that not only expand opportunities to vote, but that actually and effectively boost turnout.

Surveys of political attitudes consistently reveal widespread support for the idea of a duty to vote. In many Western democracies, upwards of 90 percent of survey respondents affirm claims that voting is a civic duty, an essential component of good citizenship.[8] And studies that ask citizens similar questions about other forms of political participation reveal that this way of thinking is unique to voting. Affirmation of the duty to vote is not just a proxy for general attitudes about the value of political participation. Voting, specifically, is more tightly linked to models of good citizenship than other participatory acts. In one of the broadest surveys of political attitudes in contemporary democracies, the 2014 ISSP citizenship module, respondents were asked how important it is for a good citizen to "always vote in elections." In all but one of the countries or regions included in the survey, over 50 percent of respondents rated the importance of "always voting" a 6 or a 7, on a 7-point scale.[9] By contrast, the percentage of respondents who rated "keeping watch

8. Though the rate of belief in the duty to vote has declined slightly over time, in the US and Canada, endorsements of the idea of the duty to vote remain very high ("Trends in Political Values and Core Attitudes: 1987–2007"); Blais, *To Vote or Not to Vote?*, 94–98). In Europe, belief in the duty to vote is falling somewhat faster, though a majority of citizens in many countries still report belief in a duty to vote (Carlsson and Johansson-Stenman, "Why Do You Vote?," 507; Furlong and Cartmel, "Social Change and Political Engagement"; Goerres, "Why Are Older People More Likely to Vote?"). In a 2010 survey of Korean voters, when asked to select their main reason for voting among several options, 70 percent selected "Voting is a citizen's duty." The second most popular response was "to support my candidate," selected by 13 percent of respondents (Achen and Hur, "Civic Duty and Turnout," 58).

9. ISSP Research Group, "International Social Survey Programme: ISSP 2014—Citizenship II Variable Report." Most of the studies were conducted at the country level, but results were reported separately for East and West Germany, for three regions of Belgium (Flanders, Wallonia, and Brussels), and for Arab and Jewish Israelis. The Slovak Republic is the one country where fewer than 50 percent of respondents rank "Always Voting" in the top two categories of

over the government" in the top two categories of importance exceeded 50 percent in only 20 of the 38 countries studied. And the percentage of respondents who similarly rated "being active in social and political organizations" exceeded 50 percent in only two. These results suggest that the widespread belief in the duty to vote is not just one example of a more general belief in a duty of political participation. Rather, citizens regard voting as a uniquely required form of participation.

Studies that have delved more deeply into the nature of citizens' attitudes toward voting reveal that the difference between how citizens view voting compared to other forms of participation is not merely a difference of degree, but of kind. Russell Dalton has argued that popular beliefs about the norms of good citizenship place voting in a "Citizen Duty" framework, whereas other activities intended to influence political decision-making fit together within a "Citizen Engagement" framework. Citizens' attitudes toward voting are more similar to attitudes toward obeying the law or paying taxes than to engaging in other forms of participation.[10] Characterizing the findings of a series of studies of American citizenship, David Campbell presents a more nuanced picture of voting norms. Voting, Campbell argues, occupies a unique space at the overlap of civic and political activities. Voting is motivated *both* by a desire to contribute to community functions and by a desire to influence public decision-making by exercising political voice.[11] Taken together, these studies show that although many different kinds of political participation may be considered indicative of good citizenship, voting is the only participatory act widely thought to be a *necessary* component of good citizenship.

Other research on political behavior supports the idea that citizens think very differently about voting than they do about other forms of participation. In their seminal study of political participation, for example, Verba,

---

importance. In general, former communist-bloc countries tend to rate all of the participatory actions as being of lower importance compared to democracies in other regions (consistent with other research suggesting a more fragile commitment to democratic governance in these countries: Anderson et al., *Loser's Consent*). But ratings of the importance of voting have *increased* in a number of former communist countries since the last time the ISSP citizenship module was conducted in 2004 which suggests that belief in the duty to vote is at least correlated with democratic consolidation (see ISSP Research Group, "International Social Survey Program: ISSP 2004—Citizenship I Variable Report").

10. Dalton, "Citizenship Norms and the Expansion of Political Participation."

11. This unique duality of voting is revealed most clearly in the "U-shaped" curve representing the relationship between political heterogeneity and voter turnout. Campbell, *Why We Vote*, esp. 34–35; 157–176.

Shlozman, and Brady assert that "on every dimension along which we consider participatory acts, voting is *sui generis*."[12]

What is it about voting that leads citizens to bind the idea of good citizenship to voting? One possible explanation, proposed by Anthony Downs, is that citizens view voting as a form of "social insurance" against the potentially destabilizing possibility that *no one* votes in an election.[13] Setting aside questions about whether this way of thinking would reflect an accurate picture of the importance of elections relative to other institutions that depend on voluntary participation, survey research suggests that this is not an accurate explanation for how citizens think about the point of voting. In fact, one of the questions on a classic index measuring a sense of civic duty in the United States asked whether respondents believe they ought to vote even when they anticipate that many other people will vote.[14] In a more recent survey of Canadian students, over 90 percent of respondents agreed with the statement: "in order to preserve democracy, it is essential that the great majority of citizens vote."[15] Moreover, the way that citizens act on their sense of duty also seems inconsistent with Downs' account. Citizens often exhort others to do their duty by voting. Some devote a great deal of time to organizing non-partisan "get out the vote" efforts, and many wait in line, sometimes for hours, to cast their own votes. None of these practices would make much sense if the duty to vote existed simply to ensure that someone votes. Belief in the duty to vote reflects a belief that it is important that everyone—or at least nearly everyone—votes.

These studies of individual attitudes provide important information about the distinctiveness of popular voting, but the public, shared practice of voting is not reducible to a collection of individual attitudes. For one thing, there is plenty of heterogeneity in the extent to which citizens have internalized the duty to vote—that is, in how much it motivates them and under what conditions. Social desirability bias undoubtedly plays at least some role in producing the extremely high rates at which survey respondents affirm a duty to vote. When people respond to questions about civic duties, they may say what they think they are supposed to say, even if this does not

12. Verba, Schlozman, and Brady, *Voice and Equality*, 24. This quote comes at the conclusion of a discussion in which the authors argue that it is not possible to draw general conclusions about participation from looking at research on voting. Among other differences, Verba, Schlozman, and Brady observe that the motivations for voting are different from other forms of participation.

13. Downs, *An Economic Theory of Democracy*, 261–68.

14. Campbell, Gurin, and Miller, *The Voter Decides*, 195.

15. Blais, *To Vote or Not to Vote?*, 95.

reflect the beliefs that really motivate them when no one is watching. This can be seen in studies that attempt to eliminate or reduce social desirability bias. One set of studies in the US and Canada found that the proportion of survey respondents who have internalized the duty to vote is around half.[16] This still reflects striking affirmation of the importance of voting, as compared to other forms of political participation, but it is less staggering than the numbers reported in typical surveys.

Even when survey respondents just say what they think is the socially desired response, that still provides useful information about how people understand the norms of the community. When it comes to things we do together, like voting, we often rely on a set of shared norms that we all accept as the norms that we will use to govern our shared activity, even if we do not necessarily endorse or internalize them. This possibility—that individuals can recognize and accept the role of shared norms they do not personally care about—makes collective action much easier to carry out. The widely recognized standard of universal participation on occasions for popular voting shapes the practice even when many citizens have not internalized a sense that they have a duty to vote. As a number of "get-out-the-vote" experiments have shown, the belief that they will be held accountable to the public norm of universal voting can motivate citizens to turn out who might not otherwise.[17] Public norms also shape how citizens view the point of voting practices and their role within them. And public norms provide standards that govern electoral administration and form the basis for justifications and critiques of administrative policies as well as citizens' actions.

The expectation of universal turnout operates as a public norm that shapes election administration as well as private activity and public discourse around elections. In many countries, the public belief that elections entail universal participation is formalized in law. Twenty-nine democracies have some form of compulsory voting law on the books, including, for example, Australia, Belgium, and Argentina. In some of these countries, the duty to vote is enshrined in the constitution.[18] Alternatively, some political communities codify the standard of high voter turnout by invalidating elections or referenda that do not achieve a specified turnout minimum.[19]

16. Blais and Achen, "Civic Duty and Voter Turnout," 484.

17. Gerber, Green, and Larimer, "Social Pressure and Voter Turnout."

18. Birch, *Full Participation*, 36.

19. The practice is most common in former communist-bloc countries, transitional democracies, and in constitutional referenda (Malkopoulou, "Lost Voters," 6). The practice of minimum turnout requirements resembles the requirement of quorum in other decision-making bodies.

Even where the expectation of universal participation does not yield enforceable, legal mandates to vote, the effort and expense devoted to administering elections dwarfs any other public effort to elicit political participation. Administering a single federal election can cost a typical US county hundreds of thousands of dollars,[20] and measures to increase the convenience and accessibility of voting have contributed to a rapid rise in costs for many jurisdictions.[21] India's 2014 parliamentary election required nearly a million polling places and over 10 million government personnel to ensure that all eligible voters, even those in the most remote parts of the country, would be able to vote.[22] The energy and resources devoted to bringing all citizens to the polls (or to bringing the polls to all citizens) reflect the publicly shared belief in the importance of *mass* participation in elections.

The activities of non-governmental organizations and associations also reflect the public norm of universal voting. This can be seen in (at least facially) non-partisan get-out-the-vote drives, like "Rock the Vote," which aims to increase turnout among young adults and other groups with historically low voting rates. It is not uncommon for companies trying to cultivate a "public-spirited" image to issue public service advertisements linking the company's brand to an exhortation to vote.[23] These kinds of campaigns do not explicitly promote a particular position; rather they build on and reinforce the public norm, implying that "whoever you vote for, we can all agree that it's important to vote."[24] And, of course, the significance of a standard

20. Montjoy, "Changing Nature and Costs." Using election spending data from 26 states, the MIT Election Data + Science Lab estimated a lower bound on the cost of election administration in United States at 8.10 US dollars per voter (Mohr et al., "How Much Are We Spending").

21. Giammo and Brox, "Reducing the Costs of Participation." Most reforms to make voting more convenient and accessible increase costs because they increase administrative burden. One exception to this is universal vote-by-mail, which appears to reduce costs ("Cost and Participation—Statewide Elections").

22. Vyawahare, "A Primer on India's Parliamentary Elections."

23. Google's Election Day "doodles," and Facebook's "voter button" represent prominent (and sometimes controversial) examples, but many other brands also collaborate with voter turnout campaigns. An example of this is the footwear company Kenneth's Cole's "Stand Up, Show Up, or Shut Up" advertising campaign in partnership with "Rock the Vote" (Mejia, "Kenneth Cole & Rock the Vote").

24. This quote paraphrases the result of an exchange between a Democratic campaign manager (Will Bailey) and a group of children on an episode of *The West Wing*. The children, promoting a public service Election Day message encouraging turnout, make a sign that says: "It doesn't matter who you vote for, make sure you vote." Bailey suggests that the children revise their sign to say: "*Whoever* you vote for, make sure you vote." The point, of course, is that it does matter who you

of approximately universal participation is reflected in, and reinforced by, persistent handwringing over "low" turnout rates, even when half of eligible citizens participate.[25] It is hard to imagine any other participatory practice where a 50 percent participation rate would seem very low. The way we talk about voting reflects a widely recognized belief that something has gone wrong when turnout rates deviate too much from the benchmark of universal participation.

Momentousness and Aggregative Equality

The expectation of universal participation is not the only essential feature of popular voting. In this section, I outline two additional aspects of voting that distinguish it from other participatory practices: the creation of decisive participatory *moments*, and the application of an aggregative interpretation of equality. Together with the expectation of universal turnout, these two features of popular voting contribute to important democratic functions and to the realization of democratic values.

While the expectation of universal turnout is a distinctive feature of popular voting, the application of aggregative equality, and to a lesser extent, the creation of distinct democratic moments, are common across different types of voting practices (including, for example, voting within a legislature or judicial body). The discussion in this section builds on existing work that illuminates the democratic value of decisive moments and of aggregative equality. But to this point, democratic theorists have largely discussed these features without specific attention to how they operate in the context of *popular* voting. While some of the virtues of voting procedures are common across many different applications, they also take on additional significance when combined with the character of mass participation in popular voting and the expectation of universal turnout.

---

vote for. But, crucially, Bailey's revision maintains the idea that the importance of voting does not depend *just* on the content of your vote (Alex Graves, "Game On").

25. News coverage on the 2016 US presidential election, much of which emphasized a decline in turnout relative to 2008 and 2012, despite turnout rates remaining close to 60 percent, illustrates this (see, e.g., "What Does Voter Turnout Tell Us about the 2016 Election?"). This kind of coverage of turnout rates in the neighborhood of 50–60 percent is common across many democracies (for similar coverage of recent French, Mexican, and Israeli elections, respectively, see Adler, "Turnout Sharply down in French Election"; "Participación del 1 de julio no rompió récord"; Rahman, "Why Did Arab Voter Turnout for Israel's Election Plunge?").

POPULAR VOTING CREATES POLITICAL MOMENTS
AROUND SHARED DECISION-MAKING

The practice of popular voting creates salient, shared political moments. These moments are constituted by clearly delineated occasions when citizens cast their votes, when votes are counted, and when election or referendum results are publicized and certified. These results are understood as constituting a collective *decision*. The results of a popular vote are not primarily viewed as informative or expressive. The point of these occasions is to resolve some question about what is to be done. Usually, this question is one about who will hold particular offices, but occasions for popular voting also sometimes settle substantive matters of law or policy.

The discreteness of these decisive occasions distinguishes participation in popular voting from other forms of political participation. Many of the avenues through which citizen activity affects political outcomes involve diffuse acts of influence that accrue over time. Thus, even if our model of citizen participation includes other practices—like deliberation, for example—that all citizens are expected to participate in at some time, in some way, voting is unique in calling for citizens to participate in a particular way, at a particular time. And voting generates an immediate causal link between these participatory occasions and the political decisions they produce. Of course, voting follows a long process of agenda-setting and campaigning in which diffuse acts of participation influence the set of possible outcomes. But occasions for popular voting create clear, pivotal moments when political outcomes hinge on identifiable instances of popular participation.

In part because popular voting involves clearly delineated occasions for participation and decision, it creates distinct moments in which the political community is rendered salient to its members. For large polities, national votes represent the most significant, if not the only, truly shared collective moments. These moments help to constitute and reinforce the foundations of political community—the sense that citizens share not only an identity, but a common project. Nations may occasionally experience other shared collective moments, like national tragedies or victory in international sporting events. But popular voting creates collective moments around the experience of doing something together, of governing together on equal terms. Because it defines decisive participatory occasions, the practice of popular voting creates moments of unity that help constitute the people as a *democratic* political community.

Another key aspect of the participatory moments created by popular voting is their predictable recurrence. Popular voting in contemporary democracies is not simply a one-off event. Some referenda (for example, the Brexit vote) may, in some respects, appear as unique participatory events, but in most established democracies, even these special referenda fit within a broader practice of popular voting. Generally, citizens can expect to vote many times in their lives. At a minimum, citizens in established democracies can expect to be called upon to vote at intervals of four to five years, but popular votes in many polities occur at a much greater frequency. As I will argue in the fourth section, this predictable recurrence of voting contributes to its functional role in establishing a democratic political culture.

POPULAR VOTING APPLIES AN AGGREGATIVE INTERPRETATION OF EQUAL PARTICIPATION

The third key feature of popular voting that I want to highlight involves the nature of the decision-procedure itself, i.e., how it translates the inputs of citizens' acts of participation into a decisive, collective outcome. Voting applies an *aggregative* interpretation of what it means for individuals to participate equally in making a collective decision. The aggregative interpretation of equality characterizes a decision-procedure with certain properties: 1) the procedure presents all participants with a choice set; 2) participants communicate their preferences over the options in the choice set; 3) these expressed preferences (votes[26]) are counted and aggregated according to a predefined function (voting rule) that translates the profile of votes into a single decision; 4) the profile of votes and the voting rule jointly determine the electoral decision; 5) the voting rule treats votes equally and satisfies plausible conditions of collective rationality.

To understand what is distinctive about the aggregative interpretation of equality, it is worth taking a moment to contrast it with another interpretation. In the aggregative interpretation of equal participation, equality among participants is realized through symmetry: symmetry in the nature

26. Aggregative equality does not always involve a voting procedure. Sometimes the presentation of choice set, solicitation, expression, and aggregation of preferences is broken down with other procedures—most notably idealized bargaining or auction procedures. For the purposes of simplicity, I characterize aggregative procedures in voting terms, but these procedures share with other decentralized public choice procedures, like bargaining, a common approach to treating participants equally, and a common understanding of how the value of collective decisions qua aggregative outcomes can be derived from the value of participants' individual choices.

of participation and symmetry in the way that a rule treats those acts of participation. This symmetry makes the aggregative interpretation of equality impersonal and anonymous—it is not responsive to features of individuals, only to their actions (votes). Not all interpretations of equal participation involve this sort of symmetry. For example, classic accounts of equality in democratic deliberation may allow for asymmetric treatment of individual participatory acts depending on their content (e.g., proposals or reasons with greater merit are weighted more heavily). Some also allow for asymmetry in the form of participation (e.g., some people may speak more than others). On these accounts of deliberative equality, equal participation is realized through the disposition of citizen participants to treat each other as equals in their deliberations.[27] The *im*personal character of aggregative equality, then, contrasts with the *inter*personal character of deliberative equality.[28]

Skeptics of the value of voting might argue that the aggregative interpretation of equality is too thin to support the normative weight of democracy. The symmetry of treatment required by aggregative equality makes the decision-procedure inflexible and unable to respond to all aspects of individual and social agency that ought to be involved in collective decision-making.[29] Symmetry of treatment also requires aggregative decision-procedures to be agnostic toward the content of citizens' preferences and dispositions, even when their preferences are themselves inegalitarian or otherwise repugnant to democracy.

The aggregative interpretation of equality does have important features, though, that contribute to the democratic value of popular voting. Here I will just briefly characterize these virtues of aggregative equality, but in the following sections, I will say more about how they contribute to the value of popular voting as a practice. First, aggregation entails a *concrete* and *transparent* form of equality in the equal weighting of votes. Citizens can recognize when a voting rule treats votes symmetrically. The deliberative interpretation of equality that I described above cannot be fully transparent.

27. See, e.g., Cohen, "Procedure and Substance," 164.

28. Some versions of deliberative democracy call for sensitivity to individual participants' experiences, perspectives, personalities, and capabilities in sharp contrast to the anonymous and symmetric treatment of participants under aggregative equality (e.g., Young, *Inclusion and Democracy*).

29. Perhaps the most serious problem for the aggregative interpretation of equality involves the existence of persistent minorities when a group of citizens has highly correlated preferences across a range of issues. The aggregative interpretation of equality does not provide a satisfactory diagnosis or response to our intuitions about this problem.

It depends on the mental states of citizens—attitudes of reciprocity, and an openness to the deliberative contributions of fellow citizens—which are unknowable to others. While citizens and political leaders can *signal* that they possess the appropriate mental states for deliberative equality, their fellow citizens still must trust that they are acting and reasoning in good faith and are not unduly influenced by unconscious biases.

Second, applications of aggregative equality are replicable. Precisely because deliberation is more flexible and more sensitive to a wider range of relevant factors than voting, it may be harder to rerun a deliberative procedure if some doubts arise about its legitimacy. Since aggregative equality is sensitive to far fewer features of participants or their contexts, it is easier to reproduce the conditions of an aggregative decision-procedure to replicate parts of it in an audit.[30]

Third, applications of aggregative equality are scalable. The same voting rule can be applied whether the electorate contains 100 or 100 million citizens. Scaling up the procedure does, of course, entail some practical difficulties in counting ballots and calculating the outcome based on the votes, but modern societies have already learned to surmount these practical difficulties. Scaling aggregative procedures does not radically change the nature of the procedure, and importantly, does not undermine the basis for aggregation's transparency and replicability.

These three virtues do not mean that the aggregative interpretation of equality is superior to alternatives. But it does mean that applications of aggregative equality can help realize some facets of democratic values that other forms of equality may not. There are good reasons to have institutions that apply a transparent, scalable, and replicable form of equality operating alongside institutions that apply other forms of equality in the same democratic system.

Popular Voting Instantiates Democratic Values

These three key features of popular voting—the standard of universal participation; the creation of recurrent, decisive, participatory moments; and the application of aggregative equality—together constitute a practice that contributes to the realization of democratic values in unique ways, especially

---

30. The transparency and replicability of aggregative equality may be particularly important for allaying suspicions, and securing acceptance of dissenters in contexts where collective decisions are made despite residual disagreement and conflicting interests. On the merits of voting vs. deliberation when consensus is unavailable, see Warren, "A Problem-Based Approach to Democratic Theory."

in large, modern polities. In this section, I will discuss how the practice of popular voting instantiates democratic values. Then, in the following section, I will discuss the functional roles that popular voting plays in supporting a healthy democratic culture.

Broadly speaking, the creation of discrete moments constituted by approximately universal participation and the application of aggregative equality, renders simultaneously salient two essential aspects of democracy: that democracy is a collective undertaking of *all* citizens, and that democracy is founded in the equal agency of *each* citizen. It can be hard to mentally reconcile the value of massively shared collective agency—the popular sovereignty of the citizenry as a whole—with the value of any particular individual contribution to that whole. Occasions for popular voting, though, represent rare moments where this reconciliation is achieved. Though these moments cannot bear the full normative weight we attribute to democracy, they nevertheless constitute an important part of a democratic *system* that can.

A SYSTEMIC PERSPECTIVE ON DEMOCRACY

No single institution or participatory practice can adequately realize the full value of democracy, especially in a large society. Fortunately, though, many institutions, norms, and practices operate simultaneously within democratic systems and together can more completely realize democratic values. Appropriately evaluating democratic practices like popular voting, then, calls for adopting a *systemic* perspective. That is, it calls for appreciating the purposes of a practice as it fits within a more complex political system.

Systemic approaches to evaluating institutions and practices hold that particular practices will have strengths and weaknesses relative to particular functions within a broader system. No individual practice or institution can be expected to solve all of the problems we need a democratic regime to solve.[31] A political institution or practice may also contribute to the realization of democratic values because of the way it supports or interacts with other parts of the system. And this can be true even if, when viewed in isolation, the institution seems to violate one or more democratic principles.[32] Institutions

31. See esp. Warren, "A Problem-Based Approach to Democratic Theory."
32. Mansbridge et al., "A Systemic Approach," 3, 18; Vermeule, *The System of the Constitution.* The reverse is also true. Particular institutions that have laudable democratic credentials when viewed in isolation can undermine or displace other beneficial parts of a democratic system (Mansbridge et al., "A Systemic Approach," 3).

that promote descriptive representation for particular disadvantaged groups provide a clear example of this. Viewed in isolation, these institutions seem to violate formal requirements of political equality. Viewed in the context of a democratic system as a whole, though, they can be seen as equalizing democratic representation, and ensuring that representative institutions function as they should. This functional approach to evaluating practices within a democratic system sheds light on the value of popular voting, as I will argue in the last section of this chapter.

Adopting a systemic perspective does not mean that practices and institutions must be viewed exclusively in functional terms, though. Some practices and institutions—including popular voting—still instantiate democratic values in themselves, even though they must always do so incompletely. The human values that are bound up in ideals of democracy—equality, autonomy, individual and collective empowerment—are rich and multi-faceted, which is why they are best realized by complex interactions among many different institutions and practices. At the same time, though, distinct practices that instantiate some aspects of democratic values can and should be valued in their own right.[33] Popular voting is one such practice. The constellation of features involved in voting creates singular moments that embody democratic values in unique ways. I do not mean to claim that these moments best or most completely instantiate democratic values, but simply that they do so in ways that other democratic practices, including deliberative and contestatory practices, do not. In combination with other components of modern democratic systems, popular voting allows for a richer and more complete realization of democratic values.

CONCRETELY ESTABLISHING THE EQUAL AUTHORITY OF ALL CITIZENS

Elections and other occasions for popular voting establish concrete moments of ultimate authority for the whole citizenry, and of equal authority for everyone within it. Most decision-making about how public power is to be exercised in modern democracies is delegated and diffuse. Individuals or small groups of people represent the community, deliberating, deciding, and acting on its behalf. This occurs through the formal procedural delegation

---

33. That is not to say, of course, that they are valued for their own sake. On the difference between how we value the practices that constitute democratic values and what we value about them, see Beerbohm, *In Our Name*, 34–35.

of political power to elected officials and appointed administrators. And it also occurs through the informal delegation of political influence to groups of citizens who engage in discretionary participatory activity like lobbying, petitioning, and demonstrating. The kinds of things we want modern political communities to be capable of achieving would be impossible without this kind of representation. Still, it is an imperfect and incomplete presentation of the people.

Popular voting, too, is an imperfect and incomplete presentation of the people, but it presents a different, and differently valuable, face of the polity. Popular voting as a practice reserves some particularly weighty political decisions for the entire citizenry. Just as a company's bylaws might allow for a great deal of delegated decision-making, and yet reserve some decisions to be made by an ultimate decision-making body, such as a board of directors or assembly of shareholders, modern political communities reserve a few decisions to be made by the ultimate democratic authority—all of its citizens. The discreteness and decisiveness of voting occasions are particularly important to this role of voting, as is the expectation of universal participation. What makes voting different from other participatory practices is precisely that it is not supposed to be delegated to a subset of the people. Popular voting designates decisions that are meant to be directly attributable to the body of the people as a whole. Insisting upon a quorum when attributing decisions to a particular group of people is a familiar practice, and it is no less sensible when the group is very large. Most systems for popular voting do not impose formal quorums, but the standard of universal participation reflects the idea that the results of a vote are meant to be attributable to the citizenry as a whole. The more citizens abstain, the more questionable this attribution may be. Under such conditions, voting looks less like the special exercise of the ultimate authority of the citizenry, and more like yet another instance of delegation.

It is true that even the voting body of the citizenry is only one possible representation of the people as a political community or collective agent. Voting procedures are, in some important ways, contingent, if not altogether arbitrary. The outcome of a vote in any group of people will depend on the agenda, as well as the rule for aggregating votes into a collective decision, not to mention the way that citizens form their political preferences and judgments. The processes that determine these features of a voting procedure will themselves be governed by a different operation of democratic values. Still, voting represents an important moment in democratic life because it is an occasion when the ultimate decision-making procedure includes *each and every* member of the polity on manifestly equal terms. The democratic values of inclusion and equality may be instantiated differently in other institutions, but popular voting creates the only occasions on which they are reconciled so concretely.

RENDERING THE RELATIONSHIP BETWEEN INDIVIDUAL AND COLLECTIVE AGENCY TRANSPARENT

Because popular voting creates discrete moments of participatory decision-making, characterized by approximately universal turnout on approximately equal terms, it also renders the role of individuals in contributing to the collective empowerment of the community *transparent* to citizens. Skeptics of the value of voting often lament the minimal influence of individuals in elections, complaining that individual votes do not matter, particularly because any one vote almost certainly will not swing an election. And yet, the collective result of an election is constituted by individual contributions in a salient and transparent way.

The traceability of collective decisions to individual inputs—especially as exemplified in voting procedures—distinguishes modern liberal democracy from mob rule. The counting—and in some cases, recounting—of ballots makes it clear that the collective agency of the community is compatible with and depends on the individual dignity of separate persons. Melissa Schwartzberg has argued that voting initially emerged as a decision-procedure in contexts where it was important to recognize the epistemic dignity of individual judgments and to preserve their discreteness. Voting came to replace acclamation as a decision-procedure in large, democratic contexts when individual citizens were recognized as having judgments worthy of individual recognition.[34] Acclamation is a decision-procedure that is appropriate where only the collective voice is valued. Voting is a decision-procedure that is appropriate where collective agency is valued, in part, because it is derived from individual agency.

The optics of voting help to reconcile individual and collective agency in the minds of voters. Popular voting is a massive collective undertaking. It is salient to citizens as such, particularly through media coverage of elections, which conveys a sense of the scale of the enterprise—hundreds of thousands of poll workers, hundreds of millions of voters, truckloads of voting machines, and boxes of cast ballots shown in hours and hours of election

---

34. Schwartzberg, "Shouts, Murmurs, and Votes."

coverage.[35] Voter turnout is also a regular subject of election coverage. And even where low turnout is predicted, headlines often still emphasize the scale of the event, proclaiming that millions are expected to make their way to the polls.[36]

At the same time, individual votes are treated with a certain dignity and importance that represents a surprising contrast to the optics of voting's scale. Perhaps nothing illustrates this so powerfully as iconic images from the contested 2000 US presidential election, in which judges and election officials scrutinize individual ballots with a magnifying glass during a Florida recount.[37] Though often imperfect, vote tallies are held to a standard of precision and validation unmatched by other formal or informal channels of citizen participation.[38] This standard also reveals itself in cases when actual election administration fails to treat individual votes or voters with appropriate dignity, when public outrage or legal consequences censure such behavior as departures from the ideals of voting.

The act of voting contrasts with other forms of collective participation, like demonstrations or rallies, in which individuals' voices are subsumed into the whole. And, especially in systems that require ballots to be cast in person, the act of voting also contrasts with those—like signing a petition or contacting one's representative—in which the context of the act masks its character as a contribution to the *collective* activity of democracy. Popular voting makes salient both of these aspects of participation—the equal and discrete value of the individual contribution, and the collective whole of which it is a part—creating a participatory experience in which citizens can regularly recognize and internalize their *equally shared collective* agency.

Popular voting creates singular moments that simultaneously manifest a concrete form of equality, massively shared collective agency, and individual dignity. These moments play an important functional role in large, complex polities. Among other things, they help to socialize citizens into their role in

---

35. Highlights from CNN's televised coverage of the 2016 US election provide a paradigmatic example of this formula for election reporting: *Relive Election Night 2016—CNN Video*.

36. For example, the first line of CNN's online coverage of the 2018 midterm election states "millions of Americans headed to the polls" (Ries et al., "Election Night in the US"). This trope is not limited to coverage of US elections by popular American news media. See, for example, the headline from an article in *The Conversation* about the February 2019 Nigerian elections: "What to expect as 84 million Nigerians go to the polls" (Ajala, "What to Expect").

37. King, *Judge Robert Rosenberg*.

38. Thirty-eight states and the District of Columbia in the US require some form of post-election audit to check for fraud or systemic errors in vote-counting. Most post-election audits require time-consuming manual inspection of ballots or paper records ("Post-Election Audits").

a democracy. But the way that popular voting reconciles various democratic values in the minds and emotional experiences of voters also has value in itself. Voting moments help to constitute a relationship between citizens and the collective project of democracy in which their own role is manifest to them. In these moments, citizens can see the relationship of parts to the whole, adopting the perspective that is appropriate for the co-creators of a democratic project.

THE COLLECTIVE EXPRESSION OF EQUAL RESPECT

In addition to establishing instances of ultimate, equally shared authority for the entire citizenry, and creating moments in which collective and individual agency are transparently reconciled, popular voting also constitutes an important practice of collective expression. The optics of mass participation in elections and the formal and concrete equality of citizens qua voters lend popular voting communicative value. In *Just Elections*, Dennis Thompson characterizes the expressive effects of elections, which both "enable citizens to express attitudes about the political process" and "express the polity's attitude toward its citizens."[39] Thompson explains that when individuals go to the polls along with so many of their fellow citizens, "visibly and publicly participating in the same way in a common experience of civic engagement, they demonstrate their willingness to contribute on equal terms to the democratic process."[40] The practice of popular voting reinforces a public recognition of the equal political authority of all citizens by calling upon us to perform our own authority and enact our respect for the equal authority of our fellow citizens. Popular voting conveys a vivid reminder of what democracy really is: a collective activity of self-rule undertaken by a community of equals.

Critics of the idea that voting ought to occupy a central role in our models of democratic citizenship have raised doubts about whether expressive features of voting can explain its value, and especially about whether the expressive character of voting grounds an expectation of universal participation, or a duty to vote. Geoffrey Brennan and Loren Lomasky acknowledge the value of expressive acts, and even acknowledge that the act of voting may have some expressive value. Voting, they argue, might express valuable sentiments like concern for the community and "assent to the legitimacy of the

---

39. Thompson, *Just Elections*, 22–23.
40. Ibid., 34.

public enterprise."[41] However, Brennan and Lomasky ultimately reject the idea that the potential for voting to carry this expressive content is enough to warrant the expectation that everyone participate in it. They argue that while active political engagement may have some expressive salience, the mere act of occasional voting is insufficient to demonstrate meaningful involvement in the community's public life.[42] Voting, according to Brennan and Lomasky, is too infrequent and too easy to provide a strong signal of citizens' commitment to the political community. It is cheap talk.

By focusing on what individuals express or communicate about themselves through their discrete acts of participation, though, Brennan and Lomasky neglect important features of voting that contribute to its expressive value. First, the unique context for the act of voting gives it expressive significance. The expectation of universal participation, combined with the formal equality of votes, and the miniscule influence this affords to any one individual, provides voters with an unparalleled opportunity to express and perform their willingness to participate as one among many in a *shared* project of democratic governance.

Second, Brennan and Lomasky evaluate voting as purely an individual expressive act. By voting, though, citizens do not just engage in individual expressive acts, but also contribute to a vital form of collective communication. Seana Shiffrin has argued that humans face an imperative to belong to a community "that communicates to its members their inclusion as equal members."[43] One source of the value of democratic institutions and practices is their ability to communicate some essential ideas—like inclusion and recognition of status—that individual acts of expression cannot adequately convey.[44] Voting is not the only democratic practice with this communicative potential, but in its conjunction of universal participation, concrete and formal equality, and the optics of voting moments, voting allows the community to affirm distinctive aspects of citizens' equal political agency. Moreover, the expectation of universal turnout means that the community calls on its citizens to regularly participate in the collective demonstration that the community values, and values equally, the contributions of each and every citizen.

41. Lomasky and Brennan, "Is There a Duty to Vote," 81.
42. Ibid., 82.
43. Shiffrin, "Speaking Amongst Ourselves," 152.
44. Ibid., 149.

Popular Voting Performs Valuable Functions
in Contemporary Democracies

The value of popular voting is located partly in how it instantiates unique facets of democratic principles like equality and popular sovereignty. This does not exhaust the value of the practice, though. Popular voting also has instrumental value because of the functions it performs in sustaining a healthy democratic culture. These functions, which include creating favorable conditions for mobilization and organization, socializing citizens, and disciplining public officials, are essential for enabling modern democratic systems to realize the values we attribute to them. Insofar as the practice of popular voting helps perform these functions, then, it contributes to the realization of democratic values beyond those it immediately embodies.

The functional and the intrinsic aspects of voting's value are nevertheless closely linked, as voting's ability to perform its functions also depends on the way that it instantiates democratic values. The functions of voting that I will describe here arise from the effects of anticipating, participating in, and witnessing moments of collective decision-making that have the characteristics and instantiate the values I have described in the first three sections of this chapter. If a system of voting does not actually instantiate these values—if it is an empty ritual—then voting will likely not have the same effects on the psychology or rational incentives of citizens and political leaders. In conjunction with voting's constitutive contributions to democracy, though, its instrumental functions enrich the value of voting as a democratic practice.

CREATING FAVORABLE CONDITIONS FOR MOBILIZATION, ORGANIZATION, AND POLITICAL INNOVATION

The practice of popular voting, through the creation of discrete moments of collective decision-making, and the expectation of approximately universal participation, creates favorable conditions for democratic political activity. First, voting performs a coordinating function for emerging or under-resourced political groups that might otherwise face difficulty organizing for coordinated political action. Knowing that they can expect their fellow citizens to vote increases the expected benefits to citizens of attempting to pursue a common political goal with likeminded compatriots. Organizing political action generally involves not only convincing citizens of the worthiness of a cause, but also overcoming disincentives to participate and coordinating on the time, place, and manner of participation. If citizens know that others with similar interests or concerns are already likely to vote, though, then would-be organizers need fewer resources to mobilize citizens to vote with common purpose.

The expectation of universal participation and the special weight placed on voting in public conceptions of citizenship also create favorable conditions for more inclusive political mobilization. Political parties, activists, and other political agents strategically deploy their resources to mobilize potential supporters into action, taking into account both how likely they are to get a favorable response and the costs of off-setting any barriers to the participation of those they might mobilize.[45] Individuals who are already likely to undertake an activity are more likely to be targets of political mobilization strategies because it is easier (i.e., less costly) to nudge them into taking action. Often this fact has inegalitarian consequences. Some people are harder to mobilize than others. This may be because they face higher barriers to participation or because they are positioned on the margins of social networks, making it more costly to reach them.[46] Both of these factors are often present among the most under-represented groups in political participation—low income, low education, and young adult citizens. The result is that political agents economizing on their organizational resources are less likely to try to mobilize these groups, leading to uneven rates of political participation. Patterns of voter mobilization are less skewed, though.[47] The expectation of universal participation makes mobilization strategies that target a broader range of citizens more attractive because it is easier to take citizens who already feel some pull to vote, and just give them a little extra nudge over the edge. The more social resources are devoted to lowering the costs of voting and increasing its benefits (including social and psychological ones), the more political agents are able to spread their mobilization resources over a larger and more inclusive group of citizens.

Finally, because it creates special moments that direct public attention toward democratic politics, popular voting creates an environment favorable

45. For a classic account of how elite mobilization strategies drive participation, see Rosenstone and Hansen, *Mobilization, Participation, and Democracy in America*.

46. Mobilizing individuals at the margins of social networks is not just more costly, it is also less valuable to political actors, since these mobilization efforts are less likely to spill over to others, whereas mobilizing individuals at the center of social networks will tend to yield greater gains as these individuals can, in turn, mobilize many of their connections (ibid., 31–33). On the role of network position in political mobilization, see also Campbell, "Social Networks and Political Participation"; Verba, Schlozman, and Brady, *Voice and Equality*.

47. Rosenstone and Hansen, *Mobilization, Participation, and Democracy in America*, 238.

to both political organization and innovation. In the period leading up to a vote, the mass public is more attuned to political messaging than they might otherwise be.[48] Those hoping to spread new political ideas, consolidate support for old ideas, or simply to publicize information about the government need to expend fewer resources to reach the same number of people in such an environment.[49]

Of course, the nature of popular voting moments will also shape the kinds of political messaging that citizens are attentive to. One concern about this claim might be that the salience of status competition among parties might crowd out attention to substantive political issues, making it harder to draw an audience for issue-specific messaging. Scholars of affective polarization have hypothesized that the relative importance of status competition versus ideological commitment in motivating political engagement and participation varies depending on proximity to elections. The relative importance of partisan status competition around elections need not mean that partisans are necessarily unreceptive to messaging about particular issues; this environment might provide an opportunity for activists to reframe what counts as a victory for the party by grafting new issues onto the party platform or identity. Nevertheless, thinking about how elections shape not only the level of political energy and attention, but also where it is directed, should shape how we understand voting's place within a democratic *system*. One potential upshot of this consideration is the importance of establishing temporal and symbolic boundaries around voting occasions to create space for non-electoral modes of political attention.

SOCIALIZING CITIZENS

The practice of popular voting, when characterized by an expectation of universal participation, also performs crucial functions related to the socialization of citizens. Perhaps the best way to appreciate these functions is to

---

48. Gallup polling shows regular spikes in attention to political news among US respondents during election years (Auter, "Number of Americans Closely Following Politics Spikes"), and Google Trends data shows a similar pattern in internet searches for "politics" (Google Trends Ngram, "'Politics' (Searches in the United States, 2004–Present)"). For an overview of research on media environment during elections outside of the US, see Van Aelst, Thorbjørnsrud, and Aalberg, "The Political Information Environment during Election Campaigns." For discussions of the content of political coverage during election campaigns, see, e.g., Strömbäck and Dimitrova, "Political and Media Systems Matter."

49. E.g., Huddy, Mason, and Aarøe, "Expressive Partisanship."

imagine what a model of citizenship might look like without the expectation that everyone votes. Modern democracies involve many sites of political influence, and healthy democracies undoubtedly depend on citizens' engaging in a variety of forms of political participation. Skeptics of the special importance of voting have argued that this complexity of modern democratic systems calls for a more pluralist model of citizen participation, which treats voting as just one among many ways that citizens can exercise their political agency.[50] A fully pluralist model of citizenship would call for citizens to actively engage in politics when they happen to encounter issues of personal significance to them, and it would call for citizens to engage only in those participatory activities that grant them a relative advantage over their political adversaries, or that are otherwise strategically useful in pursuing their goals. An upshot of this pluralist model of participation is that citizens who lack strong political preferences can signal their satisfaction with the status quo by not participating. Another upshot is that citizens may choose to informally delegate political authority to their fellow citizens with greater motivation, stronger preferences, or more political savvy.

The pluralist model of citizen participation may initially seem amenable to a systemic perspective on democracy; it seems appropriate for a system in which democratic values are realized through the combination and interaction of a plurality of political institutions and practices. Nevertheless, a *strictly* pluralist model of citizen participation cannot plausibly sustain a democratic system—at least not under the social conditions of large modern societies. The pluralist model of citizen participation depends on a certain view of what citizens are like: citizens must have not only the resources and opportunities to participate in politics, but also a set of "citizen" attitudes and dispositions that affect how they recognize and interpret opportunities for participation, including a sense of efficacy, political interest, and a commitment to democracy. A democratic system, therefore, must include practices that socialize citizens into their role, inculcating the kinds of attitudes that are necessary for citizens to view themselves and their fellow citizens as equal political agents, co-authors of their public life. Even a systemic view of democracy, then, requires modifying the pluralist model of citizen participation at least enough to ensure that all citizens take part in practices that socialize them into the citizen's role and inculcate democratic attitudes. This is a function of the expectation of universal participation associated with popular voting.

50. See, e.g., Brennan, *The Ethics of Voting*; Chalmers, *Reforming Democracies*; Lever, "Compulsory Voting: A Critical Perspective"; Olsen, *Participatory Pluralism*.

One of the main apparent virtues of a strictly pluralist model of citizen participation, as I have described it, is that it seems to be desirably undemanding, respectful of the burdens on citizens' time and mental energy that constrain our capacity to understand and participate in governing a complex society. The pluralist model allows citizens who are satisfied with the status quo or who wish to defer to their fellow citizens to participate by omission, influencing the direction of public life through their choice not to intervene.[51]

Even if democracy does not require all citizens' active participation, however, it does require that they view their non-participation as a choice. Any non-minimalist account of democracy requires that citizens see themselves as rightful and potentially effective political actors. Evaluations of democratic participation, then, must be sensitive to the observational equivalence between intentional, inactive participation and a lack of political efficacy. This is especially true since empirical research on citizen attitudes has suggested that non-voting is often better explained by citizens' failing to regard themselves as effective political agents, than by their adopting a pluralist model of participation.[52]

A democratic model of citizen participation cannot take citizens' sense of efficacy or levels of political engagement and motivation as given. Individuals' political interest and engagement depends on features of their political environment that may be distributed unequally, including access to information about politics, and "networks of recruitment" for encountering opportunities to participate and for developing the kinds of "civic skills" that enable citizens to participate in influential activities confidently and effectively.[53]

Levels of political engagement are also likely to be self-reinforcing. Individuals' existing political inclinations affect how they filter environmental

51. This can be understood as a form of "virtual control" as described in Pettit, *A Theory of Freedom*. That abstention can be incorporated into a model of contributory influence is also a feature of some models of voting, as in Al Goldman's characterization of elections in terms of "vectorial causal systems" (Goldman, "Why Citizens Should Vote").

52. In their classic study of political attitudes, Gabriel Almond and Sidney Verba distinguish between two sets of political attitudes. Some individuals see themselves as "citizens," able to exert influence over their political circumstances, while others see themselves primarily as "subjects," passive recipients of law and government actions. Almond and Verba find that non-participants tend to demonstrate subject attitudes (Almond and Verba, *The Civic Culture*, 117–18). Other classic survey research similarly confirms that habitual non-voters tend to have a substantially lower sense of political efficacy than voters (see, e.g., Miller, Miller, and Schneider, *ANES Data Sourcebook*, 321).

53. Verba, Schlozman, and Brady, *Voice and Equality*, 3–16.

stimuli; unless individuals are already inclined to be active in politics, they are not likely to pay attention to the kind of information that might motivate them to *become* politically active. This is all the more serious as individuals increasingly obtain their information from websites and services that tailor content for individuals based in large part on what their past behavior predicts they will find interesting. Individuals' political engagement also depends on whether they or others in their social networks care about the kinds of issues or conflicts that have already become politically salient. There is no reason to suspect that the kinds of issues that might be important to a particular group of citizens will enter political discussion unless that group can be brought into the political arena.[54]

Just like any other habit or lifestyle, political disengagement has a kind of inertia. Without some external impetus, or significant occasion, it can be very difficult to choose a moment to change our behavior, even if we know that we would like to do so at some point. The practice of popular voting performs an important function, then, that would be missing in strictly pluralist model of citizen participation: it creates significant occasions that can help to overcome that inertia precisely because they seem sufficiently momentous to warrant a change in behavior.

Any plausible model of citizen participation will allow for citizens' levels of political engagement to vary across our lives. Whether it is because we become preoccupied with more immediate and intimate concerns like caring for young children or weathering a personal financial crisis, or because we are responding to changes in the political environment, most citizens will, at some point in their lives, largely check out of politics. And in any democratic system that resembles those we have now, many citizens will keep political activity at arms-length for most, if not all of their lives. Popular voting, though, creates a kind of backstop against total political disengagement. Periodic occasions on which all citizens know they will be called upon to participate help citizens to keep a foot in the door of politics. At the same time, these occasions also offer citizens vivid reminders of their equal share in ultimate political authority.

The strictly pluralist model of participation is a model for the political life of the already engaged citizen. It does not offer guidance for overcoming or avoiding political disengagement, marginalization, or alienation. This orientation of the pluralist model of participation might be appropriate for the classic descriptive version of pluralist democratic theory which aimed

54. Schattschneider, *Semisovereign People*, 100–109.

primarily to explain the stability of democratic regimes.[55] A model of citizen participation for democracies aimed at realizing the value of collective empowerment on equal terms, though, cannot be insensitive to the possibility of widespread alienation and habitual disengagement.

In existing democracies, the extent to which citizens tend to participate depends largely on whether their political environment enables them to cope with the complexity of modern politics and presents them with easy and accessible ways to develop skills and habits of political involvement. An effective model for socializing politically engaged and efficacious citizens must ensure that citizens regularly encounter opportunities to participate which are clear, accessible, and salient, and which activate their attention.

Placing periodic moments of approximately universal participation at the center of our political culture can help cultivate the attitudes and create the political environment necessary for an otherwise pluralist model of citizenship to work. Voting offers citizens a starting point for political engagement. Political learning can be practically oriented toward the specific decisions on which citizens are expected to vote. Moreover, the expectation of widespread participation in elections can improve citizens' information environment as they make these decisions, creating incentives for political entrepreneurs to disseminate their political messages while citizens are most attuned to them.

Proponents of a strictly pluralist model of participation might worry that carving out a special role for voting as a way of socializing citizens into political agency is ultimately self-defeating if voting becomes a substitute for other forms of political participation. Some democratic reformers have argued that the popular focus on elections diverts citizens' efforts and attention away from issues they might really care about and from more efficacious modes of participation or more pressing reform needs.[56] But there is little evidence to support this claim.[57] Polities with mandatory voting, for

55. E.g., Dahl, *A Preface to Democratic Theory*; Lipset, *Political Man*.

56. E.g., Chalmers, *Reforming Democracies*.

57. Some research reveals a different set of participatory norms and attitudes undergirding voting and those undergirding other forms of participation (especially online activism), as well as an apparent generational shift from attitudes associated with voting toward those associated with other forms of participation (e.g., Dalton, "Citizenship Norms and the Expansion of Political Participation"). This research might seem to suggest that there is such a substitution effect; but behavioral evidence does not seem to support such a claim and other work has suggested that aggregate trends in participation (i.e., simultaneous decline in voting rates and increases in some other forms of participation) are more likely caused by correlated social changes (e.g., contemporaneous increases in education and decreases in social connectedness) than a direct substitution effect (Rosenstone and Hansen, *Mobilization, Participation, and Democracy in America*, 217).

example, do not appear to suffer from reduced non-electoral participation.[58] In fact, high turnout may make voting's limitations much clearer, disabusing citizens of what Sarah Birch has called "the illusion of an unfulfilled potential efficacy"[59] and the belief that realizing the "true popular will" only requires mobilizing a silent majority.

By establishing a minimal level of active political participation, an ethic of participation that calls for universal voting helps to mitigate cycles of disengagement. Regular voting in elections gives citizens a chance to perform their political agency and to develop a sense of themselves as competent political actors. Voting can also serve as a gateway to further participation if, in the process of learning about an election, citizens discover information that motivates them to become involved in other ways.

In addition to creating an environment conducive to political efficacy and engagement, the expectation of universal participation in popular elections helps citizens to internalize commitment to democratic norms. When citizens vote in high-turnout democratic elections, they participate on manifestly equal terms with their fellow citizens. When they vote, citizens not only perform their own agency, but they do so in a context in which the realities of massively shared agency are salient. The expectation of universal participation in elections thus offers citizens a regular opportunity to reaffirm their commitment to pursuing political goals within the constraints imposed by democratic equality.

This function of popular voting might not initially seem essential when adopting a systemic view of democracy, since political equality may be an emergent phenomenon, arising from the interactions of many different political practices that may not all aim directly at it. We might imagine that in a well-designed system we can all pursue our own particular interests or goals using any and all means that are strategically rational, without having to worry about how to accommodate our fellow citizens. Such a system might align citizens' strategic incentives and opportunities to ensure political equality, and therefore, might not seem to require that citizens themselves affirm a commitment to political equality.

Even this thin understanding of democracy, though, requires that citizens remain committed to resolving conflict within accepted democratic institutions and processes. A democratic system, even one the incorporates a pluralist model of citizen participation, thus benefits from practices that

58. Birch, *Full Participation*, 69–72.
59. Ibid., 69.

periodically raise the salience of this commitment.[60] Moreover, because it is impossible to design perfect institutions or practices that are immune to capture or breakdown over time, a sustainable democratic system requires that citizens internalize at least enough of a commitment to democracy to defend and reform political institutions as necessary to maintain their compliance with democratic norms of political equality.[61] Insofar as they are characterized by universal participation and command public attention, popular elections periodically remind citizens that they are part of a political community—a people—engaged in a shared project of democracy.

So far I have discussed the socialization functions of popular voting as they apply to the ongoing socialization of citizens throughout their lives. Popular voting plays an additional role in the socialization of young people by defining a clear age of political maturity. The age of political maturity is the age at which citizens are expected to become fully equal participants in a democracy. Democracy calls for granting all adult citizens equal political status, and it calls on adult citizens to regard one another as equal political agents. But this requires a publicly recognized definition of political adulthood. Modern societies typically lack discrete moments that mark individuals' full entry into adulthood. Instead, we have a disaggregated series of legal indicators of adulthood that occur at different ages. Moreover, many informal social indicators of adulthood, such as home-ownership, completion of formal education, marriage, and having children, are occurring later in life or declining in importance, and some are also increasingly unavailable to a large number of young adults. Because popular voting is uniquely characterized by an expectation of universal participation, and because it defines discrete political moments, the voting age can, and to a large extent does, serve as a widely recognized signifier of political adulthood.[62] The voting age marks

60. In a classic statement of the descriptive theory of pluralism, *Political Man*, Lipset argues that democracy requires more than just a variety of channels for citizens and groups to seek political influence; democracy also requires "integrative" institutions that encourage citizens to recognize their membership in the political community and to pursue their political goals within the community's legitimate decision-making processes. Lipset suggests that elections may be valuable integrative institutions (*Political Man*, 31).

61. We might be skeptical whether it is psychologically stable for citizens to maintain this commitment without also cultivating more demanding attitudes of reciprocity and civic love (see Allen, *Talking to Strangers*), but my description of the minimal conditions for democracy is certainly not incompatible with such ideas (and, in fact, I am sympathetic to them).

62. In the 19th century in the United States, when turnout among the eligible population—especially among young adults—was very high, the occasion of voting for the first time, casting one's "virgin vote," served as an important coming-of-age ritual for many young men (Grinspan, *The Virgin Vote*). Though first-time voting may not have quite the same ritual importance it once

a turning point in the life of a citizen, representing the point when political engagement is no longer supererogatory, but rather is a matter of fulfilling the responsibilities of an adult citizen.

DISCIPLINING PUBLIC OFFICIALS

Finally, of course, the practice of popular voting plays an important functional role in democracy by disciplining public officials to remain attentive to the political agency of all citizens. Political activists and interest groups have many ways to exert pressure on public officials besides voting,[63] but only a small subset of the population will use these strategies. The standard of universal turnout makes voting uniquely valuable as a way of directing the attention of political leaders to the collective capacity of the entire citizenry. Most of the time, public officials only have to worry about satisfying an active, organized minority. But in a system characterized by periodic moments of approximately universal participation, elected officials know that at least occasionally, they will need to make their case to the entire citizenry. Empirical scholarship on the effects of elections has given rise to many debates about how responsive politicians are to public opinion or to the real interests of voters. But there is no doubt that politicians do change their behavior in response to electoral incentives,[64] and how they perceive their electoral incentives is shaped by whom they expect to vote.[65]

Of all the functions of popular voting, this one has received by far the most attention from political theorists and political scientists. It is worth dwelling on it for a moment, though, because skepticism about the effectiveness or value of this function has underpinned recent radical criticisms of electoral democracy. Proponents of replacing popular elections with

---

did, the voting age still seems to mark a turning point in how we perceive and talk about political activity among young people.

63. Public shaming is one strategy, another is to hijack officials' efforts at public messaging (e.g., demonstrating at public appearances to affect media coverage of them), a third is to make it difficult for elected officials to fulfill the responsibilities of their office without responding to the demands of activists (through, e.g., sit-ins in public buildings or demonstrations that disrupt the provision of public services).

64. For a review of much of this literature, see Ashworth, "Electoral Accountability."

65. Griffin and Newman, "Are Voters Better Represented?"; Martin, "Voting's Rewards." On how compulsory voting appears to affect the substance of party platforms, see Fowler, "Electoral and Policy Consequences of Voter Turnout."

lottocratic institutions often argue that electoral accountability does not work.[66] They link rising distrust in and dissatisfaction with governing institutions to evidence of agency slack[67] and the outsized influence of wealthy elites. These theorists conclude that elections do not effectively constrain representatives to govern in accordance with citizens' wishes.[68]

There is no doubt that elections are imperfect tools for disciplining public officials, and they are certainly inadequate on their own to secure everything we want from democracy. But focusing on the limitations of elections often obscures the real achievements of electoral accountability. The prospect of re-election makes officials work harder for their constituents and reduces corruption.[69] The mere fact that an election will draw attention to their actions can make officials work harder even when they don't care about re-election, so long as they do care about their public reputations.[70] Parties and candidates do tend to take positions that align with voters' preferences;[71] when they don't, voters tend to punish them.[72] Scholars have also shown that electoral accountability is at least partially responsible for the democratic peace.[73] Widespread distrust in electoral institutions is undeniable and worrisome, but it is far from clear that we should attribute it to out-of-touch politicians or failing electoral accountability. The disciplining function of elections is certainly flawed, but it is not trivial. And like the other functions I have described in this chapter, different voting systems can perform the disciplining function better than others.

66. Guerrero, "Against Elections"; Van Reybrouck, *Against Elections*; Landemore, *Open Democracy*.

67. Agency slack is a term of art among scholars of politics and organizations. This term is associated with "principal–agent models," which characterize relationships where one person or entity (the agent) is empowered to act on behalf of another (the principal). Principal–agent models are commonly used to characterize the relationship between elected representatives (the agents) and their constituents (the principals). Agency slack refers to the extent to which the agent is able to get away with acting in a way that principals would not approve of.

68. Van Reybrouck, *Against Elections*.

69. Alt, Bueno de Mesquita, and Rose, "Disentangling Accountability and Competence"; Ferraz and Finan, "Electoral Accountability and Corruption."

70. Micozzi, "Does Electoral Accountability Make a Difference?"

71. Thomassen and van Ham, "Failing Political Representation or a Change in Kind?," 413–14.

72. Canes-Wrone, Brady, and Cogan, "Out of Step, Out of Office"; Hall, "What Happens When Extremists Win Primaries?"

73. Conconi, Sahuguet, and Zanardi, "Democratic Peace and Electoral Accountability"; cf. De Mesquita, Koch, and Siverson, "Testing Competing Institutional Explanations of the Democratic Peace."

Before concluding, I want to emphasize that the value of the disciplining effect on public officials created by popular voting does not depend on its serving as a direct instrument of popular control, especially not an all-purpose one. Democracy is not fully realized in any single moment or through any single political institution or practice. Rather, democracy is realized in a complex system involving myriad interactions among citizens and between citizens and their government.

To the extent that proponents of lottocracy or other participatory democratic reforms aim to create more effective opportunities for more citizens to influence more areas of public life, their aims are compatible with mine.[74] The value of elections' disciplining function will be enhanced by empowering citizens in areas where there are especially large gaps between the interests of politicians and the interests of the public, such as legislative redistricting. The value of elections' disciplining function will also be enhanced by giving more citizens more fine-grained ways to communicate with their representatives. An important precondition for democracy to emerge from a participatory system is that political representatives who wield broad and substantial power take themselves to be acting on the authority of the entire citizenry, and as such, are solicitous of the interests, concerns, and opinions of all citizens. The disciplining effect of elections, thus, may be only partially about the rational incentives it creates. It is also about making certain aspects of the job salient to representatives, shaping how they view themselves and their role, and creating certain dispositions or habits of attention. When elections are characterized by approximately universal participation, they create vivid moments in which elected officials are reminded that they are empowered at the behest of all citizens. Those who wish to fulfill the duties of their offices, and indeed to keep their offices, should be responsive to petitions from all sectors of society and look for ways to understand and address the concerns of different communities in their political programs.

Conclusion

In characterizing the distinctive role that popular voting plays in the realization of democratic values, one of the goals of this chapter has been to vindicate certain aspects of contemporary voting practices that have been

---

74. For examples of lottocratic institutions that strengthen or supplement, rather than replace electoral representation, see Fishkin et al., "Deliberative Agenda Setting"; Neblo, Esterling, and Lazer, "Politics with the People."

underappreciated—and sometimes scorned—by academic scholarship on democracy. These include the folk belief in a singular, specific duty to vote and in the value of high turnout, as well as the general spectacle of voting and the amount of attention it garners relative to other occasions for participation. I have argued in this chapter that these aspects of how we think about voting should not be understood as *responses* to the value of voting, but rather as *features* of the practice itself. Together with the formal properties of voting procedures, the expectation of approximately universal participation and the treatment of voting as a spectacular democratic moment constitute the practice of popular voting, and this constellation of features is what creates the democratic value of the practice.

The celebration of these underappreciated aspects of popular voting is only one of the purposes of this book, though. In characterizing the core features of popular voting and their value, I aim to provide normative guidance for how voting practices can be maintained and improved to more fully realize their potential value. Declining voter turnout rates have been a source of mild public concern for decades. This account reinforces the idea that preserving the democratic value of popular voting requires reversing this trend. Other significant threats to the value of popular voting are less widely recognized but come into view with a clear account of voting's distinctive purposes in contemporary democracies. In later chapters, I take up the task of articulating some of the concrete normative guidance that my account of voting's value provides for citizens, political leaders, and democratic reformers.

The nature of popular voting as a practice and the role it has come to play in contemporary democracies is in many ways contingent. The account of voting's value that I have offered is not derived from a top-down interpretation of what democratic values require, and I do not mean to suggest that democracy logically or practically entails a practice of popular voting with the characteristics and value I have described. The practice of popular voting and its role within contemporary democratic systems have developed over the past few centuries as a result of public and private deliberation, elite negotiations, social struggle, legal battles, and a wide range of contingent historical processes. The practice of popular voting represents an important piece of how our present-day political communities have, to this point, attempted to realize democratic values.

Because of this contingency, skeptics might doubt whether this account of voting's value and purposes can really ground normative claims about how we ought to design or reform our institutions, or about how citizens ought to conduct their lives. In chapter 6, I respond to this sort of radical criticism, demonstrating that there are reasons internal to most democratic theories to assign normative weight to existing practices. In that chapter I also sketch out a theory of democracy as shared agency to give shape to the role that existing practices play in our practical deliberations about the ethics of democracy.

Before taking up these questions about the normative implications of my account of voting, though, it is important to address some more immediate concerns about voting that might generate skepticism about whether popular voting can really bear the values I have attributed to it. In the next chapter, I address two concerns about voting associated with what is now often called "democratic realism." I call these two concerns the "inputs" and the "outputs" problems. These concerns have featured prominently in skepticism about the value of popular voting and have contributed to the marginalization of voting within normative democratic theory. I argue that a systemic view of democracy allows us to respond to these concerns without de-emphasizing the place of voting in our models of citizen participation. Nevertheless, sensitivity to these two problems must play an important role in evaluations of and reforms to voting systems.

2

Democratic Realism
and the Value of Voting

In chapter 1, I argued that popular voting plays a distinctive and important role in realizing core democratic values. Voting instantiates unique aspects of democratic values by creating spectacular moments of participatory collective decision-making on concretely and manifestly equal terms. And voting also serves functions that support the realization of democratic values in other institutions or practices.

Skeptics of the value of voting might wonder, though, whether popular voting isn't ultimately all just smoke and mirrors. Over the past century, a number of political theorists have argued forcefully that popular voting does not, and realistically cannot, constitute true collective decision-making, at least not of the sort that can be said to realize democratic values. These arguments have focused on two kinds of potential problems with voting procedures. One kind of problem concerns the value of the *inputs* to voting procedures: citizens' votes, some critics have argued, do not actually reflect the things that we think should matter for our public decision-making.[1] The second kind of problem concerns the value of the *outputs* of voting procedures: even if individual votes do have some value, there is no procedure for aggregating these votes in a way that preserves and transfers their value to the aggregated outcome. If individual votes are melodic musical solos,

1. E.g., Brennan, *The Ethics of Voting*; Brennan, "Medicine Worse Than the Disease?"; Caplan, *The Myth of the Rational Voter*.

the aggregation problem suggests that there is no way to combine them to make a symphony. Instead we only get noise.

Concern about these two problems has yielded two divergent responses within democratic theory. The minimalist response maintains the identification of voting and democracy, but argues that we should treat the concept of democracy as an analytical category rather than a value-laden ideal. The more common approach, though—at least among normative political theorists and philosophers—has been to maintain a normatively rich concept of democracy by adopting a systemic view of democracy in which voting plays only a small role. Voting can be understood as a valuable exercise of collective agency because of a wide range of democratic deliberative processes and complex relationships of representation that shape electoral agendas and the preferences citizens express with their votes, and that decrease the normative weight that formal properties of voting procedures must bear.[2]

My own account of voting's connection to democracy fits squarely within the second approach. But, I argue, mainstream systemic approaches to democratic theory are still in need of some correction—at least when it comes to their treatment of popular voting. It is perhaps a consequence of contemporary democratic theory's emphasis on complex deliberative processes and discursive practices (what been called the "deliberative turn" in democratic theory) that voting seems to have become marginalized within democratic theory. The centrality of voting in popular beliefs about democracy and in democratic aspirations may seem at odds with a view of democracy as a complex system in which popular voting is only one part.

The goal of this chapter is to show that the account of popular voting's distinctive role in contemporary democracies that I offered in chapter 1 is compatible with a clear-eyed and sophisticated systemic view of democracy. The special treatment that voting receives in popular models of citizenship does not depend on either a naïve "folk" conception of electoral democracy, nor on a stripped-down minimalist conception. It can be justified by appreciating the core features of popular voting practices and how these features contribute to the realization of democratic values within a democratic system, including one that involves complex processes of deliberation and representation.

This chapter proceeds in four sections. In the first section, I introduce the potential problems with meaningful aggregation and describe the scholarly debate over their prevalence and significance. In the second section,

2. Cohen, "Deliberation and Democratic Legitimacy," 28.

I argue that the minimalist response to these problems with aggregation is both unnecessary and untenable. In the third section, I describe the more appropriate response: adopting a systemic view of democracy. In this third section, I build upon the key insights of the "deliberative turn" in democratic theory to explain how aggregative procedures can play a meaningful role in a democratic system against the right discursive backdrop. Finally, in the fourth section, I address some potential remaining concerns about the compatibility of my account of popular voting's central role in modern democracy with a robust deliberative democracy.

Two Potential Problems with Vote Aggregation

I have argued that voting is an act of collective agency. Part of the distinctive value of popular voting as a practice is that it creates moments in which citizens are able to see how their individual agency (their own votes) contribute to collective agency (electoral outcomes). As I argued in chapter 1, aggregative equality plays a critical role in how we understand the results of a vote as a product of collective agency. Aggregative equality characterizes decision-procedures where the combination of individuals' votes and an appropriate voting rule jointly determine the collective decision or outcome. If we are to interpret voting as a valuable act of collective agency, then, two propositions need to be true: 1) the inputs to aggregation—individual votes—reflect some value of individual agency that is worth aggregating; and 2) the rule that is used for translating votes into electoral outcomes incorporates those votes in appropriate ways. How we understand what it means for a decision to incorporate votes in appropriate ways depends on why we think votes reflect the value of individual agency. Standardly, that reason has something to do with the *information* that votes contain about citizens' preferences over potential options.[3]

To appreciate the significance of these two propositions, it may be useful to consider some (intentionally far-fetched) hypothetical decision-procedures. Instead of voting to make decisions for our community, we might simply ask every citizen to flip a coin. I suspect that in most situations where we use voting to make decisions, we would find the coin-flip procedure objectionable. If voting is preferable to a random coin flip, it is presumably because voting gives people the opportunity to make the outcome dependent on information about their preferences. Alternatively, we might

---

3. See, e.g., Ingham, *Rule by Multiple Majorities*.

imagine surveying citizens on whether they prefer pizza or hamburgers and electing candidate A if pizza is preferred by more people and candidate B if hamburgers are more preferred. In this case, the outcome does incorporate information about citizens' preferences, but not about preferences that are relevant to the decision at hand.

Other decision-procedures might solicit relevant information about individual preferences but incorporate that information in perverse or inappropriate ways. For example, we might choose an outcome that receives the *fewest* votes from individual citizens. Or we might count all votes cast before noon four times, and all votes cast after noon only once. In both of these examples, the collective decision-procedure incorporates individual preferences expressed in votes, and the outcome depends entirely on how people vote, but there is something wrong about the *way* the outcome depends on the vote.

Criticisms of the value of voting as a democratic decision-procedure have disputed both of the propositions needed to describe voting as an act of collective agency and to explain its value. Some critics have argued that the kind of information that gets expressed in citizens' votes does not actually reflect valuable aspects of individual agency. Critics have also argued that even if individual votes are valuable acts of individual agency, voting procedures do not aggregate those votes in a way that preserves their value and transfers it to the outcome. In the remainder of this section I will discuss these two kinds of challenges, beginning with the challenge to aggregation procedures (and consequently to voting's "outputs"), then turning back to the problem with voting's individual "inputs."

THE "OUTPUTS" PROBLEM: SOCIAL CHOICE AND THE IMPOSSIBILITY OF PERFECT AGGREGATION RULES

What is the appropriate way of translating individual votes into collective outcomes? The two examples of inappropriate procedures I offered above point to two generic principles that voting rules should comply with, at least if voting is to constitute an instance of equally shared collective decision-making, as I argued in chapter 1. First, voting rules should treat all votes equally. Second, voting rules should be such that outcomes depend on votes in non-perverse ways, i.e., in accordance with norms of rationality. In the next chapter I will discuss in greater detail how to define these principles and apply them in evaluating voting systems. But this simple and generic formulation is sufficient here to explain the potential "outputs" problem with voting procedures.

The outputs problem refers to the possibility that voting procedures may not translate a set of votes into an electoral outcome in a way that transfers the value of individual votes to that outcome. Unfortunately, we cannot avoid this problem just by designing really good voting rules.

A proper appreciation of the outputs problem is essential for understanding the conditions under which voting procedures contribute to the realization of democratic values. But the nature and extent of the problem is often misunderstood, so it is worth taking some time to explain.

The most significant characterization of the outputs problem comes out of the field of social choice theory. Social choice theory aims to understand how we can make collective decisions in ways that appropriately incorporate information about individual preferences. Social choice theorists characterize properties of decision rules that formalize and standardize our intuitions about what it means to treat individuals' preferences equally and non-perversely. They then examine different aggregation rules—i.e., formulas that determine how a given set of individual preferences translates into a particular collective choice—to determine whether and when different rules exhibit these desirable properties.

The kinds of aggregation problems and formulas that social choice theorists examine operate at different levels of abstraction. Many aggregation rules discussed in social choice theory are not practicable as voting rules. This is because social choice theory serves two purposes: the first purpose is conceptualizing the requirements of aggregative equality (or other values like fairness or coherence); the second is developing tools for evaluating real-life voting or decision rules. These two tasks are related, though—how we evaluate voting rules depends on how we conceptualize aggregative equality. The outputs problem with vote aggregation is a conceptual problem revealed by social choice theory that turns out to have massive implications for the practical task of designing and evaluating democratic voting rules.

A version of the outputs problem with preference aggregation can arise whenever a group of people is trying to choose among more than three options, and when each group member's preferences over the options are taken to have discrete and equal value. When there are only two options, majority rule emerges again and again in democratic theory as the presumptively best decision rule.[4] But majority rule's attractive properties do not straightfor-

4. E.g., Waldron, "The Constitutional Conception of Democracy"; Shapiro, *Politics Against Domination*, 40–44, 50; see also Dahl, *A Preface to Democratic Theory*, 37–38. Majority rule has intuitive appeal, perhaps because, despite its mechanical character, it still resonates with organic metaphors of the body politic (see, e.g., Locke, *Second Treatise of Government*, 52). But majority

wardly generalize when a group faces more than two choices. And true binary choices are rare. Political communities face an inconceivable array of distinct options for exercising public power and arranging our public lives.

When we face collective choices among more than two alternatives, majority rule no longer applies. And it turns out that there is no procedure for aggregating preferences over more than two options that exhibits all of the properties that make majority rule attractive. A large literature in the field of social choice theory includes numerous demonstrations of a general trade-off between equality and collective rationality in preference aggregation.[5] When there are more than two options in a choice set, we cannot even conceptualize, let alone practically implement, a voting rule that will reliably treat individual preferences equally and non-perversely. At least not unless we place restrictions on the kinds of preferences citizens are allowed to express in their votes.

The most famous of these demonstrations is Kenneth Arrow's proof of what he calls the "General Possibility Theorem" (now more commonly known as "Arrow's Impossibility Theorem"). Arrow specified several conditions that we should expect a democratic function for aggregating individuals' preferences over a set of options to meet. First, the aggregation function should yield a complete and transitive social preference ranking. That is, it must identify which outcomes are favored over others. An attractive *democratic* aggregation rule should also satisfy democratic conditions related to how it produces a social preference ranking based on individual inputs. Arrow specifies some minimal conditions that plausibly capture democratic values of equality and collective rationality. These can be labelled: unrestricted domain, independence of irrelevant alternatives (IIA), pareto efficiency (aka unanimity), and non-dictatorship[6] (I will explain the significance of each of these conditions below). In his proof of the General Possibility

---

rule's appeal is not just intuitive. Social choice theorists have repeatedly demonstrated that majority rule exhibits important formal properties that reflect our concerns about the equal and non-perverse treatment of votes. The most important statement of this is May's theorem (May, "Simple Majority Decision").

5. See Austen-Smith and Banks, *Positive Political Theory I*, 25–56 for this formulation of the problem and demonstrations.

6. There are a few variations on Arrow's theorem which specify the conditions somewhat differently. In the first edition of *Social Choice and Individual Values*, Arrow proves the theorem with respect to the conditions of unrestricted domain, IIA, non-dictatorship, positive responsiveness (sometimes also called monotonicity), and non-imposition (Arrow, *Social Choice and Individual Values*, 22–31). However, in the second edition, he includes a note observing that the impossibility condition also holds if monotonicity and non-imposition are replaced with the weaker condition of pareto efficiency. Pareto efficiency captures the underlying concerns of both (in fact, pareto efficiency implies non-imposition) and is also more intuitive and weaker than the monotonicity condition.

Theorem, Arrow shows that for groups of more than two people with more than two options, any preference aggregation rule that reliably yields a complete and transitive social preference ranking will have to violate one of these conditions. What this means is: there is *no* preference aggregation rule that can be relied upon to incorporate preferences in a way that is both equal and non-perverse.

Arrow's assertion that a democratic preference aggregation rule should satisfy all four of these conditions is a reasonable interpretation of what aggregative equality requires. Unrestricted domain formalizes the intuition that an ideal democratic aggregation rule should apply to any set of preferences people might have. IIA and pareto efficiency formalize the idea that an ideal aggregation procedure should be resistant to agenda-manipulation, be positively responsive to changes in citizens' expressed preferences, and ensure victory for any outcome that is unanimously preferred. Finally, non-dictatorship formalizes an extremely minimal version of the desiderata that everyone's preferences be treated equally. If Arrow's conditions do represent necessary minimum conditions for an ideal aggregation procedure, then we are forced to accept that no ideal procedure exists. More importantly, though, it turns out that the trade-off between equality and collective rationality that Arrow's theorem reveals remains even with alternative formalizations of these conditions,[7] and even with weaker requirements on the kinds of outcomes that aggregation procedures must be able to produce.[8]

These results from social choice theory have significant implications for how we understand the value of voting as a collective decision-procedure, and for how we evaluate voting rules. The impossibility of designing a decision rule that reliably exhibits properties of equality and collective rationality means that there is no single benchmark that we can use to assess our voting rules. The outcomes of a vote cannot be fully justified by the voting rule's tendency to track the outcomes that we would get from an ideal decision-procedure, because there is no such procedure.

---

7. Austen-Smith and Banks, *Positive Political Theory I*.

8. Probably the most influential impossibility theorem after Arrow's is the Gibbard–Satterthwaite theorem. Gibbard-Satterthwaite shows that for any group with three or more individuals with well-behaved (complete, transitive) preferences over a choice set with three or more options, there does not exist a rule for aggregating these preferences into a single collective decision that satisfies the normatively desirable conditions of unrestricted domain, non-dictatorship, and strategy-proofness. See Gibbard, "Manipulation of Voting Schemes"; Satterthwaite, "Strategy-Proofness and Arrow's Conditions." Though Arrow's theorem is more famous, Gibbard–Satterthwaite is oriented toward more immediate practical concerns about voting rules.

Some political theorists have argued that the impossibility of defining a perfect aggregation rule means that the outcomes of popular voting simply cannot ever be interpreted as collective decisions, and that we should greatly downgrade the normative significance we attribute to electoral outcomes.[9] I will address these arguments later in this chapter. For now, let me assert that this pessimistic conclusion is too hasty. *The real implication of social choice theory's impossibility theorems is that evaluating voting rules is a messy, contested, and context-dependent process.* Evaluating voting rules, then, is much like evaluating any other political institution. The impossibility results of social choice theory can seem shocking when we first encounter them because voting has so often been justified as a form of either pure or perfect procedural justice.[10] Social choice theory shows us that voting cannot be justified in this way. But the same is also true for most of our political institutions.

In the next chapter, I will say more about how to evaluate voting rules in light of my account of voting's purposes. Here let me say a bit more about how the potential outputs problem pushes us to examine how voting rules operate within a particular context, especially in conjunction with the components of a democratic system that shape electoral agendas and citizens' preferences over them.[11] There is no aggregation rule that can reliably satisfy important democratic conditions of equality and collective rationality regardless of the views that citizens hold. What this means is that it is not possible to take a random group of individuals and use aggregation procedures to determine what choice would most democratically reflect the preferences of that group. But this does not mean that vote aggregation cannot ever instantiate democratic values or yield decisions attributable to the *members of a community*, who are related to one another in many other ways in a complex democratic system.

One possible upshot of evaluating procedures in the context of specific systems is that we can relax one of the conditions on democratic aggregation rules that gives rise to the outputs problem. That is the condition of unrestricted domain. Many political theorists have argued that unrestricted domain is unnecessarily demanding. Recall that an aggregation function satisfies unrestricted domain when it is applicable (and continues to satisfy

9. Riker, *Liberalism Against Populism.*

10. For a comparison of pure, perfect, and imperfect procedural justice, see Rawls, *A Theory of Justice,* 74–75.

11. Mark Warren refers to this as the "collective will formation" problem of democracy, and argues that deliberative practices are particularly important for addressing this problem ("A Problem-Based Approach to Democratic Theory").

other desirable conditions) across any possible set of individual "preference profiles" over the relevant options. Unrestricted domain holds that an aggregation procedure must be able to treat preferences equally and non-perversely for any logically possible set of preferences that citizens might have. But some democratic theorists have suggested that this condition is too strict. Perhaps a satisfactory aggregation rule need only be applicable over the sets of preference profiles that individuals actually have or are likely to have.

For example, when it comes to political questions, the members of a community often seem to exhibit what are called "single-peaked" preference profiles. To understand what this means, imagine that all the options are arranged along a single line, and each person's first choice is represented as a point on that line. This first choice is called the "ideal point." If a person has a single-peaked preference profile, then for any two options to the same side of their ideal point, they will never prefer the option that is farther from their ideal point.[12] A community can be said to have single-peaked preference profiles when all of its members have single-peaked preferences over the same ordering of options along a line. The idea that describing someone's position on a left–right or progressive–conservative political spectrum helps us predict their political preferences on many issues assumes that people typically have single-peaked preferences. When conservative voters prefer conservative candidates to moderate ones, and moderate candidates to those further to the left, while progressives have the opposite ranking and moderates prefer more centrist candidates to those at either extreme, we can say that they have single-peaked preference profiles.

As it turns out, there is a decision-procedure, known as the Condorcet Rule, that will satisfy IIA, pareto efficiency, and non-dictatorship over a domain restricted to single-peaked preference profiles; in fact, it is a rule that happily extends the intuitively appealing idea of majority rule.[13] If enough individuals in a community do have single-peaked preferences, then it is possible to identify a way of aggregating those preferences that treats them all equally and non-perversely. If we think citizens usually have single-peaked

12. Single-peaked preference is sometimes described more straightforwardly in terms of distance from the ideal point (i.e., a person has single-peaked preferences if they always prefer options that are closer to their ideal point over options that are further away). But this definition is unnecessarily narrow. Single-peaked preferences can be asymmetric. That is, I might have more tolerance for deviation from my ideal point in one direction over the other.

13. Black, *The Theory of Committees and Elections*, 14–34. But see also Moulin, "Generalized Condorcet-Winners for Single Peaked and Single-Plateau Preferences"; Dasgupta and Maskin, "On the Robustness of Majority Rule."

preferences, then we might think that voting rules designed to approximate the Condorcet Rule are justifiable procedures to resolve political disagreement.

The domain of single-peaked preference profiles is just one example of a domain of preference profiles for which it is possible to design a voting rule that treats votes equally and non-perversely, though it is the most intuitive and probably the most politically relevant. The idea that policies, parties, or candidates can usually be coherently located on a common left–right political spectrum seems to enjoy wide acceptance, as does the idea that voters will usually prefer policies or parties that are closer to their "ideal point" on that ideological spectrum than those that are farther away. To the extent this is true, then voters' preferences can be described as single-peaked. When the presence of multiple salient issue or value dimensions in a society makes it hard to place candidates and parties on a single political spectrum, though, it is less likely that citizens will have single-peaked preferences.

Single-peaked preferences do not eliminate the potential outputs problem with aggregation. Rather, they reveal one way in which context may matter a lot for evaluating voting rules. But scholars debate whether we can reliably expect citizens to have single-peaked preferences over political outcomes, especially since political outcomes and issues can be evaluated on many dimensions. As I will argue later in this chapter and in subsequent chapters, there may be reasons for thinking that single-peaked preferences can be induced with appropriate background conditions, but it is extremely implausible that they will emerge naturally or invariably. This is especially true since political entrepreneurs will generally have an incentive to destabilize single-peaked preferences when they do exist by introducing new issues or new ways of framing issues that enable popular support to shift to different alternatives.[14]

Furthermore, there may be countervailing reasons to avoid maximizing the prevalence of single-peaked preferences. There may also be good reasons not to choose decision rules that do the best job of picking Condorcet winners or otherwise satisfying Arrow's conditions. Some things that we might want from a voting rule, such as sensitivity to intensity of preference, may introduce more risk of some violations of collective rationality. In the next two chapters, I will dive further into these questions about how we navigate these and other trade-offs when we evaluate voting rules (chapter 3), and preference-formation and agenda-setting processes (chapter 4).

---

14. Miller and Schofield, "Activists and Partisan Realignment in the United States"; cf. McKelvey, "Intransitivities in Multidimensional Voting Models."

The potential outputs problem with aggregation does not mean that voting isn't a valuable exercise of collective agency. But it does set limits on the normative weight we can expect voting to bear, and once again, reveals why a *systemic* perspective on voting's connection to democracy is essential. Whether, and in what way, vote aggregation contributes to democracy depends not only on the formal properties of the voting rule, but also on how that rule performs in a given democratic system. Voting procedures and practices cannot stand alone. They must contribute to and mesh with, among other things, democratic processes of agenda-setting and preference formation.

THE "INPUTS" PROBLEM: INAPPROPRIATE, UNINFORMED, INAUTHENTIC, OR UNSTABLE PREFERENCES

At the beginning of this section, I suggested that two propositions must be true if voting is to be understood as a valuable act of collective agency. First, individual votes reflect the value of individual agency, and second, the rule that is used for translating votes into electoral outcomes incorporates individual votes in appropriate ways. I have just described a challenge to the second proposition arising from social choice theory's impossibility theorems. As I have argued, this challenge need not be interpreted as a falsification of that proposition. Rather, it helps us understand the conditions under which it might be true.

A different set of concerns about the value of voting calls into question the other proposition crucial to the justification of voting as a collective decision-procedure: that individual votes reflect the value of individual agency. The claim here is not just that some information about citizens' preferences is relevant to democratic decision-making. This proposition makes the stronger claim that citizens' votes contain the relevant information about their preferences. This proposition is the foundation for the belief that democratic decisions can be built from individual votes, taken as they are. Unlike other participatory acts or expressions of public opinion, we do not expect that citizens' votes will be filtered, tempered, completed, rationally reconstructed, or even "refined and enlarged"[15] before they are brought to bear on public decisions.

---

15. Madison, "The Federalist Number 10." Madison argued that elected government acts to refine and enlarge public opinion "by passing them through the medium of a chosen body of citizens." But when it comes to the decision of who should govern, and any other decisions on which citizens vote directly, no such refinement occurs.

The challenge to the proposition that citizens' votes contain valuable information about their preferences comes primarily from empirical scholarship on political behavior. At the extreme, skeptics of the value of voting argue that when we really understand what kinds of things affect how people vote, we cannot affirm the proposition that individual votes bear the value of individual agency. Consequently, we should be more cautious about interpreting electoral outcomes that are constructed from individual votes as products of collective agency or of attributing value to them.

Most accounts of the value of human agency allow that not everything people do reflects that value equally. Common sense would suggest that deciding to murder someone is not a valuable act of human agency. Nor is deciding to surrender my wallet to a mugger at gunpoint or deciding to assist a terrorist organization after months of psychological torture and indoctrination. More controversially, impulsive decisions that violate my self-imposed policies, or that are at odds with my deeply held values, might also fail to represent valuable acts of human agency. At least they seem to reflect less valuable forms of agency than decisions that better align with my more reflective judgments. When I mindlessly snack on whatever food is in front of me despite my resolution not to do so, or when I give in to my toddler's whining despite my belief that he needs firmer boundaries, these actions do not reflect my agency in the same way as when I consciously choose snacks for pleasure or nourishment, or when I discipline my child in ways I believe to be in his long-term best interests. Many skeptics of the value of voting have argued that the kinds of preferences that get expressed in people's votes are analogous to one or more of these examples—they do not actually reflect what it is we value about human agency.

Scholars of democracy have raised a variety of concerns about the value of individual votes. These concerns can be grouped into four categories. First, some critics of voting have argued that individual votes lack value insofar as they reflect *bad* values or preferences.[16] Some people simply hold racist or otherwise bigoted views about how society should be run, and these views shape the decisions they reach at the ballot box. The democratic election of the Nazi Party in Weimar Germany, for example, shows that individuals' votes may reflect preferences or judgments so vile that they simply have no value and need not be accounted for in collective decision-making. While this is sometimes pitched as an argument against democracy in general, it is a particular challenge for voting. Voting is based on the proposition that

16. Brennan, *The Ethics of Voting*, 68.

individual votes, taken as they are, should determine outcomes. The treatment of votes does not depend on their content or motivation. Other democratic practices, such as deliberation, do not adopt such a neutral stance toward the content of citizens' contributions, and so are less vulnerable to this kind of concern.

Second, some scholars point to a *misalignment* between the decisions that individuals express in their votes and the deeply held values or goals they aim to promote with their votes.[17] This misalignment can occur when citizens' voting decisions are based on irrelevant or false information, or when significant cognitive biases affect their interpretation of the information they do have. Research in political behavior has demonstrated that misinformation, cognitive bias,[18] and seemingly irrelevant cues like name-recognition,[19] ballot order,[20] inferred ethnicity,[21] and attractiveness[22] probably affect some voting decisions. Skeptics of the value of voting point to this research to argue that even if we think that our processes for collective decision-making ought to respect and accommodate citizens' ability to act in pursuit of their own values or goals, this does not give us reason to value individual votes.[23]

Scholars debate the frequency and severity of these apparent irrationalities in voter decision-making.[24] Many have also argued that features of the political environment and the design of political institutions affect citizens' ability or incentives to learn about politics, and to effectively use the political knowledge that they do have.[25] Some of the concerns about citizens' competence to make voting decisions that align with their deeply held values are overstated. Others are, at least in principle, remediable. In any case, this

17. E.g., Caplan, *The Myth of the Rational Voter*.

18. Huber, Hill, and Lenz, "Sources of Bias in Retrospective Decision-Making"; Healy and Lenz, "Substituting the End for the Whole."

19. Kam and Zechmeister, "Name Recognition and Candidate Support."

20. Ho and Imai, "Estimating Causal Effects of Ballot Order."

21. Thrasher et al., "Candidate Ethnic Origins and Voter Preferences."

22. Banducci et al., "Ballot Photographs as Cues."

23. Brennan, "Medicine Worse Than the Disease?," 42–46.

24. E.g., Fowler and Hall, "Do Shark Attacks Influence Presidential Elections?"; Prior and Lupia, "Money, Time, and Political Knowledge."

25. In some conditions, voters may be able to effectively use heuristics and cues to cast meaningful votes with little information (see, for example, Bowler and Donovan, *Demanding Choices*). Other scholars have demonstrated that institutional context can affect citizens' ability and incentives to acquire political information (Shineman, "Effects of Costly and Incentivized Participation"). And vote-choice is more likely to reflect policy preferences, rather than other (seemingly irrelevant) factors when parties' policy decisions are more differentiated (Ansolabehere, Rodden, and Snyder, "Strength of Issues").

debate illuminates the key point that the value of voting as a democratic decision-procedure always depends on the character of the background context in which citizens form their political preferences and judgments.

A third kind of concern that has been raised about the value of individual votes relates to their *authenticity*. Experimental research on how people form political beliefs and preferences suggests that they might be easily manipulated by political elites. Citizens often seem to adopt positions on policies or even adopt ideological labels in response to cues from political elites (especially party leaders).[26] Elites can also manipulate citizens' political decisions indirectly through their influence over the information environment. Even without censoring information or circulating false propaganda, political elites can affect citizens' political decisions if they are able to determine how questions are framed, or successfully "prime" citizens to focus on certain aspects of the questions, or to evaluate them from certain perspectives, such as partisanship.[27] If citizens are unconscious of the role that cue-taking or priming plays in their political decision-making, or if they are unable to resist it, then it might seem that the value of the agency reflected in individual votes is at least attenuated.

The opportunity for elites to manipulate voters' judgments is also, in principle, somewhat remediable. But that manipulation is possible in the first place points to a fourth concern that skeptics have raised about the value of voting's inputs, which is the *instability* of people's preferences. Most citizens do not seem to have stable preferences about many of the political issues that come before us.[28] Ask us a similar question with different wording or in a different context, and we may give very different answers. Unstable and context-dependent political preferences are not just a practical result of incomplete information or susceptibility to elite manipulation. Context-dependent preferences are probably just more endemic to human decision-making than traditional models of rationality allow. Humans simply cannot consider all feasible options nor all relevant dimensions of evaluation simultaneously.[29]

26. See esp. Lenz, *Follow the Leader*; cf. Achen and Bartels, *Democracy for Realists*.

27. Chong and Druckman, "Framing Theory"; Slothuus and de Vreese, "Political Parties, Motivated Reasoning, and Issue Framing Effects."

28. Although the extent of preference instability on salient and long-standing political issues has probably been overstated (Ansolabehere, Rodden, and Snyder, "Strength of Issues").

29. Moreover, in value pluralist frameworks, it turns out to be formally impossible for individuals to identify a stable and justifiable ranking of alternatives when there are multiple dimensions of evaluation because of a problem analogous to the social choice problem (Patty and Penn, *Social Choice and Legitimacy*).

Our preferences then appear context-dependent because in different contexts we are prompted to consider different aspects of the choice.

The prevalence of unstable preferences sharpens traditional complaints about tyranny of the majority. Electoral majorities cannot justify public decisions to those who disagree with them simply by demonstrating that minority objections are outweighed by the judgments or preferences of the greater number. Electoral outcomes depend in part on how political questions are framed, in what order they are considered, and myriad other factors that shape how people think about their voting decisions. Those who find themselves in the minority might reasonably complain that their preferred outcome would have prevailed had the deliberative environment been just a little different. And crucially, this complaint will always be available so long as humans' preferences remain sensitive to context and framing.

It might be tempting to regard unstable preferences as a lamentable limitation of human cognition, but this would be a mistake. Flexible and context-dependent political preferences can also grease the wheels of human interaction. When we form our preferences in ways that are responsive to our social context we are better disposed to act together with others, and better able to converge on a shared course of action. Malleable preferences facilitate collective action in practice. They allow for the emergence of agreement without the time-consuming, arduous, and often futile process of rational persuasion. And even when we don't agree, our preferences can shift into forms that are more comprehensible to each other and even more amenable to meaningful aggregation.[30]

We should not interpret concerns about the objectionability, irrationality, manipulability, or instability of citizens' preferences as conclusive evidence that voters' expressed preferences have no value. But these concerns do point to a deep, unavoidable question that any account of the value of voting must answer: why should we allow the aggregation of any particular set of votes determine the political outcomes we all must live with?

Once again, answering this question depends on an appreciation of popular voting's place within a democratic system, and the way that voting procedures interact with the other democratic practices and institutions that compose this system.

Individuals cannot be assumed to have complete, coherent, and stable preferences over the full range of possible courses of action a polity might

---

30. List et al., "Deliberation, Single-Peakedness, and the Possibility of Meaningful Democracy."

pursue. But given the challenges of acting together, that might be a good thing. Meanwhile, individuals can and do form meaningful preferences over a narrower (and more cognitively manageable) agenda, especially when considering a small set of widely recognized evaluative criteria or issue dimensions. In the right sort of discursive environment (the characteristics of which I discuss in chapter 4), we can affirm these preferences as valuable reflections of individual agency. Under these conditions, the aggregation of citizens' preferences as expressed in their votes can instantiate a valuable form of collective agency and provide a justifiable foundation for public decision-making.

The potential challenges to the value of voting's inputs and outputs that I have canvassed in this section must be taken seriously by anyone who wishes to preserve and enhance the value of modern electoral democracy. But taking these challenges seriously does not require denying the value of popular voting as an application of aggregative equality and instantiation of collective agency. Instead, as I have argued in this section, these challenges help us to better understand *how* we should evaluate voting institutions and practices. In particular, they show that we cannot refer to a universal ideal voting procedure as the benchmark against which electoral institutions and practices are assessed. The value of any particular voting procedure will depend on the political context in which it is applied. Evaluating voting procedures and practices, then, cannot be done in isolation. When considering, for example, how to reform our electoral institutions, we must always do so with an eye to the democratic system of which they are a part. Furthermore, as I will argue in the remaining chapters of this book, an appreciation of the potential problems with voting's inputs and outputs is necessary to understand *how* we should assess the democratic character of agenda-setting and preference-formation processes and their relationship to the practice of popular voting.

Against Minimalism

Some democratic theorists have argued that the challenges to the value of democratic voting procedures that I discussed in the previous section reveal the popular association between voting and "rule by the people" to be untenable, posing an apparent dilemma for democratic theorists. If we wish to articulate a conceptually coherent definition of democracy, they argue, we may keep either the traditional, value-laden idea of democracy as rule by the people or the particular institutional arrangements and practices that have come to be identified with modern democracy, but not both. In this section I briefly critique the "minimalist" response to this dilemma, most famously articulated in the works of Joseph Schumpeter and William Riker. Minimalists like Riker and Schumpeter respond to the challenge of specifying the relationship between voting and democracy by retaining the popular identification of democracy with elections, but jettisoning most of democracy's normative content. Voting in elections, on the minimalist view, is the most important practice of democracy, but this is not because it enables collective self-rule or any related value.

In *Capitalism, Socialism, and Democracy*, Joseph Schumpeter argues that the "classical doctrine of democracy" is fundamentally flawed because it defines democracy as both a goal—"to achieve the common good"—and a method for achieving that goal—"through the will of the people expressed in elections."[31] But, Schumpeter argues, the method of elections cannot achieve the goal of realizing the common good. Schumpeter anticipates many of the findings of late 20th- and 21st-century political science research in his criticism of ordinary citizens' political competence. Because political decisions are so far removed from their everyday lives, he argues, ordinary citizens don't have the incentive or opportunity to form rational preferences about political questions. Rather, citizens' political preferences tend to be indefinite, irrational, impulsive, and easily manipulated by political elites.[32] Under these conditions, Schumpeter argues, the classical doctrine of democracy is simply untenable.

While Schumpeter rejects the "classical" account of democracy because voters are manipulable, William Riker rejects it because voting systems are manipulable. Since electoral outcomes often depend on which voting rule is used, and since there is no ideal aggregation process against which voting rules can be assessed, the choice of voting rules (including, for example, rules for weighting votes, districting, and agenda-setting) may reflect the strategic considerations of political elites, more than any thoughtful consensus on appropriate democratic procedures. Consequently, Riker argues, it would be inappropriate to imbue any particular electoral outcome with normative weight as "the will of the people."[33]

31. Schumpeter, *Capitalism, Socialism, and Democracy*, 250.

32. Ibid., 256–63.

33. Riker, *Liberalism Against Populism*, 236–38. Riker draws two conclusions from his discussion of the social choice literature: first, that "outcomes of voting cannot, in general, be regarded as accurate amalgamations of voters' values" (236) and second that "the outcomes of any particular method of voting lack meaning because often they are manipulated amalgamations" (238). He

Having dispensed with the normatively loaded idea that the will of the people is expressed through elections, Schumpeter observed a need to develop a clear definition of democracy that could be evaluated, like any other institution, according to its effects. Schumpeter thus argues that democracy ought to be understood exclusively as a method, proposing to define it as: "that institutional arrangement for arriving at political decisions in which individuals acquire the power to decide by means of a competitive struggle for the people's vote."[34] Likewise, Riker proposes a renewed emphasis on electoral institutions without the normative baggage of "rule by the people." According to Riker, what is left of democratic elections in the wake of social choice theory is simply "an intermittent, sometimes random, even perverse, popular veto."[35] Elections might occasionally result in the removal of a corrupt or tyrannical official, but this removal should not be attributed to an act of collective agency on the part of citizens. According to Riker, the removal of would-be tyrants is best attributed to the element of randomness introduced by any election.

Minimalists' basic criticisms of the idea that vote aggregation alone is sufficient to reveal or create a popular will are sound. But minimalists are wrong to conclude that *any* account of voting's relationship to an ideal of collective self-rule must be incoherent.[36] Aggregation on its own cannot bear the full normative weight of democratic ideals. But aggregation need not stand on its own, and democratic theory has offered a wide array of alternative models to the "classical" or "populist" interpretations of democracy that Riker and Schumpeter critique.

Readers with minimalist sympathies might argue that the minimalist move of rejecting the value-laden ideal of democracy as rule by the people is motivated as much by a set of practical political concerns as by the demands of theoretical coherence. Both Schumpeter and Riker worried that, in the absence of well-defined institutional content, the ideal of democracy as rule

---

concludes: "Social choice theory forces us to recognize that the people cannot rule as a corporate body in the way that populists suppose" (ibid., 244).

34. Schumpeter, *Capitalism, Socialism, and Democracy*, 269.

35. Riker, *Liberalism Against Populism*, 244.

36. Riker explicitly acknowledges a limited conclusion by framing his argument as a rejection of the populist "interpretation of voting." By delimiting his conclusion in this way, Riker leaves room, in theory, for the possibility that the people might meaningfully be said to rule through other democratic institutions. But it is clear from Riker's discussion of the centrality of voting, in which he claims that meaningful elections are a sufficient condition for democracy, and that the three core values of democracy should be understood as things that make elections meaningful (*Liberalism Against Populism*, 5), that he thinks the normative significance of democracy rests on the normative significance of voting.

by the people was vulnerable to misguided (and often dangerous) populist interpretations; populist leaders could then claim a democratic mandate to justify curtailing liberal rights. Schumpeter observed that terrible acts of violence have been committed under the banner of democracy. Contemporary democratic theories that might be characterized as minimalist also join Schumpeter and Riker in the view that the pursuit of a vague and overdemanding ideal of democracy could jeopardize the real accomplishments of electoral institutions.[37]

The minimalist argument for abandoning the concept of "rule by the people" is most plausible when it is based on the practical consequences of using such a concept, rather than on a critique of the concept itself. But this practical argument also fails for two reasons. First, that a value-laden concept may be distorted and abused to justify harmful, even evil, political programs is not sufficient reason for abandoning the concept. That the ideal of democracy can be used in this way is due to its attractiveness as an ideal. Anything that people believe has enough value to be worth sacrificing for can become a banner under which we transgress or dismantle other things of value. This practical argument for revising the concept of democracy, then, still depends on the minimalists' argument that the ideal of "rule by the people" is incoherent or so unrealistic as to be normatively useless or in fact, not worth sacrificing for.

Second, theorists cannot simply get rid of democracy's positive valence by fiat. Even if common usage of the term shifts toward the minimalist definition focused on electoral institutions, the word democracy retains its normative baggage. Minimalists may hope to offer a purely descriptive definition of democracy, allowing an objective assessment of the merits of democratic institutions. But even if, in theory, the minimalist definition of democracy is value-neutral, in practice, people still read normative significance into the word. Consequently, the electoral institutions it refers to get saddled with a normative weight that they cannot bear alone.

Voting at the Margins of Democratic Theory

Democratic minimalism is only one response to the apparent dilemma posed by the two challenges I discussed in the first section of this chapter. In responding to concerns about the inputs and outputs of aggregation, some democratic theorists have ended up grasping the other horn of the dilemma.

---

37. See, e.g., Cain, *Democracy More or Less*; Rosenbluth and Shapiro, *Responsible Parties*.

These democratic theorists focus on interpreting the idea of "rule by the people" and the values it contains while rejecting, or at least de-emphasizing, their association with electoral institutions and the practice of popular voting. In the past decade or so, systemic analyses of democracy, like those I alluded to in the previous chapters, have revived discussions of voting and elections within academic democratic theory. But at the same time, explicit and radical skepticism about voting's democratic value has become increasingly widespread and mainstream. Though voting skeptics still represent a minority of democratic theorists, academic democratic theory has not really provided a satisfactory counter to this skeptical position. It is worth, then, taking a moment to appreciate why popular voting was neglected by political theory for some time and what is missing from existing defenses of voting. The aim of this section and the following is to dispel remaining doubts that the practice of popular voting as I described it in chapter 1 can continue to play a central role in a sophisticated conception of democracy.

The most striking feature of normative democratic theory in the past half century has been a shift in attention toward political speech and discourse. This trend has been called the "deliberative turn" in democratic theory.[38] This renewed focus on political speech within democratic theory has often been framed through a contrast with a traditional or popular focus on voting.[39] Early and influential contributions to deliberative democratic theory, while never denying the value or importance of voting, conspicuously chose to de-emphasize this practice in their theories. Instead, they highlighted underappreciated, but equally essential discursive practices. The deliberative turn, then, simultaneously offered a corrective to a simplistic identification of democracy with voting and an answer to minimalist skepticism about democracy's status as a normative ideal.

38. For a brief intellectual history of the deliberative turn, see Floridia, "The Origins of the Deliberative Turn."

39. Even though deliberative democratic theorists have recently embraced a more systemic perspective, the rhetorical contrast between voting and speech, or between deliberative and aggregative conceptions of democracy, still appears in work by prominent scholars. In her recent Tanner Lectures, for example, Seana Shiffrin highlights the limitations of elections relative to a free speech culture. She does not argue that elections are without value, but argues that their limitations must be emphasized "as a corrective to the fixation on elections as the sine qua non of democracy" (Shiffrin, "Speaking Amongst Ourselves," 147). And in a recent article, Simone Chambers, in characterizing "deliberative constitutionalism," asserts: "this view of democracy places imperative emphasis on the public sphere as the locus of legitimacy rather than voting" (Chambers, "Democracy and Constitutional Reform," 1123).

Efforts to elevate political speech within theoretical and popular conceptions of democracy, and to loosen the identification of democracy with popular voting, are motivated by two kinds of arguments which respond to the limitations of voting as democratic practice. For one thing, as I argued in the first section of this chapter, the democratic value of vote aggregation relies on the background conditions against which it takes place. Both the value of individual votes and the democratic character of voting procedures—their ability to simultaneously satisfy equality and collective rationality—depend on the communicative processes by which citizens form their political preferences.

Shifting attention to political speech (and especially to deliberation) provides a way of avoiding the minimalist conclusion that democracy is an incoherent political ideal.[40] Proponents of a deliberative conception of democracy, for example, have argued that the social choice problem is less troubling when judgment aggregation follows a democratic process of judgment formation. When citizens' preferences or judgments are formed in a process of deliberative justification, they incorporate a concern for political equality into the content of citizens' preferences *before* they are aggregated.[41] Electoral minorities have less reason to complain about the arbitrariness of aggregative procedures if their equal political standing has already come into play, restricting the range of potential outcomes to those that can be justified on the basis of reasons acceptable to all.

Even when we have adequately addressed concerns about aggregation's inputs and outputs, though, aggregative equality still has its limitations, and some democratic theorists argue that the aggregative interpretation of equality is too "thin" to bear the normative weight of democracy.[42] A second impetus behind the deliberative turn, then, was a desire to theorize democratic practices that reflect alternative conceptions of political equality. Alternative interpretations of political equality, including the version of deliberative equality I described in chapter 1, may operate in the attitudes that citizens have toward one another, or in more complex patterns of social

40. On deliberative democracy as a critical response to minimalist democratic theories, see Floridia, "The Origins of the Deliberative Turn," 46–47.

41. In response to Riker's criticism of popular democracy, Joshua Cohen argues "once the deliberative institutions are in place, and preferences, convictions and political actions are shaped by them, it is not clear that instability problems remain so severe as to support the conclusion that self-government is an empty and incoherent ideal" (Cohen, "Deliberation and Democratic Legitimacy," 28).

42. E.g., Young, *Inclusion and Democracy*, 20–21.

relationships. Unlike the aggregative interpretation of equality, alternative interpretations of equality do not necessarily require symmetry in the treatment of individuals, as epitomized in the equal counting of votes. They might then be better able to assess a complex array of political relationships that citizens have with each other.

It is also worth noting that efforts to focus more on political speech and to de-emphasize voting are not limited to theories of deliberative democracy. Many contemporary democratic theorists who reject the deliberative ideal of reasoned justification similarly critique the narrow focus of aggregative conceptions of democracy. Theorists of "agonistic" democracy, for example, who believe that deliberative democratic theory does not give enough weight to the centrality of conflict in politics, often argue that democracy requires giving attention to the character of the processes by which conflicts become politically salient. For agonistic democratic theorists, political equality does not necessarily turn on the exchange of reasoned justifications or the content of citizens' political judgments, but it does require space for citizens to contest and politicize dominant social narratives.[43] Like deliberative democrats, then, agonistic democrats turn the critical gaze of normative democratic theory away from voting to examine the character of a broad range of institutions and environments that affect political speech acts.[44]

The rhetorical effort to distinguish democratic discourse from voting and to hold up alternatives to aggregative equality has pushed voting to the margins of political theory. Though most democratic theorists acknowledge that popular voting and elections are an essential part of a democratic system—as a way of supporting and structuring deliberation[45] or dealing with "residual disagreement"[46]—the nature of that role and the evaluative standards we should use to assess voting practices have been substantially

43. See, e.g., Disch, "Toward a Mobilization Conception of Representation"; Disch, "Democratic Representation and the Constituency Paradox"; cf. Mouffe, *The Democratic Paradox.*

44. See Wingenbach, *Institutionalizing Agonistic Democracy.* Many theorists of agonistic democracy argue that agonism is inherently resistant to institutionalization. This does not mean that the quality of agonistic democracy does not depend on the character of political institutions; rather it means that it is difficult to formulate a list of attributes agonistic institutions should have, since any given set of political arrangements will always exclude some lines of contestation.

45. Joshua Cohen, for example, suggests that expecting deliberation to end with voting can mitigate the pressure to reach consensus for the wrong reasons (Cohen, "Reflections on Deliberative Democracy," 331). Henry Richardson has also suggested that voting can provide a valuable form of closure "firming up and formalizing an implicit agreement" arising from deliberation (Richardson, "Democratic Intentions," 366).

46. Cohen, "Deliberation and Democratic Legitimacy," 23.

undertheorized. Even where they are discussed, the standards for assessing voting practices are largely treated as an afterthought. For example, in their classic deliberative democracy text, *Democracy and Disagreement,* Amy Gutmann and Dennis Thompson claim that majority rule will still "have a prominent place in a deliberative perspective." But to defend this, they simply gesture at the aggregative interpretation of political equality to justify such a voting procedure, and offer no discussion of the serious concerns around constructing, let alone applying, such a standard.[47] Most seriously, insofar as deliberative democrats acknowledge the necessity of voting procedures, it is not clear that they mean to defend popular voting; discussions of voting within deliberative democratic theory often fail to distinguish between the role of voting in legislatures or other representative bodies, and the role of *popular* voting.[48]

The lack of a clear theoretical account of the role of popular voting in modern democracies has consequences for the kind of normative guidance contemporary democratic theory has to offer citizens and political leaders. At the extreme, it opens the door to radical criticisms of electoral democracy and claims that we should not, in fact, value popular voting. One proponent of participatory pluralism, citing many of the same concerns that motivated the "deliberative turn," asserts "mass enfranchisement as a form of political participation is virtually meaningless in modern societies."[49] More recently, in defending a new paradigm of "open democracy," Hélène Landemore has argued that "elections may legitimately be seen as preventing rather than facilitating genuine rule by the people."[50] Similar sentiments can be found in other popular and academic defenses of lottocracy.[51]

---

47. Gutmann and Thompson state simply that "no one has yet proposed a decision-making procedure that is generally more justified than majority rule (and its variations)" (Gutmann and Thompson, *Democracy and Disagreement,* 131). Joshua Cohen similarly appeals to traditional accounts of the virtues of majority rule to justify majority-rule voting as the appropriate way to end deliberation in the absence of consensus (Cohen, "Deliberation and Democratic Legitimacy" 23). Thomas Christiano has criticized this move, arguing that—given the conception of political equality they are working with—deliberative democratic theory does not provide a convincing account of why minorities should accept the outcomes of aggregative procedures when reasoned deliberation does not result in consensus (Christiano, *Rule of the Many,* 38).

48. Gutmann and Thompson do implicitly make this distinction elsewhere when they discuss the value of electoral accountability. But it is not clear that popular voting for elected representatives is meant to play the same "prominent role" in democracy as voting that settles residual disagreement (Gutmann and Thompson, *Democracy and Disagreement,* 142–51).

49. Olsen, *Participatory Pluralism,* 5.

50. Landemore, *Open Democracy,* 43.

51. E.g., Guerrero, "Against Elections"; Van Reybrouck, *Against Elections.*

The emergence of radical skepticism about voting's value demonstrates why political theorists must not take voting for granted anymore. It is absolutely true that voting cannot do all of the normative work it is sometimes expected to do in a democracy. It is likewise true that popular voting is not the only, nor even the most important, political practice in modern democracies and that the democratic value of voting procedures depends on the background conditions—especially the speech environment—against which they take place. But if we think that voting and elections will continue to play a vital role in large democracies, even as we strengthen deliberative practices, we need to better understand how voting—given its distinctive strengths and limitations—can fit within the rich and sophisticated models of discursive democracy that contemporary democratic theorists favor.

In the previous chapter I described the value that popular voting practices contribute to modern democratic systems. The two challenges to aggregative equality have led some critics to question voting's democratic credentials. But as I have argued in this chapter, acknowledging that popular voting's role is embedded within a democratic system and relies on a democratic discursive environment can make the special role of popular voting compatible with a clear-eyed account of democracy that acknowledges the challenges to aggregations inputs and outputs.

It is worth taking a few pages, though, to acknowledge some potential worries that may remain about whether the central role for popular voting that I have just described really is compatible with non-minimalist democratic theories. In the next section, then, I revisit some of the major features of the account of popular voting I offered in chapter 1 and show how they are consistent with the key insights of the deliberative turn in democratic theory.

Voting in a Democratic System

In this book, I argue for adopting a systemic approach to understanding and evaluating democratic institutions and practices like voting. The full value of democratic practices cannot be appreciated by viewing them in isolation. Democratic systems contain numerous institutions and practices that complement each other by instantiating different facets of democratic values and by reconciling them in different ways. Some democratic practices also create preconditions for other practices to work as they should, and some counteract the weaknesses of other practices. Democratic institutions and practices that seem incomplete or flawed when viewed in isolation can, when viewed as part of a democratic *system,* still be understood to contribute to a full and rich realization of democracy's value.

In the first chapter, I argued that a systemic approach to evaluating democractic institutions reveals how voting's valuable role within contemporary democratic systems is constituted by some of the very features that reform-minded democratic theorists have found most objectionable. Democratic theorists have criticized the popular norm of universal participation, and the special attention devoted to elections in the public eye. These aspects of the contemporary practice of voting, they claim, can only be justified by an untenable belief that voting is more important to democracy than other forms of participation or democratic practices. I have argued, though, that these features of popular voting are essential to the practice and enable it to contribute to democratic values as it does. Voting creates recurrent, salient moments in which citizens experience themselves as parts of the whole, as standing on equal terms with their fellow citizens and contributing to a collective project. Voting cannot realize the values associated with this experience, nor contribute to the functions that it serves, if it is unable to reliably elicit widespread participation and serve as an object of shared attention.

Maintaining a special and central place for voting in an ethic of citizenship and in popular conceptions of democratic participation can be compatible with—and, in fact, strengthen—a broadly pluralist conception of democratic participation. The practice of popular voting instantiates aspects of democratic values that may be missing from other modes of participation. Moreover, the practice of popular voting, as constituted by an expectation of universal participation, performs essential functions even within a complex, pluralist democratic system. These functions include: socializing citizens into their role as equal political agents; creating an environment that is favorable toward mass mobilization and organization; and disciplining public officials to be attentive to the entire citizenry.

As recent systemic approaches to democratic theory have begun to recognize, these functions are no less essential in conceptions of democracy that emphasize speech and deliberation. Even if our ethic of citizenship prizes participation in deliberative or contestatory discourse, citizens must somehow be socialized into the role of active citizen. Citizens must internalize the belief that politics is *for them* and develop a disposition to pay attention to, think, and talk about politics. A discursive democracy also requires an environment that enables citizens to translate talk into political action. That is, a discursive democracy requires an environment that facilitates mobilization and organization. And, of course, a discursive democracy requires representatives disciplined to listen to political discourse across all sectors of society.

The fact that voting's centrality in popular conceptions of citizenship performs functions that are vital in a discursive conception of democracy is not yet sufficient to demonstrate that a special status for voting is compatible with discursive views of democracy. It remains to be shown that the practice of popular voting accomplishes these functions in a way that fosters valuable forms of democratic discourse. Theorists of discursive democracy might worry that the special emphasis on voting socializes people into a model of citizenship that is ill-adapted to their preferred conception of democracy, or that it disciplines public officials to be attentive to the wrong things.

Concerns of this sort can be sorted into two broad categories. First, some have argued that the special emphasis on voting constructs and perpetuates a conception of citizens as consumers (choosers) rather than producers of democratic governance.[52] Second, some might worry that voting casts citizens as self-interested egoists. Both of these concerns suggest that even if voting does perform the functions I described in chapter 1, it does so in a way that actually undermines a full and complex realization of democratic values in a political system. The role into which citizens are socialized and the political environment created by moments of popular voting might be too narrowly tailored around an aggregative conception of equal citizenship.

Minimalist theories of electoral democracy lend credence to these concerns, especially to the first, as they often explicitly compare voters to consumers.[53] But these two concerns are also fundamentally rooted in the formal features of voting procedures. The worry that voting casts citizens as consumers emerges because voting always involves evaluating a fixed agenda. The worry that voting encourages an excessively individualist, even egoist view of citizens is grounded in the fact that voting procedures uncritically accept individual contributions. It might, then, seem that citizens are not expected to *internalize* democratic values like equality. Critics worry that placing a practice with these features at the center of our models of citizenship stacks the deck in favor of individualist or consumerist understandings of democratic citizenship.

The model of democratic citizenship that popular voting promotes depends on more than its formal properties, though. In chapter 1, I argued

---

52. See, e.g., Cohen, "Money, Politics, and Political Equality."

53. Schattschneider, *Party Government*, 60; Schumpeter, *Capitalism, Socialism, and Democracy*, 263; see also Pateman, *Participation and Democratic Theory*, 13–14.

that the practice of popular voting in modern democracies is constituted by three essential features: the application of aggregative equality, the expectation of universal participation, and the creation of spectacular participatory *moments*. We cannot evaluate voting practices without appreciating how these three features operate together to create a singular democratic experience for citizens.

Once we adopt this holistic view of voting as a practice, the concern that voting socializes citizens into an excessively individualist model of citizenship seems less plausible. While it is true that formal voting procedures impose no requirements on the content of democratic votes, the expectation of universal participation, the reality of high turnout, and the salience of mass participation on Election Day counteract the apparent individualism of the vote.[54] It simply doesn't make sense for individuals to view voting as an egoistic act. The reality of mass participation constructs voting as thing that is done with many others. And viewing voting as a means of achieving political ends requires citizens to consider the kinds of ends that can unite a winning coalition. That citizens in fact do reason about voting in this way is revealed by the prevalence of strategic voting on the basis of candidate or party viability. Moreover, survey evidence suggests that people think of voting more in sociotropic than egocentric terms,[55] and that citizens who exhibit more sociotropic thinking are more likely to vote.[56]

Some deliberative democratic theorists may still worry that voting practices do not encourage citizens to cultivate attitudes of reciprocity. Deliberative democrats view reciprocity as a core component of an ethic of democratic citizenship. In common language, reciprocity indicates a moral attitude of give and take—a willingness to make return for what has been given. Gutmann and Thompson argue that reciprocity in a democracy requires that "citizens recognize and respect one another as moral agents."[57] Deliberative democratic theory interprets the principle of reciprocity to mean that citizens owe each other reasoned justification for the exercise of power:[58] being responsive to my fellow citizens as co-creators of democracy requires offering them reasons that they can understand and might be able

---

54. Of course, this demonstrates how much the experience of voting matters to its functions!
55. Bruter and Harrison, *Inside the Mind of a Voter*, 193.
56. Ibid., 133.
57. Gutmann and Thompson, *Democracy and Disagreement*, 14.
58. Ibid., 14.

to accept, and in turn, to consider the reasons they offer me.[59] The lack of content requirements, and the privacy of the actual act of voting may make it appear that voting does not cultivate democratic reciprocity.[60] Since individuals don't have to offer reasons for their votes, they may vote on the basis of reasons that do not respect the free and equal status of their fellow citizens.

Deliberative reason-giving is not the only way that citizens express and that communities reinforce democratic reciprocity, though. Reciprocity entails a willingness to give and take, and in a democracy in particular, this means a willingness to participate on equal terms with each other. Nowhere is this willingness put to the test more than in popular voting. The chance of a single voter changing an electoral outcome approaches zero very quickly as the size of the electorate increases. Some democratic theorists decry voting because it entails such minimal individual influence, but it is precisely this minimal influence that makes voting a good opportunity to exhibit democratic reciprocity. In many forms of participation, individuals may hope to be more influential just because their fellow citizens are less influential. When I vote, though, I know that this will not be the case. Voting thus offers a clear opportunity for me to exhibit reciprocity by embracing the manifestly equal agency of my fellow citizens.[61]

Of course, the extent to which popular voting avoids promoting an egoistic conception of citizenship depends on what the practice of popular voting actually looks and feels like to citizens. One of the main arguments of this book is that conversations about electoral system design and reform need to be more attentive to the way that citizens experience Election Day and the act of voting. Democratic theorists who imagine changing popular attitudes toward voting with the hope of creating space for more deliberative or collaborative modes of participation should recognize that doing so will also change the experience of voting. Eroding the expectation of universal participation and diminishing the public attention that voting receives may well have the perverse effect of reducing the salience of collective activity in the practice of voting. Efforts to displace voting from the center of popular

59. Other democratic theorists follow Gutmann and Thompson in identifying reason-giving as core to reciprocity. Corey Brettschneider, for example, defines reciprocity as "a commitment to reason giving as a central obligation and entitlement of citizens" (Brettschneider, *Democratic Rights*, 25).

60. For a critique of secret voting on these grounds, see Brennan and Pettit, "Unveiling the Vote."

61. Joshua Cohen argues, conversely, that in voting, we count the interests of others, "while keeping our fingers crossed that those interests are outweighed" (Cohen, "Reflections on Deliberative Democracy," 335). There is a difference, though, between hoping that most other citizens share my judgment and hoping that I will somehow be able to exert unequal influence on political life.

conceptions of citizenship could result in making it *more* like the egoistic experience its critics believe it to be.

The second concern—that voting socializes citizens into a consumerist model of citizenship—is probably more apt than the first. The core of this concern is that placing a practice in which citizens merely choose from among a set menu of options reinforces a belief that the creative work of politics is rightly limited to an elite group of political "producers." These political elites invent and market political products—candidates, policies, platforms, ideologies, and slogans—and citizens' role is to decide which of these products to vote for, just as consumers decide which products to buy. Some democratic theorists have argued that this is a good model for democratic citizenship.[62] The problem is that, in light of the potential input and output problems with voting that I described at the beginning of this chapter, such a consumerist model of democratic citizenship is not adequate to justify the exercise of public power, one of the core purposes of a conception of democracy. If democracy is to adequately justify public decisions to those who disagree, it must extend beyond the aggregation of votes and also say something about the conditions in which political agendas and preferences are formed.

Many democratic theorists (including myself!) believe that the ideal of democracy requires that citizens must have real opportunities to contribute to the creative work of politics. This requires first and foremost an open society with a free speech culture and elected officials disciplined to attend to a broad range of concerns and to emerging political claims and ideas. Beyond merely formal opportunities, a robust, thriving democracy requires that citizens be socialized into a conception of citizenship in which they see it as appropriate and possible that they might become involved not merely in making a choice among a set of options, but also in defining the choice set and helping to shape the public meaning of political decisions. I argued in chapter 1 that voting plays a crucial role in this socialization by ensuring that citizens keep a foot in the door of politics. But critics might worry that the way this socialization is achieved reinforces an idea that voters are only choosers and not producers.

This concern, I think, cannot be entirely avoided, especially in a large and liberal society. But as with the concern about egoist voting, it might be mitigated by different voting practices. When it comes to creating a popular voting practice that socializes citizens into a more-than-consumerist model of citizens, it will be crucial to think about how electoral systems shape and

---

62. E.g. Schattschneider, *Party Government*; Rosenbluth and Shapiro, *Responsible Parties*.

interact with party systems. A number of democratic theorists have recently argued that party politics—and particularly practices of partisanship—are crucial to understanding how citizens relate to the processes of agenda-setting and preference formation that make collective decision-making possible, meaningful, and democratically justifiable.[63] Yet despite the intimate link between electoral systems and parties—and between voting and partisanship in empirical political science—recent normative theory on party politics has had relatively little to say about voting. In subsequent chapters, I bring this book's theory of voting into conversation with recent work on partisanship. In chapter 4, I discuss the normative frameworks that we should use to evaluate democratic party systems, arguing that we should prize party systems and forms of party organizations that mobilize a broader range of citizens into political action. In chapter 5, I argue that the visibility of parties and party politics on Election Day helps create a voting experience that enables citizens to see themselves not just as choosers, but as active political agents.

Conclusion

In chapter 1, I argued for adopting a systemic approach to evaluating democratic institutions and practices, like popular voting. This chapter has shown that the value of voting cannot be understood *except* through a systemic perspective on democracy. Voting procedures justify political outcomes to those who dislike them because the procedures are thought to instantiate key political values. More specifically, voting procedures are thought to justify political outcomes because the procedures reconcile equality and popular sovereignty. But whether a voting procedure can, in fact, reconcile these two key values of democracy through the aggregation of individual votes depends on the context in which it is applied. The democratic value of voting (and the justifiability of electoral outcomes) depends on two things: 1) the agenda-setting processes that determine which options will appear on the ballot for citizens to vote on; and 2) the discursive environment within which citizens form their political preferences. Adequate attention to the democratic system within which we practice popular voting can alleviate concerns about the value of electoral inputs and outputs that I discussed in the first section of this chapter. But the value of voting practices and our ability to attribute electoral outcomes to citizens' exercise of equal agency

---

63. E.g., Muirhead, *The Promise of Party in a Polarized Age*; Rosenblum, *On the Side of Angels*; White and Ypi, *The Meaning of Partisanship*.

depends on a background of democratic discourse that enables citizens to form meaningful political judgments and that is not dominated by illicit forms of political power.

Many democratic theorists have argued that these insights mean that popular attitudes toward voting—which treat voting as the central participatory practice in a uniquely justifiable form of political rule—are untenable. Some scholars have suggested that this means we must revise our beliefs about the normative weight that democracy can be expected to bear. Others have argued that we must redirect public attention toward other sorts of democratic practices, especially practices of deliberative or contestatory discourse.

I have argued that both of these approaches to voting are mistaken. The special place of voting in popular conceptions of citizenship is defensible not because it *reflects* the importance of voting, but because it helps to *constitute* a practice that instantiates unique values and performs essential functions in modern democracies. It is true that voting's value is greatly attenuated without robust practices of democratic discourse. At the same time, though, the democratic value of political discourse is greatly attenuated without the functions performed by a practice of popular voting with the key features I have described.

Popular voting and discursive practices are mutually supporting in a democratic system. Democratic deliberation and other forms of democratic speech are essential for making the aggregation of votes reflective of democratic values. At the same time, voting performs vital functions by socializing citizens into their role as a democratic agents and by creating favorable environments for political campaigns aimed at informing, persuading, organizing, and mobilizing the mass public.

Of course, this mutually supporting relationship isn't guaranteed. It requires that democratic practices and the institutions that support them be maintained so that they best fulfill their purposes within this democratic system. In the next three chapters of this book, I turn to the tasks of evaluating and improving voting practices. Chapter 3 synthesizes the arguments from the first two chapters to outline some key principles for would-be reformers. Chapter 4 takes up the question of how we should think about agenda-setting processes that make voting meaningful, with a special focus on the evaluative standards for party politics. Chapter 5 discusses how elections should be administered to provide an optimal voting experience. In the conclusion I raise some questions that we should consider as we think about the future of voting in a rapidly changing social and technological environment.

3

Evaluating Voting Systems

The first chapter of this book provided an account of the core features of popular voting and showed how the civic ritual that is constituted by these core features contributes to the realization of democratic values in modern societies. Moments of mass popular voting dramatize simultaneously the dignity of *each* citizen's contributions to democracy and the collective agency of *all* citizens acting together. They do so by cultivating an expectation of universal participation—that all citizens contribute to collective decision-making at the same time, in the same way—and by employing a concrete and transparent, aggregative form of equality. Elections, and other occasions for popular voting, mark special moments in which acts of collective agency on equal terms become important objects of shared attention for the entire community.

Taken together, these aspects of popular voting constitute a practice that contributes to the realization of democratic values in unique and important ways. Elections provide predictable, periodic, and salient occasions for individuals to perform their roles as citizens, and for the community to express its endorsement of an ideal of equal and shared political agency. The distinctive expectation of universal participation in elections also performs essential functions that support other parts of modern democratic systems. These include socializing citizens, mobilizing new or underserved constituencies, and creating a favorable environment for inclusive organizing and political innovation. I have argued that this account of popular voting's distinctive purposes provides a normative grounding for many contemporary practices surrounding voting. In particular, it explains and justifies the special attention that elections receive in popular discourse about democracy.

At the same time, my account of popular voting's role in modern democracy also offers resources for critical evaluation of the way we vote. This account allows us to better understand what kinds of electoral institutions and practices enable popular voting to best fulfill its distinctive purposes. The next three chapters of this book take up this critical project. In this chapter, I discuss in broad terms some of the considerations that should shape how we evaluate voting practices and reform projects. Then, in chapters 4 and 5, I demonstrate how these evaluative tools can illuminate specific normative questions about the design of electoral institutions and the administration of elections.

The first three sections of this chapter are organized around the three core features that I have argued constitute the practice of popular voting in modern democracies: the expectation of approximately universal participation; the application of aggregative equality; and the creation of spectacular democratic "moments." Focusing on each of these features in turn brings to the fore different considerations that are relevant to evaluating existing and proposed reforms. It is worth emphasizing again, though, that the value of voting practices is produced by the way that these three features work together. Throughout the chapter, I highlight ways that the evaluative considerations brought to light by different features of voting interact with one another.

The first section discusses the significance of the expectation of universal participation. Here, I argue that because this expectation is a constitutive component of the valuable practice of popular voting, it provides grounds for both the popular belief in a duty to vote and mandatory voting laws. I also argue that reformers focused on increasing opportunities to vote, especially by making voting more convenient, should be more attentive to the effects of these reforms on actual turnout rates.

The second section discusses the significance of the *moments* created by voting practices. I argue that the values of popular voting outlined in chapter 1 point toward a greater need for would-be reformers and political leaders to attend to the experience of voting. The context in which citizens vote shapes our interpretation of what we're doing as much as the formal properties of the voting procedure. Where, when, how, and with whom we vote matters.

The third section discusses the application of aggregative equality. In chapter 2, I argued that evaluating voting as an application of aggregative equality requires looking at more than the formal properties of the voting rule. The potential problems with both the "inputs" and the "outputs" of voting that I discussed there mean that the value of voting as a procedure for aggregating expressed preferences, and the appropriateness of interpreting electoral outcomes as a product of collective agency, depends on how the voting rule works within the context in which it is applied. In the third section of this chapter, I discuss what this insight means for evaluating existing and proposed voting systems.

In the fourth and final section of this chapter, I briefly discuss how understanding popular voting's distinctive role in democracy might inform debates about the *kinds* of offices or questions we ought to put to a popular vote. Should popular voting be used exclusively for electing representatives, or should we also vote directly on substantive ballot measures? What sorts of choices enable the practice of popular voting to best realize its democratic value? These questions have received a great deal of attention from democratic theorists and reformers, and so I devote less time to them in this book than to other, relatively neglected, issues in electoral democracy. However, my account of voting's value can still offer important insight into these perennial questions. I discuss the different ways that popular voting's value manifests in elections versus referenda and I articulate some general principles that should guide institutional design in this area.

The evaluative considerations I discuss in this chapter are not meant to provide a blueprint for the design or reform of electoral systems. Even given the similarities in the role that popular voting plays across most large-scale democracies, this role may fit into democratic practices in very different ways. In part for this reason, many features of well-functioning voting systems are underspecified and context-dependent. This chapter aims to illuminate some underappreciated or misunderstood considerations that are relevant to evaluating voting practices in nearly all contemporary polities. But these considerations may lead to different conclusions about the merits of particular norms or institutional arrangements depending on how such reforms fit together with other aspects of a community's democratic practice.

Universality and the Distinctiveness of Voting

Perhaps the clearest normative guidance to be found in my account of popular voting arises from its emphasis on the standard of universal turnout. Understanding the value of special occasions on which all citizens are expected to participate strengthens the justification for a civic duty to vote, which has been the subject of some philosophical skepticism. The significance of universal participation also strengthens the justification for mandatory voting laws and suggests that electoral reform efforts should focus not only on access to the polls and the opportunity to vote, but also on actual turnout.

Philosophers and political theorists have offered several justifications for the widely held belief that citizens in electoral democracies have a duty to vote. Many of the most plausible quasi-consequentialist justifications, though, can only ground such a duty under narrow conditions;[1] they don't really justify anything like the ordinary view of the duty to vote. And any plausible justification for the common view of the duty to vote also seems to ground an extensive and excessively demanding bundle of other civic duties.[2] The inability of existing accounts of the duty to vote to explain why voting should be distinguished from other participatory acts as the object of a civic duty has been a significant source of skepticism about the "folk" belief in the duty to vote.[3]

The expectation of universal participation helps to constitute voting's distinctive role in contemporary democracy. This fact can explain why voting differs from other desirable forms of participation, and it can supply the grounds for a special and general duty to vote. This explanation does not rely on any claim that voting is a more important, valuable, consequential, or efficacious form of political participation, nor that voting is uniquely expressive of democratic values or commitments. The duty to vote can be justified by the value of the practice of popular voting, which is constituted

---

1. For example, according to Alvin Goldman, even if they know that their votes will not *change* electoral outcomes, morally motivated actors have reason to want to be part of a group that is causally efficacious in bringing about a good outcome. But Goldman's argument can't explain why a citizen should vote if she recognizes no moral difference among the potential electoral outcomes, or if her preferred candidate has no chance of winning (Goldman, "Why Citizens Should Vote," 217; see also Tuck, *Free Riding*, 54). Alex Guerrero's argument that individuals have a moral reason to vote to increase the better candidate's "manifest normative mandate" is subject to similar limitations (Guerrero, "The Paradox of Voting and the Ethics of Political Representation"). More recently, Julia Maskivker has argued that the singular duty to vote should be understood as an instance of a Samaritan duty—because the stakes of elections are very high and the costs of contributing to morally superior outcomes are quite low, voting is a special Samaritan duty (Maskivker, *The Duty to Vote*). This reasoning does not plausibly apply to all elections in which citizens widely believe there is a duty to vote, though.

2. See Jason Brennan's critique of a Downsian explanation for the duty to vote as a form of "social insurance" for democracy (Brennan, *The Ethics of Voting*, 24). A similar concern also applies to Eric Beerbohm's argument that voting is required for citizens to avoid complicity in the unjust actions of their representatives (Beerbohm, *In Our Name*, 76–77).

3. Brennan, *The Ethics of Voting*, 66; Lomasky and Brennan, "Is There a Duty to Vote," 82.

by an expectation of universal participation. The extent to which elections contribute to a valuable democratic system depends on how closely they achieve or approximate universal turnout, and on how well the community is able to maintain the *expectation* of approximately universal turnout over time. The civic duty to vote need not be derived directly from moral principles (democratic or otherwise). Rather, the duty to vote is one of the norms that constitutes a valuable democratic practice.[4]

A similar line of reasoning can strengthen the justification for mandatory voting laws against criticisms that they inappropriately (and inaccurately) imply that voting is uniquely necessary for democracy,[5] and that they contribute to a superstitious preoccupation of voting at the expense of other valuable forms of participation.[6] Mandatory voting laws do not rely on claims that voting is either uniquely necessary or more valuable than other forms of participation. Instead, mandatory voting laws can be justified by the particular ways that occasions of approximately universal participation contribute to contemporary democratic systems. Mandatory voting laws strengthen informal expectations of universal participation around elections. And contrary to the worries that they fetishize voting, mandatory voting laws can also highlight the extent to which voting in elections is just one piece of a broader democratic practice: when turnout is high and popular voting is performing its role well, citizens are better able to recognize that addressing remaining flaws in democracy requires attention to the non-electoral aspects of democratic practice.[7]

Justifying the imperative to vote is not the only way in which the expectation of universal participation bears on the evaluation of voting systems. Electoral reformers have a large toolkit of strategies for increasing access to the polls. Public discussions about the goals of such reforms, though, tend to focus almost exclusively on the importance of equal opportunity to vote. Reforms that have the greatest effect on diminishing the material cost of voting will be most preferred using this criterion. But while material opportunity to vote is certainly essential, realizing the full value of popular voting also depends on actual turnout. The effect of an electoral reform on actual turnout rates (both overall and among different sub-communities) should be considered one of the most important criteria for evaluating electoral reforms.

4. Chapman, "There Is a Duty to Vote."
5. Brennan, "Medicine Worse Than the Disease?," 31.
6. Lever, "Compulsory Voting: A Critical Perspective," 908.
7. For a more extensive version of this argument, see Chapman, "The Distinctive Value of Elections and the Case for Compulsory Voting."

It might seem that by prioritizing opportunity or material access, actual turnout would follow, but a cursory look at the evidence on so-called "convenience voting" belies this idea. Different sorts of reductions in the material cost of voting can have very different effects on turnout and many of these effects are small.[8] Convenience voting may sometimes even have perverse side effects that decrease turnout[9] or increase turnout only among people with the highest propensity to vote, exacerbating existing biases in the electorate.[10] I will discuss these concerns in greater detail in chapter 6. Here the point I want to make is that focusing on equal opportunity tends to lead to an overemphasis on the material costs of voting. But the costs of voting are not the only relevant factors driving participation. It is equally important to consider the positive reasons that citizens have for accepting those costs. Citizens' decisions to vote or not to vote are often influenced by factors like how voting (or citizenship more generally) fits into their personal sense of identity, how much they have internalized the belief in the duty to vote, and how much they believe that their contribution is of value to the community. These are not exogeneous features of human psychology, but may be affected directly or indirectly by electoral laws and institutions. They may also be affected by the broader political environment that electoral systems help to shape.

Attending to the *Experience* of Voting

One of the core functions of popular voting is to shape how citizens view themselves and their relationship to democracy: to help citizens develop and maintain the attitudes, perspectives, and dispositions of "citizens" rather than those of mere "subjects."[11] This means that evaluating the functioning of electoral institutions and practices requires special attention to how citizens *experience* elections and the act of voting. At their best, elections encourage citizens to perform and internalize their identities as equal agents in a shared project of democracy. The expectation and reality of universal participation discussed in the previous section play major parts in shaping this experience. But many other features that define the character of voting as a public moment can also affect how citizens experience the act of voting. These range from electoral administration policies regarding the method by

8. Blais, "What Affects Voter Turnout?"; Gronke et al., "Convenience Voting."
9. Kousser and Mullin, "Does Voting by Mail Increase Participation?"
10. Berinsky, "Perverse Conquences."
11. For the classic statement of the distinction between "citizen" and "subject" attitudes, see Almond and Verba, *The Civic Culture*.

which citizens vote and the environment in which they do so, to the common tropes in election news coverage, to the ways that employers, churches, and schools acknowledge the occasion. When evaluating voting systems we must consider how citizens experience elections as political *moments*, and the effect of these moments on citizens' attitudes and dispositions.

This argument about the importance of how citizens experience the act of voting has some parallels to "educative" arguments for democracy. Democratic theorists like John Stuart Mill and Carole Pateman have suggested that giving citizens meaningful opportunities to participate in public decision-making will lead to their having a higher estimation of their own capacity to shape their environment (a greater sense of efficacy), and to a better understanding of how human agency shapes social conditions.[12] Mill also argues that participating in government decision-making can have broad benefits for character development, leading citizens to adopt more principled and public-spirited reasoning in their deliberations.[13]

Educative arguments for democratic participation, though, tend to emphasize objective features of the decision-making power that citizens are granted, so that educative benefits of participation are viewed as increasing in the amount of control that individuals exercise over their social environment (which is a function of both the stakes of the decisions they make, and the extent to which they share control over the decision).[14] Critics of electoral democracy often critique voting as a poor vehicle for the educative benefits of democracy. While the stakes of elections may be quite high, the control over decision-making is shared to such an extent that individual citizens often feel they have effectively no control at all. Some skeptics suggest that, far from yielding Mill's imagined educative benefits, this structural feature of voting generates "rational ignorance"[15] and other pathological aspects of spectator citizenship.[16]

The primary function of voting is not to provide general educative benefits of the sort that Mill or Pateman imagined, though. Criticisms of the educative potential of elections miss the mark when they overlook the distinctive role of voting in democratic practice. First, the function of voting is not to socialize citizens into their own individual agency, but specifically into

12. Pateman, *Participation and Democratic Theory*, 35.
13. Mill, *Considerations on Representative Government*, 121–23.
14. See, e.g., ibid., 118–19.
15. Achen and Bartels, *Democracy for Realists*, 9.
16. Schumpeter, *Capitalism, Socialism, and Democracy*, 261; Brennan and Lomasky, *Democracy and Decision*, 32–41.

the shared agency of a democratic citizen. To this end, it is a feature of voting, not a bug, that individuals do not exercise meaningful control qua individuals. Elections—as moments of approximately universal participation—do not just manifest to citizens the value of their own efficacy and contributions to democracy. They also make salient how their contributions have radically equal value to those of their fellow citizens. Voting is not about what I, alone, can do, but about what we can do together.

A second problem with the critique of voting's educative potential is that, in focusing on structural features of electoral systems (and the minimal effect of individual votes), it neglects many other aspects of elections that can affect how citizens experience elections and the act of voting. If behavioral economics and psychology have taught us nothing else, they have taught us that individuals are highly sensitive to their environments. The ways that elections are conducted—when and where citizens vote; whom they vote with; what the ballot looks like; how polling places are designed; who staffs polling places—all these things may frame the experience of voting and its effect on attitudes and norms of citizenship in ways that can't be explained with traditional rational choice models.[17]

In chapter 5, I explore in greater detail how these considerations about the effect of the Election Day experience can provide concrete (and sometimes surprising) normative guidance on contemporary debates about electoral administration. Here, though, I want to emphasize that regardless of whether this sensitivity to environmental conditions is viewed as normatively good, bad, or neutral, it does appear to be an endemic feature of human psychology, and therefore something that any realistic theory of democracy should account for. One of the distinctive values of voting, as I have characterized it, is to harness citizens' sensitivities to their environments to prime the sorts of "citizen" attitudes and dispositions that enable successful democratic agency. Evaluating voting practices and reform proposals thus requires attention to the often subtle ways that they shape the experience of voting.

Aggregative Equality and the Evaluation of Voting Rules

The third key feature of popular voting practices that I highlighted in chapter 1 is the application of aggregative equality. Aggregative equality is realized in decision-procedures that invite individuals to express their preferences

---

17. Rutchick, "Deus Ex Machina"; Bruter and Harrison, "Understanding the Emotional Act of Voting."

over a given choice set and that use an egalitarian and rational decision rule for translating any set of expressed preferences into a collective decision. What distinguishes aggregative equality from other interpretations of equality (e.g., deliberative, relational, or substantive equality) is that individuals' expressed preferences and the decision rule jointly *determine* political outcomes, regardless of the content of those expressed preferences or the attitudes, and regardless of the status or other personal features of the participants.

Of the three core features of popular voting that I have emphasized in my account, aggregative equality is the only one that is common to voting practices in other institutional contexts like legislatures and juries. Perhaps as a result, discussions of voting in democratic theory have tended to focus on understanding the virtues and limitations of aggregative equality and identifying its requirements. Understanding how the aggregative interpretation of equality informs evaluations of popular voting, though, requires more than just considering the general idea of aggregative equality in voting procedures. The application of aggregative equality in popular voting interacts with its other features to produce a distinctive set of democratic values and to perform a distinctive set of functions. Evaluative standards for popular voting must be sensitive to this interaction. They must also be sensitive to versions of the inputs and outputs problems that I discussed in chapter 2 that are most likely to arise in the context of popular voting, and to how this context bears on the normative significance of these problems and the available solutions to them.

Discussions about the requirements of aggregative equality in voting have tended to focus on the formal properties of voting rules—that is, the functions that take a given set of ballots cast and translate them into an electoral outcome. Plurality rule, in which the option receiving the most votes wins, is a common voting rule. Other voting rules, like ranked choice voting, may take ballot inputs with more information, and therefore use complicated functions to determine the outcome.[18] And some voting rules, as in proportional representation systems, use relatively simple inputs but create hybrid outcomes.

As I discussed in chapter 2, it is not possible to design a perfect voting rule that always satisfies the various conditions we might want to impose on it. Evaluating the application of aggregative equality, then, requires examining how voting rules perform *in context*. Additionally, when we evaluate the

18. For a helpful discussion of "ballot structure," see Maloy, *Smarter Ballots*.

application of aggregative equality in the context of popular voting we must consider the distinctive purposes of this practice. In chapter 1, I highlighted three virtues of aggregative equality in the context of mass democracy: transparency, replicability, and scalability. Matters of electoral administration, such as voting technology, staffing and bureaucratic structure, counting practices, audits, and reporting practices can all affect the extent to which voting procedures exhibit these virtues. But formal voting rules can also exhibit these virtues to greater or lesser degrees. The operation of equality in complex voting rules may be less transparent to voters, and these voting rules may also be harder to scale (particularly if they require collecting more information on a ballot). Some voting rules may make election audits more difficult or even impossible.

In the remainder of this section, I discuss how we should approach the evaluation of voting rules in light of the particular purposes of popular voting practices. This discussion primarily concerns how to navigate the trade-off between equality and collective rationality that generates the potential outputs problem with preference aggregation. As social choice theorists have repeatedly demonstrated, voting rules that treat votes equally always have the potential to produce outcomes that are perversely responsive to citizens' expressed preferences. How often and how severely this potential is realized depends on both the formal properties of the voting rule and on how it operates within a particular context. But the potential will always be present, and so, if the aggregative interpretation of equality is to retain its democratic value and if it is to yield useful evaluative standards for popular voting procedures, we need some resources for navigating the trade-off between equality and collective rationality in voting rules. These resources can be found by looking at the distinctive features and purposes of popular voting.

I will argue that we can best navigate this trade-off between equality and collective rationality by distinguishing synchronic and diachronic aspects to the evaluation of voting rules. Synchronic evaluations are made by looking at a given application of a voting rule at a given time. Diachronic evaluations are made by looking at the performance of a voting rule across many applications over time. I will argue that some criteria for voting rules should be evaluated synchronically. That is, there are some principles that we will want our voting procedures to comply with each and every time they are used. Having some standards that a voting rule must always meet makes the operation of aggregative equality more transparent to citizens. For criteria that we think should be evaluated synchronically, it makes sense to think about how these criteria can be designed into the voting rule: that is, we will want to look for formal properties that a voting rule might have so that the satisfaction of the principles is guaranteed (at least so long as the voting rule is correctly applied).

Much of the evaluation of voting rules should take a diachronic perspective, though. Fully assessing voting rules requires looking at how they perform over time. Voting rules form part of a system in which salient agendas emerge, citizens form preferences over the agenda items, and votes are solicited and counted to generate an outcome. We will want it to generally be the case that a voting rule which treats people equally will minimize perverse outcomes, given the preferences that people tend to form over the agendas that actually emerge.[19] We will also want to consider the ways that voting rules (and electoral systems generally) shape the processes by which citizens form their preferences. The voting rule needs to operate in conjunction with other components of the democratic system so that it contributes to equally shared agency over time.

SYNCHRONIC EVALUATION: EQUALITY AND POPULAR SOVEREIGNTY

Given the trade-off between equality and collective rationality, I argue that, at least when it comes to popular voting, the satisfaction of basic equality conditions should be evaluated synchronically (and therefore should be prioritized in the formal design of the voting rule). Collective rationality, on the other hand, should be primarily evaluated diachronically.

This is not to say that equality is more important than collective rationality. Rather, it is more important to evaluate equality synchronically because *individual* violations of norms of collective rationality are usually less threatening to collective agency, and also less threatening to the value of popular voting, than are individual violations of equality. Collective agency can persist despite occasional violations of norms of collective rationality just as individual agency can persist despite occasional—even frequent—failures of individual rationality. The flexibility of citizens' preferences may also make occasional failures of collective rationality less worrisome if citizens revise their preferences in light of political outcomes. If citizens come to endorse electoral outcomes, or at least to accept them as products of their collective agency, then it seems reasonable to regard them as compatible with the polity's

---

19. To be justifiable, a voting rule must in this regard perform at least as well as non-electoral benchmarks like random chance (or the decisions of a dictator), and it must not obviously perform worse than alternative egalitarian voting rules.

collective agency, even if they came about via a process that violated norms of collective rationality. This is similar to the way that an artist might come to identify with a "happy accident." Failures of collective rationality are, of course, threatening to collective agency if they are persistent or severe and erode citizens' acceptance of electoral outcomes. But these threats can only be assessed by looking at the performance of a voting rule over time. The mere possibility that a voting rule may sometimes aggregate votes in a way that violates standards of collective rationality does not on its own undermine the value of popular voting.[20]

Failures of formal equality, though, do pose a more immediate threat to the value of popular voting. This is true for a few reasons. First, we can expect failures of equality to be more transparent than failures of collective rationality. Whether a vote-counting procedure treats individual votes equally can be assessed by looking at the outcome and at the votes cast. But when it comes to collective rationality, what we care about is not just how the procedure treats votes actually cast, but how it would respond to hypothetical vote changes. Failures of collective rationality can be harder to recognize because identifying them often requires conjecture about counterfactuals. (Consider, for example, how the significance of "spoiler" candidates in plurality-rule elections, like Ross Perot in the 1992 US presidential election, is debated.) Uncertainty around individual violations of collective rationality diminish the impact that these violations have on the social meaning and expressive value of elections.

Second, the formal possibility of violating a norm of equality casts a longer shadow than the possibility of collective irrationalities. This is because even where inequalities of influence do not actually occur, they may nevertheless create status inequalities. Consider, for example, a voting rule that assigns tie-breaking powers to the holder(s) of a hereditary office. Even if the tie-breaking power rarely needs to be exercised, the mere existence of the rule may make it harder for citizens to view the outcome of *any* election as the product of their equally shared agency. In a democratic system, various instances of unequal influence in decision-making may (in theory) balance out over time. But given voting's distinctive role in rendering salient and concrete the equal agency of each citizen and of all citizens, and given popular voting's nature as a focal point of public attention, it is particularly important that popular voting represents a transparent application of equality.

20. This is true specifically for popular voting. The value of voting procedures used in other contexts (e.g., juries and legislatures) may be less robust to individual failures of collective rationality.

To avoid the production of status inequalities, the most important formal property of a voting rule is anonymity: how the voting rule treats a particular vote should not depend on who casts the vote. This condition clearly rules out schemes like J. S. Mill's plural voting, and any other that weights votes according to hereditary office or personal characteristics. But it also rules out some more contemporary proposals that have otherwise egalitarian motivations. The anonymity condition would rule out schemes in which historically oppressed minorities are granted extra voting power or a targeted veto,[21] or in which children were extended fractional votes.[22]

Even though synchronic evaluations encourage designing equality into the formal properties of the rule, synchronic evaluations and their normative prescriptions are still sensitive to context. This is seen most clearly in the question of whether the anonymity condition rules out special districts for some minority groups (for example, New Zealand's Maori set-aside, or the mandate to create majority–minority districts in some US states). The answer to this question depends on whether we view legislative elections in systems with districts as really being many separate elections or as constituting a single national (or statewide) election with a distributed structure. If they are best understood as many separate elections, then we can think of each election as having its own rules to be evaluated separately, and we need not see the principles for drawing electoral districts as part of the voting rule itself. But if we think of legislative districts as creating a distributed structure for a single election, then we should evaluate the principles for drawing districts as part of the voting rule. These kinds of evaluations, then, will depend on broader features of the political system and public conceptions of legislative representation.

Though a full argument for this claim is outside the scope of this book, I believe that in the United States, we should view legislative elections— especially for the House of Representatives—as a single election with a distributed structure. This perspective is warranted by popular opinion and voting behavior (in which national partisanship typically dominates constituency-specific concerns). It is also warranted by the reasoning behind

---

21. E.g., Schwartzberg, *Counting the Many*, 175–79. I am not defending anonymity as a condition of *any* democratic voting rule, but specifically of voting rules used in the context of mass popular voting. Voting rules used in legislatures, special commissions, juries, or other decision-making bodies might well have different properties in light of the different functions that voting serves in these contexts.

22. Rehfeld, "The Child as Democratic Citizen."

the creation of majority–minority districts in the first place: the design of electoral districts can violate voting equality.[23]

Of course, requiring the creation of majority–minority districts is not the only way we can violate anonymity in our districting principles, and simply eliminating that requirement will not necessarily produce a voting rule more in line with aggregative equality. Racial gerrymandering to dilute minority voting power also violates the anonymity principle. So does partisan gerrymandering, and even principles that aim to promote partisan balance, proportionality, or competitiveness.[24] All of these principles call for designing a voting rule that assigns votes to different parts of its distributed structure—that treats votes differently—based on the personal characteristics of the voter or their expected vote choice. The application of a *transparent* and *concrete* standard of equality matters to the special purposes of popular voting more than it does to other democratic practices, and the anonymity principle is a key part of what makes aggregative equality so easy to recognize. This means that we have strong reason to look for alternative solutions to the inequalities created by racial and partisan gerrymandering that are consistent with the anonymity principle. One possible approach is to adopt voting rules that avoid the districting problem altogether and allow voters to sort themselves into constituencies. Lani Guinier, for example, has argued for a system of cumulative voting, which would allow intense

23. In the landmark Supreme Court case that prompted subsequent increases in the number of majority–minority districts drawn in the United States, *Thornburg v. Gingles*, the majority opinion of the court established a test for when an electoral map impairs the ability of minority voters to participate as equals in the election. The test includes consideration not only of the racial composition of a jurisdiction, but also consideration of historical patterns of racialized voting (among other things): Thornburg v. Gingles, 478 U.S. 30 (1986). Though it does not deploy the language of anonymity, the court's holding indicates that the design of electoral districts violates voting equality precisely when it violates anonymity—assigning voters to districts based on their expected voting behavior. But to diagnose and remedy these violations of anonymity, the court's test also makes reference to expected voting behavior: majority–minority districts are required where a minority group is not only large and geographically compact, but also "politically cohesive" (Thornburg v. Gingles, 478 U.S. 30 (1986), 68). Satisfying this standard, then requires that the design of electoral districts violate anonymity—assigning citizens to districts based on who they are and how they are expected to vote. Subsequent court decisions have complicated this picture of voting rights jurisprudence. For example, in *Shaw v. Reno*, the court held that race cannot be the "deciding factor" in the design of a district, in part on the basis that voters can be expected to have distinct constituent interests tied to geography: Shaw v. Reno, 509 U.S. 630 (1993). The rather muddled state of jurisprudence on redistricting and voting rights might be attributable to a muddled concept of representation underlying the system of legislative districts in the US (and other similar systems). See Guinier, *Tyranny of the Majority*, 119–37.

24. Cf. Guinier, *Tyranny of the Majority*, 127–37.

minority coalitions to concentrate their voting power to elect a favorable representative if they wished, without presuming in advance how anyone will vote,[25] while still allowing for fluidity in choice. Others have argued for more standard forms of proportional representation on similar grounds.[26]

In addition to the anonymity condition, popular voting rules should satisfy some condition(s) for the equal weighting of votes. Exactly how such condition(s) should be spelled out will again depend on how popular voting fits into the broader political system. One-person, one-vote is one example of an equal weighting condition. But other plausible conditions might aim to minimize "wasted votes" (a principle Lani Guinier calls "one-vote, one-value"[27]), or to minimize vote–seat distortions. Though there are theoretical debates over the merits of each of these principles, they ultimately depend on different conceptions of representation, and of how electoral results should translate into policy outcomes. The general account of popular voting's democratic value that I have offered in this book is, therefore, not sufficient to adjudicate among these various equality conditions. What it can tell us is that each voting rule should satisfy some plausible condition(s) for the equal weighting of votes, that the equality conditions should be concrete and transparent, and that their satisfaction should be assessed synchronically. Regardless of the electoral system or the question that voters decide, popular voting serves its purposes best when voting procedures satisfy the relevant equality conditions in every election.

Before moving on to discuss norms of collective rationality that can be evaluated diachronically, I want to briefly mention an additional value that we may want to build into the formal properties of voting rules. This is the value of popular sovereignty. Popular sovereignty is a fraught and loaded term, but as I use the term, popular sovereignty refers to the ability of a sufficiently unified and motivated public to do as it pleases, without externally imposed constraints. The most obvious violations of popular sovereignty come in the form of foreign rule or non-democratic regime forms. But popular sovereignty can also suffer from excessive procedural constraints imposed by the dead hand of the past. This does not mean that any form of proceduralism amounts to an objectionable violation of popular sovereignty. Popular sovereignty is useless without procedures that constitute and empower a people. But though it should not be assigned absolute priority,

25. Ibid., 149–50.
26. McKinney, "Keep It Simple."
27. Guinier, *Tyranny of the Majority*, 122.

popular sovereignty should play a role in the evaluation of voting procedures and practices. As I have argued, a key component of popular voting's value derives from the optics of elections as moments in which the citizenry as a whole exercises its ultimate political authority. For this reason, popular voting rules should formalize at least a minimal form of popular sovereignty by satisfying the condition of non-imposition. Non-imposition is satisfied when, for every option listed on the ballot, there must be *some* set of votes that could generate that option as an outcome.[28] This is satisfied most intuitively when the voting rule respects unanimity. This minimal condition is not sufficient to realize the value of popular sovereignty. But more demanding criteria of popular sovereignty will require diachronic assessment and looking beyond voting rules to examine electoral agenda-setting and preference-formation processes. I will discuss this more in the next chapter.

DIACHRONIC EVALUATION: COLLECTIVE RATIONALITY

Strict synchronic standards do not exhaust the normative criteria for evaluating popular voting rules. If popular voting is to effectively perform its role in democracy, then over time, popular voting procedures must produce outcomes that exhibit a general tendency of positive responsiveness[29] to citizens' preferences. Put another way, a voting rule should minimize the frequency and severity of perverse outcomes.

If citizens wanted only to make decisions with a procedure in which everyone had equal power, they might simply flip a coin. We vote not only because we want to have equal decision-making power, but because we want to be collectively *em*powered. Effective agency, whether collective or individual, requires that we can direct the effects of our actions in accordance with our preferences or intentions. To contribute to collective empowerment, a good

28. This condition is sometimes also called "citizen sovereignty," but I use the label "non-imposition," to signal that while non-imposition is related to sovereignty, it is not a sufficient condition for it. The condition acquired the term citizen sovereignty because it bears some resemblance to the "consumer sovereignty" principle in economics. Arrow, *Social Choice and Individual Values*, 28–30.

29. The term responsiveness is commonly deployed in political theory and political science to discuss either how public policy or representative behavior responds to citizens' preferences. But here I am invoking the term as it is used in social choice theory, where it refers to the positive responsiveness of voting outcomes to changes in votes. Basically it means that, if any voter switches their vote to be more favorable to option A, this will only change the outcome in a way that is more is favorable to A (cf. List, "Social Choice Theory"; for the original formulation of positive responsiveness condition, see May, "Simple Majority Decision").

voting rule should generally translate votes into outcomes in a way that conforms to intuitions about what effective agency looks like.

Social choice theorists have articulated several properties of decision rules that represent plausible formalizations of intuitive ideas about collective rationality. These properties cannot be translated into strict evaluative criteria for voting rules because they are not consistently mutually realizable alongside any plausible equality condition, at least when there are more than two options in the choice set and no formal domain restrictions.

This does not mean that social choice theory's formalizations of collective rationality are irrelevant to the evaluation of voting procedures. Social choice theorists have also demonstrated the potential normative significance of formal studies of voting rules by examining the conditions under which equality and collective rationality *can* be reconciled. As I discussed in the last chapter, this approach has led to a recovery of enthusiasm for majoritarian voting rules. When the choice set contains only two options, majority rule voting is known to satisfy a number of properties related to equality and collective rationality. And when the choice set contains more than two options, an extension of majority rule voting (known as the Condorcet Rule) satisfies conditions for equality and collective rationality over the largest domain of possible preference profiles people might have over those options,[30] including the single-peaked preference profiles thought to be common in electoral decisions.[31]

As I indicated in chapter 2, these formal defenses of majority rule are not dispositive, though. First, these formal evaluations of voting rules assume a well-defined set of alternatives and preference profiles. They abstract away from agenda-setting and preference-formation processes. And so they cannot include considerations about how a voting rule may interact with and influence these processes or the environment in which they take place. Second, and relatedly, there may be separate reasons that weigh against maximizing the conditions in which a voting rule satisfies collective rationality conditions. I will discuss these two issues in chapter 4. Third, even when a voting rule seems to satisfy conditions of collective rationality given the profile of preferences that citizens are likely to have, it is not obvious that this feature of a voting rule ought to be given strict priority over other properties that a community might desire. For example, popular voting rules like single transferable vote and instant runoff, which use ranked ballots and multiple rounds

30. Dasgupta and Maskin, "On the Robustness of Majority Rule."
31. Black, *The Theory of Committees and Elections.*

of elimination, can sometimes violate the condition of positive responsiveness. But unlike the Condorcet Rule, they can be practically implemented even with a fairly large number of options, and so they put less pressure on agenda-setting processes to narrow the choice set. Other voting rules may introduce potential violations of collective rationality in order to account for preference intensity.[32] A democratic community can plausibly decide to resolve these trade-offs by accepting the possibility of some violations of collective rationality. This is especially true if a diachronic evaluation shows that collective agency can largely be preserved without requiring a voting rule to maximally comply with formal properties of rationality.

Another set of considerations relevant to the evaluation of voting rules arises from the fact that different voting rules can affect other aspects of popular voting practices. Different voting rules can affect how citizens experience the act of voting, and thereby also affect the socialization function of voting. Consider, for example, instant runoff—a variant of ranked choice voting sometimes deployed in single-winner elections. On the one hand, expanded electoral choices, and the opportunity to express more fine-grained preferences might make voting a more enjoyable experience and give citizens a greater sense of agency.[33] On the other hand, complex voting rules might be discouraging for some citizens who find them difficult to navigate.[34] And, of course, voting rules also affect the incentives that politicians and political entrepreneurs face during election campaigns. Popular voting's effect on the political environment, including the kinds of organization and mobilization efforts that it encourages, will thus be mediated and shaped by the character of the voting rule.

Again, as always, context and implementation will affect whether and how voting rules fit into a valuable practice of popular voting. Instant runoff

32. The method of cumulative voting that I mentioned above, for example, has been defended as a way to enable intense minorities to sometimes prevail over lukewarm majorities without entrenching particular political differences. Cumulative voting does this by allowing voters to split their vote over multiple candidates in a multi-winner election. Those who strongly favor one candidate over all the others can give that candidate their whole vote. But those who do not feel as strongly can distribute their vote across multiple candidates. Cumulative voting, like other voting rules that account for preference intensity, violates independence of irrelevant alternatives (IIA).

33. Cf. Drutman, *Breaking the Two-Party Doom Loop*, 181.

34. If this effect exists, though, it is possible that this effect would fade over time. Age is the most significant demographic correlate with reported difficulty understanding instructions for ranked choice voting (Donovan, Tolbert, and Gracey, "Self-Reported Understanding of Ranked-Choice Voting"). It may well be that the complexity of ranked choice voting is most salient to those who have become accustomed to other voting systems.

voting is instructive here too. Instant runoff is widely regarded as a successful voting rule in Australia that selects broadly acceptable winners and enjoys a great deal of public support.[35] In the United States, however, where instant runoff is used in many local elections, assessments are more mixed. One of the most important justifications for instant runoff voting is that it helps ensure winners in single-member districts actually have the support of a majority of voters rather than merely a plurality. However, in many instant runoff elections in the United States, the winning candidate did not actually secure a majority, because a large number of ballots were "exhausted" before a winner emerged.[36] The prevalence of ballot exhaustion in the United States can be partly explained by implementation (e.g., rules that limit the number of candidates each voter can rank). But instant runoff's inconsistent performance in the United States may also be partly due to the broader context. The United States has a complex voting system that grants states and localities substantial discretion in the choice of voting procedures and their implementation. This complexity and the resulting variety of electoral contexts in the United States likely makes it harder for potential electoral coalitions to optimally coordinate their vote choices. It may also make it harder for citizens to learn not only the formal rules of their voting system, but also how to vote strategically within the system, since the strategy can vary so much from one locality—and even one election—to the next. This is not to say that instant runoff can't be a viable voting rule for jurisdictions within the United States, but rather, that a comprehensive evaluation and justification of the rule must take seriously how it will perform in the relevant context.

A third reason not to treat a voting's rules formal virtues as dispositive is that it is unlikely that citizens will *always* have preference profiles in the domain where a voting rule satisfies conditions for collective rationality, even when the voting rule has the largest such domain possible. The Condorcet Rule might perform well as long as citizens have single-peaked preferences. But in any large and diverse polity, with meaningful competition and at least minimally democratic agenda-setting processes, we should expect that citizens will at least occasionally form preferences that aren't so well behaved. Two things follow from this expectation.

First, assuming that no voting rule will *always* satisfy the conditions of collective rationality given the actual preferences that citizens come to have, we are necessarily evaluating the general tendencies of a voting rule. Once

35. See Reilly, "Ranked Choice Voting in Australia and America."
36. Burnett and Kogan, "Ballot (and Voter) 'exhaustion' under Instant Runoff Voting."

again, we want to evaluate these general tendencies of voting rules in their particular context. What matters is not how a voting rule performs in the space of logical possibility, but rather how it performs in the space of actual and likely political environments where it is used.

Second, when we turn our attention to general tendencies rather than infallible properties of a voting rule, it becomes harder to justify placing strict priority on *maximizing* a particular tendency relative to other things we might care about. For various reasons that I discussed above, some voting rules that are more vulnerable to violations of collective rationality may, nevertheless, create an experience that makes it easier for citizens to come to accept and even identify with electoral outcomes. Ranked choice voting schemes are often defended on these grounds. Instant runoff has been touted as an electoral solution to bitter political divisions, because it tends to disfavor polarizing candidates and discourages negative campaigning.[37] In the event that violations of collective rationality occur, voting rules must still be able to produce outcomes that citizens can view as legitimate and as a product of their collective agency. This legitimacy may be more readily secured where vulnerability to such violations is acknowledged and accepted as a trade-off for other desirable properties in a voting procedure.

When evaluating collective rationality diachronically, we aim to limit the frequency and severity of irrational or perverse outcomes over time. Here it is useful to draw an analogy to individual agency. Typical individuals often act in irrational ways that lead to unintended and undesirable outcomes. The mere possibility and occasional realization of such instances of irrationality need not generally undermine the attribution of agency to these individuals, nor the value of that agency. However, both the frequency and severity of these occasions over time does affect how we evaluate an individual's status as a self-governing agent. When I frequently act irrationally in minor matters, I might earn a reputation for being flaky or undisciplined. But particularly severe instances of irrational behavior may have a larger detrimental effect on the attribution of agency than frequent minor occurrences.[38]

---

37. Drutman, *Breaking the Two-Party Doom Loop*, 181. Some empirical studies of ranked choice voting in the United States support the claim that ranked choice voting makes for more civil campaigns (e.g., Donovan, Tolbert, and Gracey, "Campaign Civility under Preferential and Plurality Voting").

38. One or two violations of my policy not to have extramarital affairs would seem to be a more serious knock against my status as a self-governing agent than much more frequent violations of my policy not to snack on the candy in the department offices. The difference seems to be in how much of a deviation the irrational behavior produces between the resultant outcomes

A similar approach should be adopted when evaluating voting rules. Voting rules better serve their role in democracy when they lead to fewer or less severe forms of collective irrationality. There are, no doubt, different plausible ways of characterizing what makes a failure of collective rationality more severe.[39] Most likely no single satisfactory metric of the severity of a failure of collective rationality exists, and assessments of that severity will depend on a fairly ad hoc weighted consideration of a number of factors and will be the subject of political contestation. As with many other things we value, but struggle to formalize and measure, though, this should not stop us from considering the severity of failures of collective rationality in our evaluations of voting rules. A philosophical analysis of aggregative equality, unfortunately, cannot free us from frustrating debates about whether Ralph Nader "spoiled" the 2000 US presidential election (and whether it's a big problem if he did). It can only help us situate these debates within a more holistic evaluation of voting procedures.

A full examination of how to assess collective rationality is outside the scope of this book. The main point I want to make here is that, in evaluating the performance of a voting rule over time, we should consider whether some failures are plausibly regarded as more severe than others. On this account, a voting rule that frequently led to sub-optimal, but broadly acceptable, collective choices might be thought a better decision rule than one

---

and the outcomes that I intended when I adopted the policy. One or two affairs will likely impair my ability to maintain a trusting, respectful, and equitable partnership with my spouse much more than twenty extra chocolates will impair my ability to live a long and healthy life. So the violation of rationality in the prior case seems more severe. Note that our judgments about this case might look different depending on how central monogamy is to my view of what makes a healthy relationship or if I had adopted the anti-snacking policy for different reasons, such as a religious fast, or a severe food allergy.

39. Intuitively, the severity of an instance of collective irrationality might be defined in terms of the distance between the actual outcome and some superior, collectively rational outcome. There are two difficulties with this that can generate disagreement: first, how the baseline is to be defined. We know there is no clear way of defining a "true" collective preference, so how should we define the difference between perverse and non-perverse outcomes? Secondly, even if we agree on a baseline against which to establish deviation, how will we define, measure and compare deviations from this baseline that we should care about? Perhaps the most intuitive way is to think in terms of each outcome's utility, but democratic theorists are often hesitant to rely on cardinal comparisons of utility. We might also think in terms of the qualitative ways in which electoral outcomes differ from citizens' intended or hoped for results. We might also think that some kinds of failures of collective rationality are more severe than others simply in virtue of being more at odds with the idea of rational agency (violations of positive responsiveness, for example, strike me as more severe than violations of IIA).

that on rare occasions returned a result broadly deemed unacceptable.[40] And, once again, a complete evaluation of a voting rule requires looking at its actual performance (or expected performance) in a particular context, rather than simply looking at its formal properties.

Analyses of their formal properties do still have a role to play in evaluating voting rules. Voting rules are generally better, *all else equal*, when they comply with conditions of collective rationality for a broader domain of preference or voting profiles, or over a larger number of options. This greater robustness of the voting rule will generally reduce the demands on agenda-setting processes. A more robust voting rule may also better contribute to aggregative equality's virtue of transparency. Examining the formal properties of voting rules also helps us to explain why and predict when certain rules might lead to more frequent or more severe violations of collective rationality. The point I want to emphasize here, though, is that maximizing the domain of vote profiles over which a voting rule satisfies collective rationality should not be regarded as a strict priority in the evaluation of voting rules. It is one among many relevant considerations.

The democratic value of a voting rule cannot be assessed simply by looking at its formal properties. There is no voting rule that, applied to a random selection of human beings, would always produce outcomes we could plausibly describe as the democratic decisions of that group. Popular voting procedures can contribute to a democratic system of governance in a political *community*, though. This is because, in a political community, voting procedures are embedded within and interact with a broader set of democratic practices. When evaluating voting rules within the context of a democratic system, we can and should take a broader and longer view. The longer view lets us look at how a voting rule actually performs over time in a specific context. The broader view incorporates more considerations than formal analyses of voting rules typically allow: we ask how voting rules shape citizens' experience of elections and their ability to accept and even identify

40. This is perhaps the main trade-off between instant runoff and plurality rule. Citizens might typically be quite good at coordinating voting strategies in plurality systems and able to avoid perverse outcomes. But when they fail, they can fail quite spectacularly. Instant runoff rules, on the other hand, probably lead to more frequent instances where the results are sub-optimal in one way or another. But it will be unlikely to produce winners who are truly reviled by most voters. One place we can see this trade-off at work is in the switch from plurality rule to instant runoff in the Oscars vote for Best Picture. Many critics have argued that instant runoff is undesirable in that context precisely because it favors milquetoast, broadly popular films, rather than riskier, polarizing films. This resolution of the trade-off may be undesirable when identifying great works of art. But when it comes to popular elections, we may resolve the trade-off differently.

with its outcomes. These effects can be as important as the formal properties of the voting rule to our ability to regard popular voting as a valuable
exercise of collective agency.

When evaluating voting rules, we must also examine how they interact with and shape the political environment and background processes of
agenda-setting and preference formation. And we must ensure that those
processes are themselves at least minimally democratic. Aggregative equality at the voting stage can look like a farce when set against a backdrop of
authoritarian agenda-setting. The next chapter discusses how we should
think about evaluating preference-formation and agenda-setting processes
and their relationship to voting procedures. That discussion focuses in particular on a crucial driver of agenda-setting—political parties and party
systems. First, though, I want to take a brief detour to discuss the sorts of
questions best decided by popular vote.

What Should We Put to a Vote?

Perhaps what distinguishes the focus of this book from other books about
voting more than anything else is that the content of the choices that citizens
make in elections is not a central feature of my account of what makes voting
valuable. My account of popular voting as a democratic practice explains
much of the value of voting for a variety of choices that might be put before
citizens, including constitutional or legislative referenda, ballot initiatives,
and elections of representative officials. Which sorts of electoral choices
best contribute to the function of popular voting undoubtedly depends on
other specific aspects of a particular democratic system. It is worth taking a
moment, though, to discuss how this account of voting's value fits with different uses of popular voting. In this section, then, I will discuss the relative
merits of voting in elections versus substantive ballot measures. I will also
address some specific concerns about the nature of democratic representation and its relationship to different kinds of votes. Finally, I will draw out
some general considerations relevant for evaluating electoral choices and
how well they help fulfill the function of popular voting.

Throughout this book, my account of voting's role in modern democracy
has centered on popular voting in elections. In fact, I frequently use "elections" as shorthand for any and all occasions for popular voting. Elections
are the sine qua non of modern democracy. Every democracy in existence
today utilizes popular voting in elections to determine who will hold its
highest offices and wield its greatest public power. And when citizens think

of voting, elections spring foremost to mind. But popular votes on substantive ballot measures—both legislative referenda and citizen initiatives—have become increasingly common in democracies around the world. What should we make of this?

Voting in elections and referenda alike exhibits the three key features of popular voting that I have argued constitute the distinctive practice and its role in democratic systems. Elections and referenda both come with an ambition toward universal participation. Both employ aggregative equality to reach a collective decision. And both create decisive, attention-grabbing participatory moments. However, there is some variation in the way these features manifest in the practice of voting in elections and referenda that is worth discussion. The expectation of mass participation does not appear to uniformly differ between elections and substantive ballot measures. Problems with low turnout and voter roll-off—when voters vote on some measures on a ballot but leave other parts of the ballot blank—are well documented, especially where voters encounter a lot of ballot measures. But these problems can also afflict elections, especially in places like many US cities where citizens might elect dozens of officials over the course of two years. On the other hand, highly salient, constitutional referenda can garner unusually high turnout.[41] High abstention rates, then, are not a feature of voting on substantive questions per se, but rather of the over-use of voting in general.

Elections and referenda diverge more in the temporal character of the participatory moments each creates. Occasions for popular voting, whatever the question, can create arresting spectacles that dramatize the people's collective agency. How these moments fit into the broader political system differs, though. Elections recur regularly and voters revisit the same questions at regular intervals. This means that electoral moments create a rhythm or periodicity that is important to some of the functions of popular voting. Referenda on the other hand may have a more extraordinary or singular character. This is especially true when voting on referenda is infrequent and takes place on a separate day and a separate ballot. Because of these differences, voting in elections and voting in referenda no doubt realize different aspects of the values and functions I have attribute to popular voting to different extents.

To the extent that elections and referenda exhibit the core features of voting, both can instantiate the three aspects of democratic value that I elaborated in chapter 1. Whether the question to be decided is about a substantive

41. For example, though its critics lament high levels of abstention from the UK's 2016 "Brexit" vote, the turnout rate of about 72 percent in that referendum was substantially higher than typical turnout in UK elections over the past two decades ("Voter Turnout in the UK 1918–2019").

matter of law or about who will wield power in the people's name, popular voting concretely establishes the equal authority of all citizens, renders the relationship between individual and collective agency transparent, and enables citizens to participate in a collective expression of equal respect for all citizens qua political agents. Of course, elections and referenda instantiate these democratic values in different ways and one may do better than the other at some. For example, referenda might be a better vehicle for expressing equal respect for all citizens because they do not simultaneously empower some, but not others. On the other hand, elections may be a better vehicle for establishing the ultimate authority of all citizens because electoral decisions can have consequences for every aspect of public life. But these differences between elections and referenda do not matter as much as the extent to which the question to be decided exhibits some general characteristics I will discuss at the end of this section. Nor do they matter as much as the extent to which the vote exhibits the three core features of popular voting.

The differences between elections and referenda matter more for some of the instrumental values that popular voting serves. It seems likely that both can perform the functions of establishing a participation floor and socializing citizens into their role as equal agents. Because elections recur periodically, they might seem to be better suited to helping citizens develop participatory habits and civic identities. But where the experience of voting on ballot measures over time is sufficiently similar and regular, this difference may not matter much.

For the other functions of popular voting—creating an environment favorable to mobilization, organization, and innovation, and disciplining public officials to attend to the concerns of the entire citizenry—elections are essential. Elections represent more of a blank slate for political campaigns because elections determine who will wield power, not what they will do with it. The aperture of the electorate's attention, then, is likely to be wider. That is, we are more open to a greater range of political appeals and claims that seek to define the electoral choice and the political moment. And while ballot measures can be a useful tool for informing public officials about the public's sentiments, they are limited in scope and force. Electoral incentives, on the other hand, though far from perfect, have a substantial and well-documented effect on representatives' efforts to serve their constituents.[42]

Some critics have objected to substantive ballot measures on the grounds that they interfere with the popular sovereignty expressed in elections and the full operation of electoral representation, or (specifically in the American

---

42. See chapter 1 for an overview of the evidence.

context) are "alien to the spirit of the Constitution."[43] This reflects an implausible and unsustainable view of electoral representation, though, which places more normative weight on individual electoral outcomes than they can bear. Democracies can and do contain competing sources of democratic legitimation. And a systemic view of democracy holds that multiple sources of legitimation are essential for realizing the complex and multi-faceted value of democracy, especially given the diversity of modern societies and the scope of the government's mandate.[44]

Underlying the claim that ballot measures interfere with the proper operation of representative government is a subtler critique, though. Many commentators argue that referenda are more likely to be captured or to lead to bad policy.[45] These claims are more plausible and also subject to empirical verification. There is certainly no shortage of examples of wealthy and powerful interest groups who have used the ballot initiative process to their advantage. Anyone living in California in 2020 will recall being bombarded with advertisements for proposition 22. Major "gig economy" companies, like Uber, Lyft, and Doordash, spent over 200 million US dollars and succeeded in passing prop 22, which nullified legislation regulating gig labor. But these criticisms do not apply equally to all substantive ballot measures. They are more likely to apply, for example, to citizens' initiatives than to legislative referenda. And they may also be mitigated with procedural reforms that limit the number of initiatives that make it to the ballot.[46] Additionally, some substantive questions may be more amenable to a popular vote than others. Budgetary and taxation issues might be particularly poor uses of ballot measures. But procedural issues, such as redistricting reform and social issues, might be more apt.

Popular elections serve some functions that referenda do not, but referenda can still exhibit many of the virtues of popular voting and may be a salutary part of modern democracy. Much the same can be said for the different sorts of electoral contests in which citizens vote around the world. The practice of popular voting that I have characterized in this book is embedded in many different democratic systems that embody different conceptions of democratic representation. The normative guidance to be gleaned from an appreciation of popular voting's democratic purposes does not, therefore, extend to prescribing the questions on which citizens ought to take a vote

43. Broder, *Democracy Derailed*, 1, 221–43.
44. Cf. Mansbridge, "What Is Political Science For?"
45. E.g., Cain, *Democracy More or Less*; Streb, *Rethinking American Electoral Democracy*.
46. Fishkin et al., "Deliberative Agenda Setting."

or the character of the offices we elect. Attempting to extend the account in this way would run counter to the spirit of democratic democratic theory.

This does not mean, though, that popular voting will fulfill the purposes I have ascribed to it equally well regardless of the questions we vote on. There are some general criteria that electoral choices should satisfy if popular voting is to merit its place at the center of our democratic practice. I briefly enumerate these below. But I want to stress that these criteria are not determinative. They can be plausibly satisfied in many ways. Moreover, they are not the only criteria relevant for evaluating the structure of electoral choices. Instead, they must exist alongside evaluative considerations that arise from other aspects of democratic systems that may vary more from place to place.

First, and most obviously, the results of an election should decide some political question, and that decision should stand regardless of the preferences or dispositions of those in power.[47] Votes are not advisory, and public officials cannot have discretion to disregard, revise, or filter electoral results. This is the key difference between elections and many other forms of political participation. Votes are not submitted for consideration. The outcome of a voting rule settles some question related to the community's use of its collective power.[48]

Second, electoral choices should be cognitively accessible. This requires first, simply that the choice set be limited to a small enough set of options that citizens are able to form stable comparative evaluations over all of the options simultaneously. Moreover, citizens should be able, without unusual effort, to acquire at least a rough understanding of how the voting rule translates votes into electoral outcomes and of how different *electoral* outcomes translate into *political* outcomes.[49] To meaningfully participate in the exercise of democratic agency, citizens need to have some sense of how their individual votes contribute to shaping their community's public life.

What this requires of electoral choices depends on the context: we need to know something about the resources available to citizens to develop "civic" skills and to acquire information that is adequate for forming the kinds of evaluations that carry normative weight. We also need to know

47. On what sorts of counterfactuals the electoral decision must be robust over, see South-wood, "Democracy as a Modally Demanding Value."

48. None of this is at odds with the idea that political settlements—including those reached via voting—are provisional.

49. In the US, for example, cognitive accessibility would plausibly require that citizens understand that when a single party controls multiple branches of government they are usually better able to accomplish their goals than under conditions of divided government, but voters may not need to know whether the President or Congress has the constitutional power to declare war.

something about how well citizens are able to cope with cognitive limitations and maximize the usefulness of limited information.[50] These features of context are not entirely exogenous either; they may be affected at least in part by the kinds of electoral choices that voters typically face. Institutions and practices undoubtedly respond to the cognitive demands of electoral choices. Evaluating the cognitive accessibility of electoral choices requires looking at how the political system functions generally to enable citizens to reach meaningful evaluations over the options on the ballot.

Third, electoral choices must be consequential. That is, electoral outcomes should have the potential to substantially affect the character of a community's political life. This might, at first, seem unnecessary, at least for many of the functions of popular voting. One might think, for example, that the function of elections in socializing citizens into their role as equal political agents need not require that the socializing practice itself have high stakes. Consequential choices, however, add to the socializing value of elections: citizens can gain a better sense of the possibilities for collective agency by taking part in doing something substantial with others. The expressive effects of elections—the community's expression of the value of individual contributions, and individuals' expression of a willingness and a commitment to participating on equal terms—also carry more weight in the context of high-stakes decisions.

Moreover, voting serves other values for which consequential choices matter more. This is particularly true for the coordinating role that elections serve by providing occasions around which political groups face lower barriers to forming and to coordinating for political action. The value of these coordinating moments is greatly diminished if groups are not able to do much with them. And, insofar as elections establish a participatory minimum, it is important that this participatory minimum carry as much weight as possible.[51] Elections focus citizens' attention on specific participatory moments. The value of this function depends on whether those moments are worthy of citizens' attention.

Not all political questions ought to be decided by voting. If popular voting is to maintain its momentousness and its value as a special occasion for universal participation, then voting must not become too mundane or

---

50. Many political scientists and political theorists have explored the many ways citizens have of coping with the demands of voting despite ordinary cognitive limits. For a normative approach, see, for example, Beerbohm, *In Our Name*, 142–68; Bowler and Donovan, *Demanding Choices*.

51. As E. E. Schattschneider put it: "the unforgiveable sin of democratic politics is to dissipate the power of the public by putting it to trivial uses" (*Semisovereign People*, 137).

too burdensome. There is an upper limit on the number of questions that should be decided by popular vote, and priority ought to be given to more consequential choices.

The consequential choices consideration is closely related to a fourth consideration: voters should face a meaningful choice on the ballot. The meaningful choice condition requires that electoral choices correspond to salient political debates within the community. The question of what counts as a meaningful choice in an election must be sensitive to the electoral context and to the point of voting as a massively collective activity. To vote is not just to make an individual choice (for whom will I vote?), but also to make that choice within a collective context and as part of a collective decision (whom will we elect?). The conditions for a meaningful choice in the electoral context will therefore be different than the conditions that characterize a meaningful choice in other areas of life in which individual choices are decisive. Elections are massive collective undertakings. They will necessarily involve compromise, not just in the final outcome, but also in how the choice itself is defined. Voting is a way for all citizens to contribute to deciding a few questions that have been reserved for the citizenry as a whole. But the choices to be decided by elections, and the options that are to be considered relevant in those decisions, have to be worked out as part of the broader system of collective self-rule in which voting is embedded.

Conclusion

Understanding the purposes of popular voting in modern democracies should shape how we evaluate the bundle of institutions, norms, and activities that constitute practices of popular voting, as well as proposals to reform them. In this chapter, I have articulated a number of ways that my account of popular voting's purposes should inform how we evaluate electoral administration, vote aggregation rules, and the kinds of questions or options that appear on the ballot.

This set of evaluative considerations does not provide a blueprint for electoral design or reform. Many of the considerations I have described admit of a range of plausible interpretations about how they might be applied in practice, and about how they should be balanced when different considerations offer conflicting guidance. As I will argue in the final chapter of this book, there are reasons for honoring the plausible settlements that communities reach on how to structure their democratic practices. Moreover, particular voting institutions or practices may function differently in different political cultures or in conjunction with other components of communities' varied democratic systems. Evaluations of voting practices must therefore always be contextual and systemic.

Though it serves a set of distinctive and common purposes across large contemporary democracies, popular voting is not simply an accessory ritual that is layered on top of otherwise complete democratic systems. The functions that voting serves are fundamental to the operation of large-scale democracy. Occasions for popular voting structure the kinds of political interactions that citizens have with each other and with their political leaders and shape how they each relate to their shared democratic project. The background political environment in which electoral agendas emerge, in which citizens form their preferences over those agendas, and in which electoral outcomes are translated into the activities of political rule in turn give meaning and democratic significance to the practice of popular voting. For voting to effectively fulfill its role and contribute to realizing democratic values, voting practices must fit properly into the broader political system.

In the next chapter, I discuss in more concrete terms what the proper integration of popular voting into a broader democratic system entails and how it is achieved. The chapter will examine the relationship between party systems and the distinctive functions of popular voting. Modern party systems have developed concurrently with the extension of suffrage and the emergence of popular voting as a central practice of democracy. The values and functioning of popular voting and of party systems in contemporary democracies are deeply interdependent. Well-functioning party systems link voting institutions with agenda-setting and preference-formation processes and with the activities of government in ways that lend normative significance to the procedures and outcomes of vote aggregation. And voting practices, in turn, shape the character of agenda-setting and preference-formation processes through their effect on the structure of party systems. Political parties are an important part of the mechanism by which popular voting performs the functions of socializing, mobilizing, and organizing citizens that I described in chapter 1. Therefore, I defend the party system paradigm as a normative starting point for conceptualizing democratic processes for agenda-setting and preference formation. I then articulate a regulative ideal for party systems that bears on the structure of electoral contests as well as the rules governing party organization and even the administration of elections.

4

Voting with Political Parties

On November 2, 2010, Election Day, thousands of voters in the state of Maryland received a robocall telling them that the Democratic incumbent Martin O'Malley had won the gubernatorial election, and "the only thing left is to watch it on TV tonight." The call was made two hours before the polls closed. This robocall came from the campaign of the Republican challenger Robert Ehrlich, Jr., though it was scripted to sound as if it was coming from Democrats. The call went out to voters in the two largest majority-Black counties in Maryland. The script was crafted by a campaign consultant who had previously stated that the "first and most desired outcome" for the Republican campaign was "voter suppression." This Election Day robocall intended to deceive likely Democratic African American voters, apparently with the goal of keeping them away from the polls in the final hours of the election.[1]

The campaign manager and the consultant who crafted the call were both convicted of violating Maryland's election laws. The robocall was an illegal campaign tactic. But the strategy of suppressing turnout for the opposing party is all too common. One legal tactic for suppressing voter turnout frequently employed by Republican Party operatives is to challenge voter registrations on the grounds that they appear fraudulent, out-of-date, or otherwise suspicious. When these challenges are successful, they put the onus on registrants to provide proof of their continued eligibility to vote. Those who fail to do so in the designated timeframe may have their registrations removed from the voter rolls or their votes invalidated. Typically, these

1. Broadwater, "Schurick Guilty."

challenges are facially neutral, but they may target voters in disproportionately Democratic jurisdictions or use criteria that disproportionately affect
registered Democrats or likely Democratic voters.[2]

Political parties are inextricably linked to the practice of popular voting in modern democracies. Electoral institutions shape the kinds of party
systems that develop, while parties and party systems affect who votes and
how voting works in practice. It may be possible to analyze some aspects
of modern democracy without discussing political parties. Popular voting
is not one of them.

The prevalence of partisan efforts to suppress voter turnout like those
I have just described may lead to the impression that party politics should
be viewed primarily as a threat to the value of popular voting that I have
described in this book. Even parties that don't find voter suppression to be
a beneficial campaign strategy are hardly neutral in choosing sites for voter
registration drives or in choosing whom they encourage to turn out. The
idea that political parties share an ambition toward universal participation
or help citizens to view each other as equals and as co-participants in a common democratic project sometimes seems laughable.

And yet, as I will argue in this chapter, party politics has been—and
continues to be—instrumental in shaping the modern practice of popular voting, including the expectation of approximately universal turnout.
Party politics is uniquely adapted to the context of mass participation. As
one influential scholar put it, modern, electoral democracy is "unthink-
able, save in terms of parties."[3] Certain partisan practices, though—most
especially voter suppression tactics—are, indeed, a threat to the democratic value of popular voting. What is needed, then, is an account of how
popular voting and party politics work together in a healthy democratic
system that can provide purchase for critiquing pathological forms of party
competition.

This chapter has two purposes. First, this chapter illuminates how party
systems shape the background conditions in which elections can be seen as
valuable exercises of collective agency. Party politics drive the agenda-setting
processes that are crucial for meaningful applications of aggregative equality.
Second, this chapter articulates an account of healthy party politics that can
guide efforts to improve party systems, party organizations, and practices

2. For a discussion of recent uses of these tactics, see Tova, *Politics of Voter Suppression*, 85–103.
3. Schattschneider, *Party Government*, 1.

of partisanship.[4] I argue that party politics contributes to a healthy democratic system to the extent that it reflects an ideal of parties-as-mobilizers.

The chapter proceeds in three sections. In the first section, I briefly recap some of the discussion from previous chapters on the necessity of "fit" between electoral institutions and the discursive environment in which preferences are formed and electoral agendas emerge. Then I sketch some of the key evaluative criteria that should guide assessments of democratic agenda-setting processes.

In the second section, I provide an overview of empirical and theoretical literature on the role of party systems in political agenda-setting. In this section, I also discuss the virtues (and most common vices) of party-driven agenda-setting processes. This lays the foundation for the final section in which I argue for an ideal of party politics that focuses on its tendency to promote broad, deep, and durable mobilization and discuss how this ideal might bear on evaluations of party organizations and party systems.

Democracy in Agenda-setting and Preference Formation

One of the three core value-making features of popular voting is the application of aggregative equality. Voting procedures aggregate individuals' expressed preferences to generate a collective outcome via a function that treats votes equally irrespective of their content or of who casts them. Though it is not the only interpretation of political equality that matters to a healthy democracy, it does have distinctive virtues (transparency, replicability, and scalability). And when combined with mass participation and popular voting's momentousness, these virtues of aggregative equality contribute to voting's unique democratic value.

As I argued in chapter 2, if we are to interpret elections as valuable exercises of collective agency, they must be able to mitigate two potential problems with aggregation. The first is the "inputs" problem. Aggregating individual expressed preferences only produces a valuable outcome if those individual expressed preferences are themselves valuable—that is, if they reflect or correspond to valuable aspects of individual agency. The inputs problem arises when what people express with their votes does not seem to reflect the sorts of things that ought to be relevant to political decision-making. Commentators have frequently lamented that citizens'

---

4. For a further discussion of regulative ideals of partisanship and party politics, see Chapman, "New Challenges."

expressed political preferences are misinformed, arbitrary, or at odds with their deeply held values. To the extent that this is true, the value of individuals' expressed preferences is attenuated. This, in turn, diminishes the value of the electoral outcome, because its value is derived from the individual votes that determine it.

The second problem that voting procedures must overcome affects the outputs of aggregation. Even when individuals' expressed preferences are valuable, it may not be possible to combine them in a way that preserves that value and transfers it to the aggregated electoral outcome. Doing so requires that the aggregation procedure treats individual votes equally and in a way that is consistent with norms of collective rationality. But it is demonstrably impossible to design an aggregation rule that invariably does both of these things.

We cannot eliminate either the inputs problem or the outputs problem entirely, but we also need not abandon aggregative procedures as a result. As I argued in chapters 2 and 3, the background context in which voting is applied can mitigate or exacerbate these two problems. Thus, when we evaluate voting practices—including the formal rules for aggregating votes—we must examine how those voting practices fit with other aspects of the political system. In the last chapter I discussed how context affects our evaluation of a voting rule. In this chapter, I examine the link between voting procedures and discursive processes of agenda-setting and preference formation from the other side.

In this first section, I discuss these discursive processes at greater depth, and identify some of the properties that agenda-setting must exhibit to enable valuable applications of aggregative equality. In the subsequent sections I will discuss how systems of agenda-setting driven by party competition exhibit these properties and when they do so best.

For simplicity, throughout this section I use the all-purpose label "agenda-setting" to refer to a collection of different but related processes, including those that the term typically invokes as well as those more commonly and accurately described as preference formation. This broad and loose use of the term "agenda-setting" is not intended as any sort of conceptual innovation. It is simply a convenient way to label a package of discursive processes that are usefully discussed and evaluated together. We could also characterize the subject of this chapter as the components of a democratic system that perform the function of "collective agenda and will formation."[5] I use the term agenda-setting just because it is handier.

---

5. Warren, "A Problem-Based Approach to Democratic Theory," 46.

Agenda-setting processes include the political and bureaucratic procedures by which candidates, parties, or legislative proposals achieve a place on the ballot. They also include the informal discursive processes by which proposals because salient in a political community, and by which these proposals acquire particular social meanings. An example of informal agenda-setting is the process by which "Medicare for all" became not only a salient political proposal, but also a slogan for a type of progressive politics in the United States. Another example is the process by which candidates become defined by familiar campaign tropes and narratives (e.g., "establishment candidates" versus "mavericks" and "populists") and ideological "lanes."

In the way I am using the term, agenda-setting processes also include the mechanisms by which certain criteria for evaluating policies and proposals, such as individual liberty, fiscal responsibility, or economic equality, become particularly salient within a political community. And finally, here, agenda-setting includes the processes by which citizens use salient evaluative criteria to form their preferences over formal and informal political agendas.

Thus, in my usage, the bucket term "agenda-setting" includes a number of different phenomena that are logically distinct. However, these processes are all practically interrelated to some degree, and in a healthy democratic system, they must be linked in ways that are conducive to collective agency over time. Evaluating the democratic character of these various processes, then, requires looking at them conjointly.

A systemic approach to evaluating electoral agenda-setting processes involves answering two questions. First, how do agenda-setting processes support other valuable components of democratic system? For the purposes of this book, we are asking: how do agenda-setting processes (in conjunction with a particular voting rule) help to limit the frequency and severity of perverse outcomes when votes are aggregated, and how do they help citizens form and express meaningful preferences? Second, how do agenda-setting processes themselves instantiate democratic values or perform separate democratic functions? In the remainder of this section, I will discuss these two aspects of agenda-setting evaluation in turn. Because the second evaluative question has been the focus of a great deal of scholarship on deliberative (or more generically discursive) systems,[6] I will devote more attention on the first question. But the answers to both questions should inform how we think about the regulative ideals for party politics.

6. See, e.g., Mansbridge et al., "A Systemic Approach." For a discussion of deliberative agenda-setting specifically as it precedes a popular vote, see Chambers, "Democracy and Constitutional Reform."

FUNCTIONAL AGENDA-SETTING PROCESSES

The two potential problems with aggregation procedures that I outlined above can be redescribed as two conditions for meaningful aggregation. The first condition is that the inputs into aggregation—that is, citizens' preferences as expressed in their votes—must themselves be valuable. Second, the procedures for aggregating these inputs must be able to (generally) preserve and transfer their value to the electoral outcome. The more these two conditions are met, the more we can recognize aggregative voting procedures as constituting a form of collective empowerment on equal terms.

Agenda-setting processes perform an important function in modern democratic systems insofar as they facilitate the satisfaction of these two conditions. Agenda-setting processes do this by producing: 1) a relatively small set of salient proposals or potential courses of action; 2) a relatively small number of salient evaluative criteria; 3) convergence between the formal, electoral agenda and the informal, political agenda (that is, a sense that the options available on the ballot map onto salient positions in the political community); and 4) a link among citizens' preferences over the electoral agenda, so that the citizenry often has preference profiles over which the voting rule exhibits desirable properties of collective rationality, and so that citizens can make sense of how the voting rule responds to common types of vote profiles. The importance of each of these functions will vary depending on the voting rule in use, but all are relevant to some extent in any voting system.

How do these four products contribute to the conditions for meaningful aggregation? A relatively small number of salient proposals is necessary, first, for ensuring the value of inputs to aggregation. The task of evaluating alternative proposals or courses of action needs to be cognitively manageable. This means that the number of alternatives must be kept small enough for citizens to gather relevant information about all of them, to consider them simultaneously and to meaningfully compare them.

For a similar reason, a small number of salient evaluative criteria also contributes to satisfying the inputs condition. Even with relatively few salient proposals, too many evaluative dimensions means that citizens are likely to have unstable and context-dependent preferences.[7] As I argued in chapter 2, unstable preferences are not unique to politics, and should not imply

---

7. In fact, unless citizens have a strict lexical ordering among the various evaluative criteria they care about, then preferences over a number of proposals will be subject to a problem similar to the social choice problem (see Patty and Penn, *Social Choice and Legitimacy*).

that citizens' expressed preferences are necessarily meaningless or without value. However, unstable preferences open the door to problematic strategies that citizens might adopt in response to the difficulties of evaluating complex decisions. It is more likely in these circumstances that irrelevant or even pernicious factors, such as ballot order or ethnic stereotypes, end up driving citizens' decision-making. Limiting both the salient proposals *and* the criteria for forming preferences over them makes it possible for citizens to form preferences over the agenda using a reasoning process with which they can identify on reflection. This makes it more likely that citizens' votes will reflect the value of their individual agency.

Convergence between the formal, electoral agenda and the informal, political agenda is also essential to the value of inputs to aggregation. If citizens do not see how ballot options map onto salient political debates or issues that they care about, citizens are likely to feel alienated from any preferences that they express with their votes, and consequently from the political outcomes constituted by those votes.

The fourth essential product of agenda-setting processes (the link among different citizens' preferences) is primarily important for satisfying the outputs condition for meaningful aggregation—that is, for overcoming the social choice problem. Minimizing the number of alternatives on the agenda or criteria for evaluating them goes some way towards addressing the social choice problem. At the extreme, reducing the number of alternatives to two resolves the social choice problem, because majority rule (which reliably satisfies conditions of equality and collective rationality) can be straightforwardly applied. But this approach to addressing the outputs problem may make the inputs problem more severe. Citizens are more likely to feel alienated from the preferences they express over such a limited choice. Such an extreme winnowing of the agenda is not the only way to ameliorate the social choice problem, though. Interdependent processes by which citizens develop widely shared understandings of the most relevant dimensions of political debate can also help to overcome the social choice problem. These processes shrink the domain of preference profiles likely to arise in a political community, and consequently the domain of preference profiles over which voting rules need to be able to perform well. Even if these processes do not *always* nudge the citizenry's preference profiles into the relevant domain, they nevertheless help to limit the frequency and severity of perverse outcomes of voting rules.

To recap, a key function of political agenda-setting processes is to facilitate the satisfaction of the two conditions for meaningful aggregation. Well-functioning agenda-setting processes help satisfy the inputs condition when they enable citizens to form relatively stable preferences over available choices via reasoning processes with which they can identify upon reflection. Well-functioning agenda-setting processes help satisfy the outputs condition when they lead to citizens' having preference profiles that minimize the frequency and severity of perverse outcomes over time, given the existing voting rule. When agenda-setting processes function well, then individual citizens' votes reflect the value of their agency, and aggregation procedures preserve and transfer the value of individual votes to the electoral outcome

DEMOCRATIC AGENDA-SETTING PROCESSES

In addition to performing the functions I have just characterized, agenda-setting processes must also perform these functions in a way that is compatible with democratic values. If agenda-setting processes exhibit unacceptable forms of hierarchy or constraints that excessively inhibit collective empowerment, then they may undermine the value of using aggregative procedures to make decisions over the agendas they produce. Conversely, it stands to reason that more democratic agenda-setting processes will not only be more valuable in themselves, but also make the products of aggregative decision-procedures more democratically valuable as well.

What does it mean for agenda-setting processes to be democratic in their own right? Democratic theorists have given a great deal of attention to this question, so I will only briefly relay some of the most important insights from that work here. But first, it will be useful to explain which approaches will not work. From chapter 2's discussion of the inputs and outputs problem with vote aggregation, it should be clear that we cannot employ an aggregative interpretation of equality to evaluate agenda-setting processes, since valuable applications of aggregative equality depend on the functions of agenda-setting. Instead, we need to turn to an interpretation of political equality that is appropriate for discursive practices. It might seem natural, then, to turn to the alternative interpretation of equality that I characterized in chapter 1. I have called this the deliberative interpretation because it has its clearest expression in some of the canonical early theories of deliberative democracy. This deliberative interpretation of equality is realized in the exchange of mutually intelligible reasons on terms of equal respect. But while agenda-setting does often occur in the course of deliberation,[8] this

---

8. List et al., "Deliberation, Single-Peakedness, and the Possibility of Meaningful Democracy"; Fishkin et al., "Deliberative Agenda Setting."

interpretation of deliberative equality does not address the actual mechanisms of agenda-setting. The classic ideal of deliberative equality governs the *content* of reasons offered in speech and the attitudes of participants toward the reasons of others. As I have already discussed, though, agenda-setting is about raising the *salience* of particular proposals or dimensions of evaluation. It is not—it cannot be—a fully rational process. An interpretation of equality that only governs the reasons offered for or against a set of proposals does not offer the most useful tool for evaluating these agenda-setting processes.[9]

The conception of equality we need will be more complex and appropriate for open-ended, creative endeavors. Democratic agenda-setting is best understood as a creative process, rather than a deliberate choice. Elevating salient options from the full array of logical and practical possibilities requires both imagination and the ability to communicate imagined possibilities to one's fellow citizens in a way that makes them resonate. Agenda-setting occurs when citizens and our representatives appeal to familiar political identities and categories or invent new ones, when we emphasize different disagreements and conflicts, and when we construct narratives of who we are as a community and who we might be. These speech acts certainly involve choices, but they are more like the choices of an artist than the choices of a voter or judge.

In the upcoming paragraphs, I will sketch what I will call—for lack of a better word—creative equality. I do not offer this as a novel conception of equality, but rather as a synthesis of insights that have become commonplace in systemic accounts of deliberative democracy as well as more radical or agonistic democratic theories. These theories focus on whether equality is realized in access to sites of discursive influence and in the distribution of power within these sites. They also emphasize the transformative potential of the discursive environment as a crucial element of collective empowerment. When it comes to evaluating the processes that define, interpret, and raise the salience of political proposals or dimensions of evaluation, these

---

9. Efforts to identify the practical preconditions for deliberative equality may be of greater relevance. Deliberative democrats interested in institutionalizing forms of deliberative democracy have highlighted discursive norms that they understand to contribute to the realization of reciprocity and the production of reasoned discourse. These norms define, for example, who may speak, when, and for how long. They may also govern the timing and location of deliberative forums, and sometimes may aim to ensure certain targets of descriptive representation. All of these are thought to help ensure that deliberative processes are *reasonable* and reciprocal. But they more generally characterize a set of egalitarian norms for discursive environments which may be equally valuable—or perhaps even more so—when it comes to non-deliberative discursive functions.

emphases are more appropriate than the traditional concerns of aggregative and deliberative forms of political equality.

What does political equality at the agenda-setting stage require when citizens are understood as co-creators rather than co-choosers? Assessing the extent of creative equality requires looking both at how citizens are able to cultivate their creative political capacities, and at what they are able to do with them. The cultivation of citizens' creative capacities is, of course, one goal of liberal education. But formal education is for citizens what training in art history or the fundamentals of painting techniques is for artists—valuable, but no substitute for practice. Cultivating citizens' creative capacities, then, must involve drawing citizens into a practice of politics.[10] A democratic society characterized by creative equality will foster broad and deep political mobilization.

The second half of creative equality is what citizens are able to do with their creative capacities. Assessing this side of creative equality means looking at the features of the political environment that determine 1) when citizens have the *opportunity* to address proposals (or other agenda-setting utterances) to the community; 2) when and how these proposals are *amplified*; and 3) when proposals and appeals are *elicited*. Assessing creative equality also means looking at the opportunities for responding to proposals, as well as processes for amplifying and eliciting such responses. Much attention in democratic theory has been devoted to considering what it means to have equal opportunities to engage in political discourse. Though modern democracies typically grant citizens more or less equal permissions to speak publicly, some citizens seem to have more material opportunities to address proposals to the community than others. Less attention, has been given, though, to the distinction between addressing proposals and amplifying them, though this is perhaps a greater cause of unequal power to influence than mere opportunities to address the public.[11] Still less attention has been given to mechanisms for eliciting proposals and responses where appropriate.[12]

It is not enough for agenda-setting processes to be egalitarian. Democratic agenda-setting processes must also be conducive to collective empowerment. This means that democratic agenda-setting processes should also be characterized by an openness to political innovation, contestation, and

---

10. On the "educative" effects of democratic participation and this tradition of democratic theory, see the discussion in chapter 3, and especially Pateman, *Participation and Democratic Theory*.

11. See Miller, "Amplified Speech," 30.

12. But see Disch, "Toward a Mobilization Conception of Representation."

transformation. All else equal, a group of people has more collective power when it is able to influence a greater range of variables in the world.[13] The political agendas that emerge from agenda-setting processes represent only a tiny fraction of the possible courses of action potentially available to the political community. Temporarily foreclosing many potential options is necessary to enable coherent collective decision-making. But, when these foreclosures come to be seen as natural, permanent, or inevitable, something of the people's collective power is lost.[14]

Openness to transformation at the agenda-setting stage is also essential for citizens to recognize their own equally shared agency in public life, especially when they are on the losing side of significant electoral battles. When citizens are dissatisfied with the outcome of an election over a given agenda, the outcome cannot be fully justified to them on the grounds that it was the necessary result of preference aggregation, since that particular agenda will have emerged from a contingent and often mysterious process. It is easy for dissatisfied citizens to imagine that voting over an alternative agenda might have yielded a more favorable outcome. Just consider how much post-election analysis involves imagining alternative slates of candidates and counterfactual agendas—if only Bernie Sanders had won the nomination; or if only the Remain campaign had emphasized different costs of Brexit. Justifying collective decisions requires being able to say to electoral losers that they are not stuck with this agenda forever, that yes things might have been otherwise, but also that they still might be.

Two things remain to be said about democratic agenda-setting processes. First, the requirements I have just laid out are intentionally vague, and there are many plausible ways of satisfying them. They are not meant to provide a blueprint for institutional design, but rather to provide evaluative tools for understanding the strengths and weaknesses of existing political systems, emerging trends, and proposed reforms. In the next two sections, I draw on these tools to articulate the purpose and value of party systems and to develop a normative standard for democratic party politics.

Second, there is evident tension among the different requirements for democratic agenda-setting. Most obviously, we can expect that the more open agenda-setting processes are to innovation, contestation, and transformation, the more difficult it will be to achieve the functional requirements

---

13. Ingham, *Rule by Multiple Majorities*.

14. For the classic statement of this idea, see Wolin, "Norm and Form: The Constitutionalizing of Democracy."

of agenda-setting processes. This tension is sometimes viewed as a dilemma of democratic politics. Consequently, democratic theorists have often responded by grasping one horn or the other. Some minimalist (or minimalist-adjacent) theories insist that adequately satisfying the conditions for meaningful aggregation requires undemocratic agenda-setting processes (and that this is a trade-off we should be willing to make).[15] Other, radical, democratic theories view the closure associated with agenda-setting's functions as inherently anti-democratic.[16] I reject the idea that the tension between the requirements of functional and democratic agenda-setting amounts to a dilemma. Both of these sets of requirements can be viewed as scalar—they can be satisfied to greater or lesser degrees. Democratic agenda-setting processes, then, must balance these tensions, and how well they maintain the appropriate balance is best evaluated diachronically; we want to ask how agenda-setting processes perform over time. This diachronic approach is crucial to the defense of party-driven agenda-setting that I offer in the rest of this chapter. As I will argue in the next sections, competitive party systems contain mechanisms of self-correction that can help to maintain a balance among the various requirements of functional and democratic agenda-setting, but this self-correction must play out over time.

Agenda-Setting and Party Systems

Party politics drives political agenda-setting in modern democracies. Interactions among competing political parties create intelligible political debates and frame public choices from among the vast set of possibilities for collective action. In his classic text, *Party Government*, E. E. Schattschneider asserts that parties "simplify alternatives."[17] Party competition, he argues, transforms the "raw material of politics" into intelligible choices over which it is possible to reach collective decisions.[18] Other theorists of political parties have invoked different metaphors to make a similar point. Giovanni Sartori characterizes party politics as functioning like "traffic rules" which "channel" or "canalize" political expression (ensuring that it reaches its destination in an orderly fashion).[19] Most influential, perhaps is the metaphor of "cleavage." Rokkan and Lipset assert that party competition plays

---

15. Schattschneider, *Party Government*; Rosenbluth and Shapiro, *Responsible Parties*.

16. e.g. Wolin, "Norm and Form: The Constitutionalizing of Democracy."

17. Schattschneider, *Party Government*, 50.

18. Ibid., 34, 52.

19. Sartori, *Parties and Party Systems*, 37.

an essential role in "crystallizing" and organizing the social "cleavages," or dimensions of political conflict, that drive political alignments.[20] Though parties may not create cleavages out of thin air, working instead with latent tensions in public life, they nonetheless play an important role by forcing citizens "to set up priorities among their commitments."[21] The back and forth of competing partisan campaigns elevates some proposals and some criteria for evaluating these proposals. In doing so, party politics creates the conditions for democratically valuable deliberation and aggregation.

The most obvious way in which parties do this is by nominating candidates for office and pooling the effort and resources necessary to give these candidates a chance of electoral victory.[22] As a by-product of parties' dominance in formal electoral agenda-setting, parties also play an outsized role in informal political agenda-setting. Through party competition, candidates come to be associated with particular positions, narratives, or more generally, party "brands"[23] or "images."[24]

The formal and informal agenda-setting functions of party politics help to satisfy the inputs condition for meaningful aggregation. When parties nominate candidates for office and pool resources to campaign for them, they help to narrow the agenda so that it is more cognitively manageable for voters. Meanwhile, party brands and platforms raise the salience of a limited number of criteria for evaluating candidates. Finally, party brands and party organizations link different offices in a way that better enables citizens to predict how different elected officials will interact as they fulfill the functions of their various offices.

At the same time, this process also helps to satisfy the outputs condition for meaningful aggregation.[25] Shrinking the number of agenda items and

20. Rokkan and Lipset, "Cleavage Structures, Party Systems, and Voter Alignments."

21. Ibid., 93.

22. Sartori goes so far as to assert that the minimal definition of party is "a political group identified by an official label that presents at elections, and is capable of placing through elections (free or non-free), candidates for public office" (Sartori, *Parties and Party Systems*, 56).

23. Aldrich, *Why Parties? A Second Look*, 47.

24. Sartori, *Parties and Party Systems*, 293–94.

25. Some theorists of party systems have suggested that political parties initially developed as way to resolve social choice problems within legislatures. John Aldrich has argued that legislators formed "long coalitions" as a strategy for overcoming the instability associated with the social choice problem (Aldrich, *Why Parties? A Second Look*, 43). Aldrich does not claim that parties either had the goal or the effect of overcoming social choice problems in the electorate: members of the electorate (even strong partisans) do not form part of a long coalition in the same way that legislators do (18–19). Social choice problems in the electorate, though, may still be overcome as a *by-product* of legislative parties' separate function of pooling campaign resources.

salient dimensions of evaluation makes it more likely that most citizens' preferences will converge on a domain over which the voting rule performs well with respect to both equality and collective rationality. The most familiar version of this (which I discussed in chapters 2 and 3) occurs when party competition and public discourse establishes a widely accepted account of how parties and their candidates can be located on a left–right political spectrum, defined by the most important cleavage or dimension of political conflict at the time.

Recently, normative accounts of democratic parties and partisanship have also emphasized the agenda-setting functions of party systems. Many of these have focused on agenda-setting as precursor to democratic deliberation.[26] But normative theorists have also pointed to the role of party-driven agenda-setting in creating the conditions for meaningful aggregation. Russell Muirhead, for example, has argued that parties are responsible for creating the kinds of comprehensive narratives and platforms that can gain the support of a group "large and stable enough to possess democratic legitimacy."[27]

Skeptics might argue that democratic polities' reliance on party competition to drive agenda-setting processes is both contingent and sub-optimal. It is perfectly possible to imagine agenda-setting processes in which political parties—at least as we know them—play little or no role. Much popular fervor around democratic reforms in the past two centuries has been animated by a belief that the very existence of parties represents a corruption of democracy. Taking political parties as a given in a work of normative theory, then, may seem to reflect a lack of imagination or ambition. On this view, conceptualizing maximally democratic agenda-setting processes calls for a paradigm shift.[28]

There are two reasons, though, for working within a paradigm of party-driven agenda-setting to develop a regulative ideal of party politics. The first is simply that parties are so deeply engrained in modern democratic

---

26. Jonathan White and Lea Ypi have argued that practices of partisanship help create the "circumstances for justification," most notably through the "systematic generation of principled alternatives" ("On Partisan Political Justification," 385). Nancy Rosenblum has described party antagonism as the "engine of trial by discussion" (*On the Side of Angels*, 160).

27. Muirhead, *The Promise of Party in a Polarized Age*, 19, 91. Also see Rosenblum, *On the Side of Angels*, 357–59.

28. See Landemore, *Open Democracy*, 151–52. Of course, there is a substantial overlap between calls for a paradigm shift away from voting- and elections-centric models of democracy and calls for a paradigm shift in how we think about democratic agenda-setting. But some calls for rethinking electoral agenda-setting do not necessarily challenge the centrality of popular voting practices: see, e.g., Fishkin, *Democracy and Deliberation*.

politics that the kind of radical change that would be needed to supplant or circumvent them, even if possible and desirable, is extremely unlikely. In the meantime, the quality of party politics varies greatly. At the very least, we ought to have evaluative standards to allow us to identify which forms of party politics are least bad.

More to the point, though, the party paradigm *is* a good starting point for thinking about democratic agenda-setting processes. That party competition plays a leading role in political—and especially electoral—agenda-setting within modern democracies is not a lamentable historical accident. As I will argue in the remainder of this section, party systems exhibit features that help successfully navigate the tensions among the various requirements for democratic agenda-setting that I outlined earlier in this chapter.

This does not mean, of course, that party-driven agenda-setting is without drawbacks. At the close of this section, I identify some of the antidemocratic tendencies to which party politics is most susceptible. Together this sketch of the virtues of party-driven agenda-setting processes and of their most common and serious vices provides the basis for developing an evaluative ideal of party politics, which I begin in the next section.

Of course, as long as we are working with a systemic view of democracy, we need not limit ourselves to just one mode of agenda-setting. A democratic system may include a variety of agenda-setting institutions and practices that complement one another, each with its own strengths and deficiencies. I focus my attention on party politics because, as I have noted, I believe it is a useful starting point. Moreover, party politics play a major role in every electoral democracy. Democracies around the world vary greatly in the extent to which they employ formal agenda-setting bodies or encourage interest-group pluralism. But parties are universal.

THE PARTY PARADIGM OF AGENDA-SETTING

To identify the virtues of the party paradigm of agenda-setting, we first need to understand the main features of this paradigm. What *is* party politics? This question is best answered by simultaneously considering what is *not* party politics. Identifying alternatives to the party paradigm is crucial not only for understanding what the party paradigm of agenda-setting entails, but also for engaging in comparative evaluation. Since diminishing the role of party politics in democratic agenda-setting has been a major theme of reform agitation in modern democracies, it is worth considering what critics of party politics might have in mind as the alternative.

Let me identify two plausible candidates for alternative paradigms of agenda-setting, which I call the "associational pluralism paradigm" and the "mini-public paradigm." These two alternative paradigms arise from competing diagnoses of the problem with party-driven agenda-setting. Critics of party politics tend to think either that party systems impose too much structure on agenda-setting processes, or that party systems impose too little (or the wrong kind) of structure. Those who accept the former diagnosis envision a more fluid, non-partisan form of politics as an antidote to party elites' stranglehold on political agenda-setting. This vision sometimes reflects a kind of populist mysticism. There is, however, a plausible version of the non-partisan vision in which a form of interest-group pluralism dominates agenda-setting politics. This *associational pluralism paradigm* does not rest on the populist idea that agenda-setting can occur without effortful organization; rather, it envisions more fluid forms of organization. Interest groups and associated organizations wax and wane in popularity and importance. Coalitions form and disband as the moment dictates. This fluidity and dynamism of associational pluralism stands in contrast to the sticky loyalties and "long coalitions" of party politics.

The converse belief that agenda-setting processes can be improved by imposing *more* structure on them is more popular among academic democratic theorists. For those who hold this belief, the *deliberative mini-public* represents perhaps the most important paradigm of political agenda-setting. Mini-publics are institutions whose participants are selected via a random lottery. Proceedings within deliberative mini-publics are highly structured, consisting of expert presentations and moderated discussions intended to promote egalitarian, informed, and reasoned discourse. Democratic theorists have imagined many different institutional roles for deliberative mini-publics, but very often, these mini-publics are meant to perform some sort of agenda-setting function. Mini-publics have been convened for the purpose of driving informal agenda-setting (in the form of deliberative opinion polls).[29] They have also been proposed and sometimes convened for the purpose of exercising formal agenda-setting powers (in the form of citizens' assemblies that can propose ballot measures).[30]

The characteristic structure of deliberative mini-publics makes it easy to distinguish between the mini-public paradigm and the party paradigm of agenda-setting. The differences between the party paradigm and the

29. Fishkin, *Democracy and Deliberation.*
30. See, e.g., Fishkin et al., "Deliberative Agenda Setting."

associational pluralism paradigm, though, are harder to pin down. This is especially true because some theories of party politics view parties as little more than coalitions of interest groups,[31] and because party systems differ greatly from one polity to the next. Still, there are a number of features that *generally* distinguish political parties from other political associations, and that recognizably distinguish party politics from the politics of associational pluralism. In many polities, the boundary between these two modes of politics is blurrier than this discussion suggests. But what I am describing here is a *paradigm* of party politics. That is to say, this account of the differences between party politics and associational pluralism is meant to offer an intellectual starting point and framework for understanding the mechanisms that might drive agenda-setting processes and for constructing normative standards based on that understanding. Let me also reiterate here that when we adopt a systemic view of democracy, we need not necessarily view these as competing paradigms. We may believe that a healthy democratic system will involve some elements of all three, and when evaluating democratic systems in practice, we will want to consider how they function together. The distinction among these three paradigms, then, is employed here simply as a useful conceptual tool.

In the party system paradigm, political parties differ from other political associations in three crucial ways. First, parties and party competition typically have some formally constituted role in electoral agenda-setting, and often in governance as well. Second, electoral strategies are a core constitutive feature of political parties: parties seek direct control (or a share of direct control) over political institutions by nominating candidates, winning elections, and linking public offices. Third, party systems cultivate allegiances and durable party identities. These allegiances and identities connect party supporters to each other and to a political organization, and they typically survive the usual election-to-election changes to party platforms and strategies.

Electoral systems incentivize political groups to develop capacities to exploit electoral pathways to political power. In an associational pluralism paradigm, this should mean that large associations form electoral strategies, or that numerous associations form mutually beneficial electoral coalitions. In an associational pluralism paradigm, though, these strategies and coalitions remain secondary in both explanatory and normative significance. A party paradigm, on the other hand, holds that groups that form to pursue electoral

31. Bawn et al., "Theory of Political Parties."

strategies (aka political parties) take on distinctive characteristics in virtue of the functions they play in electoral politics. And these characteristics establish essential differences between party politics and other forms of associational politics.

The key difference between the associational pluralism paradigm and the party paradigm is a difference in attitude toward the empirical phenomena associated with party politics. Within the associational pluralism paradigm, party identities and loyalties that take on a life of their own beyond what can be explained by strategic coalitional politics are viewed as aberrations. If we take the associational pluralism paradigm as a normative starting point for reforming agenda-setting processes, the default response might be to try to curtail such aberrations unless they could be shown to generally contribute to the health of a broadly pluralist paradigm. By contrast, the party system paradigm would view parties' developing distinct organizational identities as an expected and welcome phenomenon. Rather than curtail them, the party paradigm from the outset explicitly aims to shape the development of parties in ways that foster functional and democratic agenda-setting processes. On the other hand, the party paradigm regards so-called parties that fail to consolidate a distinctive party identity or brand as aberrational and suspect.[32]

The core idea of the party paradigm is that political parties develop distinctive characteristics in virtue of their electoral strategy. Over time, this leads to the integration of electoral strategy into the party's core organization and even into the associated partisan identity. Insofar as parties seek to gain political power by winning elections, they are playing a numbers game. They aim to have more supporters than their opponents in the electorate and ultimately to have more supporters than their opponents in key public offices. This makes party politics distinct from other sorts of associational politics that might achieve greater influence by having fewer, but more ardent or well-resourced proponents. The party apparatus that develops to play such a numbers game is likely to diverge from other associations, then, regardless of its origins. Party politics is similarly shaped by the other major features of popular elections—the expectation of mass participation,[33] and by the regular recurrence and spectacle of popular voting occasions.

Among the most important of the phenomena that arise from parties' development around electoral strategies are sticky allegiances and durable

32. This is exemplified in recent normative theories on partisanship: see, e.g., Rosenblum, *On the Side of Angels*, 345–47.

33. On many accounts, the modern party system begins when as parties organize for mass mobilization (see esp. Aldrich, *Why Parties? A Second Look*).

identities. Parties are distinguished from temporary and spontaneous political coalitions by the existence of a recognized label and associated allegiance and identity that is only loosely tied to specific political leaders or policy platforms. That is to say, individual members might abandon the party, and individual planks of the policy platform might be dropped without the party ceasing to exist. The party label also represents at least an aspiration or pretention to durability beyond a particular election or political fight.

Classically, the meaning of the party label is cashed out in terms of general political values that are vague enough to have enduring relevance, but concrete enough to generate disagreement, and to provide some constraints on the policy platforms that a party might adopt (though the specification of these values and constraints typically evolves over time). This party label also often represents a political identity that is summative of other identities, but that functions as a social identity in its own right, characterized by affective ties, group loyalty, and in-group/out-group distinctions.[34]

Not all existing political parties exhibit or even aspire to exhibit all these characteristics. Scholars of party politics also debate the prevalence and significance of different aspects of parties and party systems that I have just described. But this account of what distinguishes political parties from other political associations—including temporary coalitions of interest groups— characterizes the party system paradigm. With this account of the distinctive characteristics of party politics in mind, I will now sketch an account of the virtues (as well as the potential pitfalls) of agenda-setting processes driven by party competition.

VIRTUES OF A PARTY-SYSTEM PARADIGM

The virtues of the party paradigm of agenda-setting arise from structural features of electoral systems and parties' characteristic electoral strategy. Party systems involve a mix of formality and informality as well as a mix of

34. In empirical studies of partisanship, these two aspects of party identity—substantive values or ideology on the one hand, and social identity on the other—are often viewed as providing competing explanations for political behavior. But while these two facets of partisanship may be in tension, it is likely that both are operative to some degree in modern party systems and that a full appreciation of the dynamics of party politics must include both elements and their interactions (Huddy and Bankert, "Political Partisanship as a Social Identity"; Huddy, Mason, and Aarøe, "Expressive Partisanship"). Much of the recent normative work on partisanship treats both the ideological and the group affiliation aspects of partisanship as valuable aspects of a democratic party politics (Muirhead, *The Promise of Party in a Polarized Age*; Rosenblum, *On the Side of Angels*).

structure and spontaneity. This mixed character of party politics enables party-driven agenda-setting processes to balance the tensions among the different requirements for democratic agenda-setting described in the first section of this chapter. Competition for political office (at least in the long run) encourages political entrepreneurship and innovation. Party leaders on the losing end of existing electoral cleavages have an incentive to find new sources of political support to increase the size of their electoral coalition. They do this by creating or amplifying new political narratives, or by politicizing new issues and identities, hoping that by changing the terms of political debates, they can peel off support from opposing parties or mobilize previously underserved voters. Parties' electoral strategy and orientation to the mass public thus represents both a spur toward agenda innovation *and* a mechanism by which that innovation can quickly gain broad uptake, suggesting a high degree of transformative potential in the party system paradigm.

At the same time, parties face competing structural incentives to clarify and consolidate political divisions and to limit the set of issues salient in political discourse. This is because parties need to form durable ties among legislators and other holders of institutional power that enable mutually beneficial cooperation over time. This is not to say that durable parties must be characterized by ideological purity at the expense of bargaining, log-rolling, and general coalition politics. But increasing numbers of salient issue dimensions increase potential incompatibilities in legislative or policy agendas, threatening the breakdown of coalitions. Moreover, reaping the benefits of pooled campaign resources that arise from party ties requires that voters can recognize and appreciate the nature of those ties and the legislative agenda, political vision, or identity they aim to advance. Thus, while competition promotes political innovation and potentially transformative politics, it also puts pressure on political parties to synthesize various upstart political issues or narratives into cognitively manageable political cleavages that map clearly onto electoral agendas.

The structure and dynamics of party politics can also promote creative equality. Numerous scholars of political parties have also observed that competitive party systems produce incentives to incorporate previously marginalized groups into mainstream politics. In one influential study, Rokkan and Valen characterize parties as "agencies of mobilization."[35] E. E. Schattschneider argues that "the enlargement of the practicing electorate has been one

---

35. Rokkan and Valen, "Mobilization of the Periphery."

of the principal labors of parties."[36] Histories of the development of modern parties often emphasize that party organization and campaigns were responsible for translating the expansion of suffrage into the expansion of turnout.[37] To the extent that parties have formalized roles in governance, these roles can be designed with an eye toward political equality, meaning that egalitarian principles may be more readily integrated into the party system paradigm than into the associational pluralism paradigm. An example of this is the imposition of gender quotas on party lists.[38]

Some defenders of partisanship have also argued that party politics plays an important role in cultivating citizens' creative capacities. Jonathan White and Lea Ypi suggest two ways that parties may do this. First, parties' efforts to synthesize political messaging for the masses mean that "sophisticated political judgments and the sometimes esoteric terms of political justification can cease to be available only to minority elites and may become part of a joint intellectual stock, available to other citizens and in turn reworked by them."[39] Second, partisan forums create spaces in which citizens can practice politics in a less antagonistic setting, allowing citizens to develop confidence in their political voice before exposing themselves to the entire citizenry.[40]

When scholars of political parties consider the pressures that parties face in virtue of their electoral strategy, they have typically focused on rational responses to structural incentives. But there are other dimensions to this story as well. The development of a political party's distinctive organizational identity around an electoral strategy need not be fully explained within a rational choice framework. Party systems arise and develop their distinctive characteristics because structural incentives interact with human psychology. Individual legislators, voters, and party agents may become strongly identified with the party and its distinctive electoral mission. By internalizing the perspective of the party, its members and supporters confer

36. Schattschneider, *Party Government*, 48.

37. See, e.g., Aldrich, *Why Parties? A Second Look*; Beer, *Modern British Politics*.

38. Even as it allows for regulation, reifying parties' role in governance can have a dark side as well. Some scholars have argued that the integration of state and party has contributed to the "cartelization" of political parties (Katz and Mair, *Democracy and the Cartelization of Poltical Parties*), which, as I discuss below, presents a danger to parties' democratic functions. The key virtues of the party paradigm stem from the hybrid status of parties as *quasi*-public entities. This is, of course, a delicate balance to maintain.

39. White and Ypi, *The Meaning of Partisanship*, 388.

40. White and Ypi, "On Partisan Political Justification," 388. See also Rosenblum, *On the Side of Angels*, 335–39.

on the party identity an independent existence that may outlive its original purposes.

In her defense of "party ID," Nancy Rosenblum has argued that a number of distinctive democratic virtues arise from partisans internalizing the party perspective. Rosenblum argues that partisans don't just want to win. They want the "moral ascendency" that comes with majority status, and they aspire to tell a comprehensive story about the public good that speaks to the entire community.[41] These aspects of partisanship may originate as electoral strategies, but Rosenblum argues that they become integral parts of what the party means to its members and supporters. Even if party leaders do not internalize these values of the party perspective, the electoral context of party politics may nevertheless make certain images of the polity salient to party leaders, affecting the kinds of proposals and programs they are able to imagine. I have argued that the electoral context makes the character of democracy as mass collective action particularly salient. The availability of this particular image may prime party leaders to think about and talk to or about the community as a whole, and to imagine what might be done with the kind of massively shared agency mobilized and made manifest in elections.

THE VICES OF PARTY POLITICS

For the reasons I have just described, the party paradigm represents a promising starting point for characterizing democratic agenda-setting processes. Competitive party systems contain institutional and psychological mechanisms that can help to perform the functions of electoral agenda-setting while also conforming to the democratic criteria of openness to transformation and creative equality.

Of course, the party paradigm also comes with characteristic drawbacks, or a particular set of vices to which it is susceptible. The two most significant of these are de facto hierarchy and factionalism. These represent respective threats to the two core values of democracy: equality and collective empowerment.

The idea of political parties often conjures images of smoke-filled rooms and gilded-age machine politics. Popular distaste for political parties springs from the notion that contemporary parties remain the creatures of corrupt bosses or out-of-touch career politicians. Parties, on this view, are simply

41. Rosenblum, *On the Side of Angels*, 357–60.

vehicles for political elites to concentrate their political power and manipulate the political agenda to serve their own purposes.

This popular image of parties is more than just the baggage of an unfortunate era in the history of democracy. It persists because it reflects an underlying reality about a common vice of party politics: de facto hierarchy. Hierarchies of power and status are common within political parties, even those that purport to have a flat organizational structure.[42] This may be due to sociological forces present within any large organization. Robert Michels' phrase "iron law of oligarchy"[43] has become a slogan for the idea that organizations the size of modern political parties will inevitably be dominated by a small subset of their members. Whether or not hierarchical organization of parties is an "iron law," it is hard to deny that it remains a persistent tendency in party politics.

The second major concern about the dynamics of party politics is factionalism. Whereas concerns about hierarchy arise because of dynamics within individual party organizations, concerns about factionalism arise because of the dynamics of inter-party competition. Democratic theorists have characterized the vice of factionalism differently, but the most generic definition of factionalism is the development of inter-group antagonisms that impede cooperation for mutual benefit, threatening the fundamental purposes of the polity.[44] Because competition among parties and the divisions or cleavages it produces are central to the party paradigm of agenda-setting, there is always a risk that these divisions overwhelm the unity of the polity. Factionalism threatens the value of equality when one group within the polity manages to exclude another from opportunities to exercise political power and/or exercises public power in a way that is neglectful or antagonistic toward some members of the polity. Factionalism threatens collective empowerment when inter-group divisions make it difficult for citizens to resolve disagreements and maintain the basic functions of collective governance.

Some degree of hierarchy and factionalism will always be present in party politics, and will always threaten to overwhelm the democratic dynamics of party systems. The task of normative democratic, theory, then, is to consider not only how to maximize the virtues of party politics, but also how

---

42. In fact, some theorists have argued that reforms to eliminate formal hierarchies are counter-productive as they end up producing organizations that are no less inegalitarian, but where emergent de facto hierarchies are no longer accountable to serving public interests (Rosenbluth and Shapiro, *Responsible Parties*).

43. Michels, *Political Parties*.

44. Chapman, "Reconsidering the Ideal of Non-Factionalism in Party Politics."

to minimize, mitigate, or manage its common vices. In the next section, I take up this task, arguing for an ideal of party politics that centers the role of parties as mobilizers.

A Democratic Standard for Evaluating Party Systems

The way I have characterized the party system paradigm is not always an apt description of how existing party systems actually operate. Party systems vary in the extent to which they exhibit the purported virtues of the party paradigm of agenda-setting. Party systems also vary in terms of how well they manage the common vices of party politics. The party paradigm is a starting point, though, for understanding how we can design or improve electoral agenda-setting processes.

Democratic reforms that shape party systems should aim to produce functional and democratic agenda-setting processes. This section explores questions about the sorts of party systems, party organizations, and partisan practices that best contribute to this aim.

Normative democratic theorists have recently articulated two distinct regulative ideals of party politics: the ideal of "responsible parties" and what I call the ideal of "parties for the common good." Each of these two regulative ideals points to a set of features that we should look for in democratic party system. I begin by briefly critiquing these two existing characterizations of ideal party politics. Then I articulate an alternative ideal for democratic party politics, based on a conception of parties-as-mobilizers.

RESPONSIBLE PARTIES

In their recent book, *Responsible Parties*, Frances Rosenbluth and Ian Shapiro argue that democracy is best served by two-party systems in which centralized, disciplined parliamentary parties compete for full control of government.[45] Such a system, they argue, produces *responsible* parties. The distinguishing characteristics of a system of responsible parties are that it concentrates power in the hands of a few party leaders and ensures that they have substantial discretion to wield political power as they choose.[46]

---

45. Rosenbluth and Shapiro, *Responsible Parties*.
46. The ideal of responsible parties is sometimes taken quite broadly to mean that parties have clearly defined positions and wield political power in such a way that makes it easy for voters to attribute responsibility to party leaders and to hold them accountable using electoral mechanisms ("Toward a More Responsible Two-Party System") but the most comprehensive and sophisticated

The only constraint that party leaders face in such a system comes from the prospect of being held responsible by voters during elections.

The case for responsible parties emphasizes how systems of responsible parties fulfill the functional requirements of political agenda-setting. The chief purported virtue of systems of responsible parties is that they tend to produce high-quality political agendas. Rosenbluth and Shapiro argue that in systems of responsible parties, leaders of competing parties have clear incentives to formulate coherent, broadly appealing platforms and messages that are easy for citizens to understand and evaluate.[47] Rosenbluth and Shapiro argue further that responsible party leaders have incentives to follow through on their proposed legislative programs and to ensure that these programs serve public interests in the medium-to-long run.[48]

Two-party competition, according to its advocates, sharpens electoral accountability by creating a unified opposition. A unified opposition improves electoral accountability by 1) providing citizens with better information about the performance of the governing party (holding the party's feet to the fire); and 2) providing a credible alternative to the incumbent party, a government-in-waiting.[49] These two functions limit principal-agent problems and give party leaders a stronger incentive to serve voters while in office. Meanwhile, the centralized and hierarchical internal organization of parties means that party leaders are better able to respond to electoral incentives, since they are not forced to satisfy the demands of party activists, or recalcitrant coalition partners.[50]

Rosenbluth and Shapiro offer an updated argument for E. E. Schattschneider's classic claim that hierarchical parties "take from the people powers that are merely theoretical."[51] Consolidating agenda-setting power in the hands of a small number of party elites might seem at odds with democratic values. But, they argue, efforts to increase popular control over political parties, or even to expand the range of options that voters face on the ballot, can perversely undermine the value of democratic elections without bringing much benefit. Attempts to dilute or circumvent the power

---

accounts of the ideal of responsible parties defend particular institutional structures that are meant to achieve this outcome by concentrating power in the hands of party leaders (see Ranney, *Doctrine of Responsible Party Government*, for a discussion of the history of the ideal).

47. Rosenbluth and Shapiro, *Responsible Parties*.
48. Ibid., 230.
49. Ibid., 37.
50. Ibid., 113, 123.
51. Schattschneider, *Party Government*, 52.

of party leaders not only prevent parties from effectively organizing collective decision-making, but also weaken the incentives for political elites to identify and serve majority interests.

The theory of responsible parties yields a concrete and measurable standard for party politics. Despite this virtue, though, we should hesitate to embrace the responsible parties model as an *ideal*. Typical arguments for responsible parties begin from an observation that the various normative criteria we might wish to apply to party politics often come into conflict. In particular, just as I suggested in the first section of this chapter, advocates of responsible parties argue that there is a significant practical tension between functional and egalitarian agenda-setting processes. They argue that party systems that more broadly distribute power to influence the political agenda will not produce the kinds of electoral agendas and public preferences that make popular voting a meaningful act of collective agency. Advocates of responsible parties assert that we should resolve this tension by maximizing the functionality of electoral agenda-setting processes. On this view, party politics should, above all else, enable the meaningful aggregation of citizens' preferences. Further, they argue that maximizing the functionality of electoral agenda-setting processes requires political institutions that entrench massive inequalities in agenda-setting power.

There are two reasons that we should be wary of embracing this approach as an ideal for party politics. First, it is not clear that the best response to tension between functional and egalitarian agenda-setting processes requires maximizing functionality to the point where egalitarian considerations are entirely abandoned. Shapiro and Rosenbluth argue that inequalities in agenda-setting power need not be worrisome so long as party leaders face strong electoral incentives to offer voters appealing options that serve "public interests" in the long run. But it is not enough for party leaders to chase electoral majorities. The absence of aggregative criteria for determining *which* majorities should prevail is what generates the need for democratic agenda-setting processes in the first place. The claim that party leaders will produce electoral agendas oriented toward public interests rings hollow if few citizens have a chance to weigh in on the appropriate balance of the public's many interests.

The second reason we should not treat the model of responsible parties as an ideal is that its value is at best contingent on a set of controversial assumptions about elites' motivations and available strategies. And, we have good reason to believe that these assumptions are often—perhaps usually—false. To begin with, it is not clear why even a unified opposition will generally find it in their best interest to help voters hold elected officials accountable to their campaign promises. Parties that have recently suffered electoral defeats may well find that the best strategy is to introduce new dimensions of conflict that destabilize electoral coalitions. To the extent this is true, so-called responsible party systems may not perform as well at maximizing the functionality of agenda-setting processes as their proponents suggest.

Another significant contingency in the model of responsible parties may make hierarchies of agenda-setting power more troubling. One prominent theory of contemporary party politics, the cartel party thesis, suggests that even in—perhaps especially in—responsible party systems, full-throated pursuit of electoral majorities may not be the best strategy for party leaders. Sometimes the better strategy for party leaders is to minimize the cost of electoral defeat, rather than to maximize the probability of electoral victory. Proponents of the cartel party thesis argue that modern economic conditions make it harder for incumbents to control their re-election prospects. At the same time, the professionalization of politics increases the costs to politicians of catastrophic electoral defeats. These trends can make no-holds-barred electoral competition less attractive to party leaders than lower-stakes electoral strategies that refrain from challenging opponents on issues where party elites may have shared interests.[52]

The portrait of elite incentives presented by the cartel party thesis presents a problem for the theory of responsible party government insofar as centralized party organizations and high barriers to entry of new parties makes anti-competitive behavior on the part of party leaders both easier and more attractive. Without constraining pressures from grassroots party activists, party elites may be more free to promote their shared personal and professional interests.[53]

Because it is empirically contingent, the model of responsible parties should not be treated as a regulative ideal. The theory of responsible parties is best thought of a just that—a theory. It offers an account of institutions that, under the right circumstances, may produce a desirable form of party politics. The observable structures of responsible parties—two-party competition,

---

52. Katz and Mair, "The Cartel Party Thesis: A Restatement."

53. Most innocuously, these shared interests may focus on suppressing competition for elite positions within parties (or competition from "outsider" parties). But anti-competitive behavior from elites of opposing parties can become more offensive to the public interest when it works to increase the rents available to office-holders (by, e.g., blocking anti-corruption laws or lobbying reform), to block access to information about government activities or suppress criticism from outside groups, or to depoliticize issues that might challenge the social hierarchies from which most politicians benefit, regardless of their party.

and centralized party organizations—are only instrumentally valuable to the extent that they produce agendas that 1) are populated with valuable alternatives; and 2) facilitate meaningful aggregation. It is possible that these structures may provide useful tools for achieving better forms of party politics, but they should not be treated as valuable in themselves, or even as necessarily good indicators of a healthy party system. This is especially true, because, as I will argue at the end of this section, there is a better alternative.

PARTIES FOR THE COMMON GOOD

The model of responsible parties does not offer a sound regulative ideal for party politics, but one argument for responsible parties implicitly contains a more promising alternative. Advocates of responsible parties argue that competition among two large, centralized parties is desirable in part because it disciplines parties to promote public interests, rather than private or sectoral interests.[54] This argument is compatible with another important strand within recent normative work on political parties, which holds that the defining feature of democratic political parties is their sincere commitment to the common good.[55]

A number of democratic theorists have argued that party politics is at its best when parties aim to advance the public interest or common good. This approach suggests that we evaluate party systems by examining the substantive or rhetorical content of the proposals that parties make and the justifications they offer on behalf of those proposals.[56] Parties, partisans, or practices of partisanship that fail to exhibit an expressed, let alone sincere, concern for the common good are criticizable. Party systems, meanwhile, can be evaluated on the basis of how well they encourage the development of party identities built on beliefs about the common good, rhetoric that employs the language of the common good or public interest, and partisans who internalize a sincere concern for the common good.

---

54. Rosenbluth and Shapiro, *Responsible Parties*, 158–59; See also Schattschneider, *Party Government*, 203–4.

55. White and Ypi, "On Partisan Political Justification," 382; Rosenblum, *On the Side of Angels*, 356–60; Muirhead, *The Promise of Party in a Polarized Age*, 19. Rosenblum's and Muirhead's accounts link this concern with the common good to parties' electoral strategies, and the goal of achieving widespread support, but in all accounts, the concern with the common good is an essential feature of the partisan identity. Partisans internalize and sincerely affirm a commitment to the common good.

56. For a particularly striking emphasis on rhetorical content in evaluating parties against the ideal of the common good, see Herman, "Democratic Partisanship."

Proponents of this ideal of party politics have defined the common good orientation as entailing equal concern for all citizens and an inclusive attitude: partisan rhetorical appeals are addressed to all citizens[57] and framed in non-exclusive terms.[58] The party identity is, in principle, open to all, and partisans hope to win over as many of their fellow citizens as possible. These egalitarian aspects of commitment to the common good are important for ensuring that party competition retains a democratic, non-factional character. Partisans recognize that a victory for the supporters of their party entails a defeat for supporters of another, so the desire to defeat one's opponents must be accompanied by the belief that such a defeat is compatible with opposing partisans' ongoing political equality.

Unlike the model of responsible parties, this ideal of parties for the common good is a genuine ideal. However, existing formulations of the ideal of parties for the common good offer insufficient critical leverage for critiquing parties and party systems in practice. We cannot assess parties' commitment to the common good by looking at the substantive content of parties' proposals, political visions, or justifications, since the substantive content of the common good is precisely the subject of partisan disagreement. This means that an evaluative standard of parties for the common good must focus on the rhetorical frames of partisan discourse or on partisans' beliefs about the inclusiveness and universality of their party's identity and vision. But this version of the ideal of parties for the common good offers no resources to critique the many ways that social positions and especially social identities affect political beliefs, affective ties to a party, and attitudes toward or treatment of opposing partisans. Social positions and identities can affect people's political beliefs in worrisome ways even when they sincerely affirm of the value of political equality.[59] Given the significant role partisanship plays in shaping partisans' regard for and treatment of fellow citizens, it is important that the principle of political equality apply not only to the content of partisan rhetoric or beliefs, but also to the causal processes that lead to the formation of party allegiances and identities and to their behavioral consequences.

Additionally, the ideal of parties for the common good does not provide an adequate basis for evaluating how party driven agenda-setting processes

---

57. Several recent normative theories of partisanship have even identified non-factional partisanship with the deliberative exchange of public reasons (see, e.g., Herman, "Democratic Partisanship"; Wolkenstein, "A Deliberative Model of Intra-Party Democracy"; Bonotti, *Partisanship and Political Liberalism in Diverse Societies*).

58. Rosenblum, *On the Side of Angels*, 356, 365.

59. Chapman, "New Challenges."

realize the conditions for creative equality I outlined in the first section. Much like the ideal of responsible parties, the ideal of parties for the common good focuses its critical attention on the products of agenda-setting processes (the content of party platforms and partisan identities), rather than the way that these products come to be. There are many plausible ways of cashing out the notion of the common good. Consequently, even political agendas characterized by competing conceptions of the common good call for democratic justification.

The regulative ideal of concern for the common good has limited value as a tool for critiquing or evaluating party systems when it is understood in terms of the content of party rhetoric. The animating concerns of this regulative ideal, though, can be given more critical teeth by emphasizing inclusive *activities* rather than rhetorical content. The ideal of parties-as-mobilizers that I propose in the remaining pages of this chapter does just that.

PARTIES-AS-MOBILIZERS

The regulative ideal of parties-as-mobilizers prizes forms of party politics and party strategies that aim to mobilize the broadest range of citizens. One of the major functions of political parties in the development of modern democracy has been to draw previously marginalized groups into mainstream political activity, especially voting. Modern parties developed alongside the extension of mass suffrage, and it was primarily because of party activities that the expansion of suffrage rights did, in fact, democratize modern government. Parties have not simply organized elite competition in emerging mass democracies. They have also mobilized majorities of citizens to make use of their new political rights. Previously excluded groups of citizens do not always come flooding into polling places upon gaining the franchise. Political parties, eager for new sources of electoral support, do not wait for new voters to come to them, though. Entrepreneurial parties reach out to newly enfranchised or long-neglected groups of citizens and draw them into electoral politics with material incentives, personal invitations, and a sense of belonging. Over time, the effects of such electoral mobilization strategies accumulate in the cultivation of political identities, citizen attitudes, and networks of political activity among communities that might otherwise remain detached from electoral politics.[60]

60. For a classic description of this process, see Rokkan and Valen, "Mobilization of the Periphery."

Of course, party systems vary in the extent to which they encourage these sorts of mobilization strategies. And modern parties sometimes find that demobilization strategies, or even voter suppression, can provide them an electoral advantage, as the anecdote at the beginning of this chapter illustrates. It is precisely this variation, though, that makes the ideal of parties-as-mobilizers an attractive and useful regulative ideal for party systems. The tendency of parties to pursue mobilization strategies is both observable and moveable. More importantly, broad mobilization is an unequivocal good,[61] affording as many citizens as possible the chance to exercise their political agency and creating the basis for collective power.

The ideal of parties-as-mobilizers is also an appropriate regulative ideal for party systems because is built on an interpretation of political equality that does not reference either citizens' preferences or a particular agenda of choices. The regulative ideal of parties-as-mobilizers thus offers critical purchase for evaluating how party systems contribute to democratic agenda-setting and preference-formation processes. The regulative ideal of parties-as-mobilizers can thus be seen as identifying how party systems create the conditions for creative equality that I characterized earlier in this chapter.

The idea of political mobilization operates on multiple levels, and the regulative ideal of parties-as-mobilizers is meant to incorporate this complexity. To illustrate the kind of normative guidance that this ideal of parties-as-mobilizers provides, I want to characterize two different registers on which we might talk about mobilization, but this is meant only as a sketch, rather than an exhaustive survey of the contours of the ideal.

The most common usage of the term mobilization in ordinary political discourse, and the most mundane way in which parties can be seen as mobilizers, refers to getting out the vote. Parties are mobilizers when they get people to the polls. The regulative ideal of parties-as-mobilizers suggests that a party system is more democratic when it encourages parties to put more resources into getting more citizens to vote. At this level, the ideal of parties-as-mobilizers doesn't necessarily distinguish between different strategies that party agents might take to get out the vote. Mobilization techniques can include stirring up enthusiasm with political advertisement, defraying the cost of voting by providing transportation to the polls, or information about how to vote, and providing social benefits or exerting social

---

61. Mobilization can, of course be achieved in objectionable ways and can sometimes lead to bad outcomes. But it is not the mobilization itself that is objectionable in these cases, but the way it is achieved or the uses to which it is put.

pressure through canvassing, rallies, and "souls to the polls"-style events. When focused on voter mobilization, the main normative guidance offered by the parties-as-mobilizers ideal is that high-turnout electoral strategies are preferred to low-turnout strategies. Party systems should encourage political parties to aim at maximizing their raw electoral support.

Party systems can encourage mobilization strategies through rules that shape the strategic incentives of party agents. Proportional representation systems, for example, tend to enjoy higher turnout rates than winner-take-all systems.[62] Other sorts of rules can increase the benefit–cost ratio to mobilization strategies. Automatic voter registration, for example, or an overlap between the registration period and the voting period (i.e., a same-day voter registration, or a so-called "golden week" in early-voting regimes), enable parties to mobilize new voters with fewer points of contact.[63] Rules that affect the costs of voting for citizens can make it easier or harder for parties to nudge citizens into voting.[64] Rules regulating Election Day party activity and contact between party agents and potential voters can also affect the relative costs of the mobilization strategies available to parties.

Political environments may also be able to move parties toward mobilization practices in ways that are not exclusively strategic incentives. Party systems give rise to varied kinds of party identities, organizational structures, and norms of partisanship. Party systems accord more with the regulative ideal of parties-as-mobilizers when party identities incorporate the goal of creating more voting supporters as an end in itself, rather than as one possible tool for electoral victory.[65] Party systems also accord more with the regulative ideal of parties-as-mobilizers when they produce a political culture that makes citizens receptive to mobilization strategies.

The ideal of parties-as-mobilizers also operates at another level, though, which is more focused on the conditions for creative equality. The ideal of

---

62. One possible mechanism for the turnout gap is that parties in proportional representation (PR) systems tend to have stronger ties to civil society associations and so may benefit more from "subcontracting" mobilization to these groups. Secondary mobilization may also be more beneficial in PR systems, since turnout is equally valuable regardless of its geographic location. And because the value of increased marginal vote share in PR systems is more consistent across time than in winner-take-all systems, parties may have more incentive to invest in mobilization capital (Cox, "Electoral Rules, Mobilization, and Turnout").

63. See, e.g., McDonald, "Return of the Voter," 5.

64. And particularly effective approaches to increasing turnout, like mandatory voting, may simply eliminate low-turnout strategies altogether.

65. The idea that partisans and party agents might internalize this goal is consistent with some of the recent normative work on democratic partisanship. See Rosenblum, *On the Side of Angels*, 357; Muirhead, *The Promise of Party in a Polarized Age*, 719.

parties-as-mobilizers links the work of getting out the vote to a deeper and weightier kind of mobilization: the activation of citizens' sense of democratic political agency. As I noted above, parties can also have short- or long-term and shallow or deep mobilization strategies. The ideal of parties-as-mobilizers favors strategies for deeper and more durable mobilization that aim not simply to get voters to the polls in a given election, but also to encourage people to develop the attitudes of an active citizen; that is, to view themselves as political agents, to reflect on how they will use that agency to advance political projects, and to consider how voting bears on those projects. For political parties, durable mobilization usually involves the creation of partisanship.

Several political theorists have recently offered compelling accounts of partisanship as a valuable mode of democratic citizenship. These theorists have characterized partisanship alternately as a practice, an identity, or a stance, but all generally agree that the hallmark of partisanship is taking responsibility for one's own political agency. Ideal forms of partisanship entail taking part in the creative work of generating, critiquing, and revising proposals for public action (not merely choosing from a set menu of options); taking sides in political conflict; and responding to and compromising with one's fellow citizens enough to be able to stand and act together with others with common purpose. Party systems that foster the widespread mobilization of this kind of active partisanship help constitute the conditions for creative equality that grant political agenda-setting processes a democratic character.

Here is another way in which the ideal forms of party politics intersect with the distinctive character of popular voting practices. The predictable recurrence of occasions for popular voting create favorable conditions for the mobilization of partisanship. Thinking about the sequence of past and future elections makes long-term political projects salient for citizens during election periods, potentially making them receptive to durable mobilization strategies. The predictable recurrence of elections grants an advantage to politicians and groups who are able to form durable sources of support; it is typically less costly for parties to induce partisans to vote than to mobilize new voters from scratch. The concentration of political attention around elections also lowers the cost of reaching out to citizens with partisan appeals. Finally, the predictable recurrence of elections, and the familiarity and consistency of the electoral environment, likely contributes to the habit-forming effect of voting for a party.

The mobilization of active partisanship is not an inevitable consequence of periodic popular elections, though, as the decline in party identification and party membership in the US and in Western Europe clearly demonstrates. "Electoralist" party forms can also emerge, providing voter mobilization services to candidates, but without establishing meaningful inter-election party identities or organizations.[66] These candidate-service parties can be expected to employ short-term voter mobilization strategies, turning out voters with messaging focused on particular candidates or issues salient in a particular election, rather than investing in the mobilization of durable partisanship. And some longer-term mobilization strategies may not cultivate very deep or active forms of political identity among citizens, instead investing in a primarily negative partisanship.[67]

The ideal of parties-as-mobilizers, then, does not stop at recommending party systems that encourage high-turnout electoral strategies. Key considerations for evaluating democratic party systems should be the extent to which they promote partisan activities that 1) help citizens recognize and appreciate their equally shared agency; 2) offer citizens clear opportunities to join with others in effective political action; 3) draw citizens into the collaborative, creative work of agenda-setting and preference formation; and 4) move beyond inclusive rhetoric to engage in concrete practices of inclusion aimed at diversifying sources of support, and especially diversifying the party's leadership.[68] Party systems that better approximate this regulative ideal of parties-as-mobilizers link periodic occasions for popular voting to projects of governance across time and reinforce the valuable socializing and mobilizing functions of popular voting. These party systems also foster the conditions for creative equality in political agenda-setting processes that lend democratic value to the outcomes of vote aggregation.[69]

Conclusion

Popular voting plays a distinctive role within modern democratic systems. Popular voting's functions bolster the value of other democratic institutions and forms of participation. In turn, other components of democratic systems affect the value of popular voting practices. This is particularly true of agenda-setting and preference-formation processes.

66. Gunther and Diamond, "Species of Political Parties."
67. Abramowitz and Webster, "Negative Partisanship."
68. On the importance of practices versus rhetoric of inclusion, and especially of diversifying party leadership, see Chapman, "Reconsidering the Ideal of Non-Factionalism in Party Politics."
69. Though a more extensive discussion of what it might look like when party systems foster these conditions is outside the scope of this book, a growing body of literature on intra-party deliberative democracy illuminates practices that are in this spirit. See, e.g., Wolkenstein, "A Deliberative Model of Intra-Party Democracy"; Wolkenstein, "Intra-Party Democracy beyond Aggregation."

In this chapter, I have argued that the party system paradigm represents the best starting point for conceptualizing democratic agenda-setting processes. Party systems have developed precisely for the purposes of organizing political competition in large electoral democracies with extensive suffrage. In part because of this, party politics contains self-correcting mechanisms that can help to navigate the tensions among the different evaluative criteria that apply to democratic agenda-setting and preference-formation processes. Rather than trying to replace, circumvent, or stymie party politics, then, efforts to improve these processes should focus on promoting better forms of party politics.

What do better forms of party politics look like? In this chapter I have argued that they look like broad, deep, and durable political mobilization, and especially the formation of active partisanship. Political parties have historically played a crucial role in voter mobilization. The expansion of suffrage rights has made a difference to democracy because parties have encouraged and incentivized citizens to take advantage of their rights. For the most part, parties continue to perform this function of getting people to the polls, though of course, different parties and different party systems do it better than others. But the ideal of parties-as-mobilizers goes beyond just getting people to the polls. Parties have different strategies for getting people to the polls, some of which may be counter-productive for long-term or inter-election mobilization. The ideal of parties-as-mobilizers suggests that when evaluating parties and party systems, we should favor those that mobilize voters in a particular way: by creating and tapping into durable partisan identities that encourage citizens to see themselves as political agents engaged in collective action and to reflect on their long-term political commitments and projects.

The value of popular voting is deeply tied to the value of party politics, and for this reason, the project of evaluating (and reforming) voting practices will always be connected to the project of evaluating (and reforming) party politics. But it is not just the mutual dependence of their value that creates this connection. Because popular voting and party politics are so closely tied, voting institutions and practices invariably affect the nature of party politics we see in a society. When we evaluate existing and proposed institutions, policies, and norms surrounding popular voting, an important component of that evaluation must examine their effect on the party system.

Most normative work in this vein has focused on the effect of electoral institutions—what J. S. Maloy calls "contest structure" and "ballot structure"[70]—on party systems. One of the most well-documented phenomena in political science is the relationship between voting rules and party systems. Systems with proportional representation tend to have more parties than those with single-member districts. In general, we expect that the rules for eliciting and counting votes and the rules for distributing political power based on those votes will affect the number and kinds of parties that develop and the kind of electoral strategies they pursue. Voting rules also affect the forms of partisanship that develop and even the extent and character of voter mobilization. It is widely recognized, then, that determining what kind of voting rules we ought to have depends in large part on what kind of party system we want.

Much less theoretical attention has been devoted to the potential effects of electoral administration on the character of party politics. As I have suggested, electoral administration policies can all be expected to shape how citizens experience Election Day and interpret the meaning of voting. Electoral administration determines where and when citizens vote or how they return ballots, how citizens demonstrate their eligibility to vote, who staffs registration and polling places, and whom else citizens may encounter when they vote. Electoral administration can thus greatly affect the environment in which citizens vote. It also affects how parties interact with citizens. Electoral administration directly affects the mobilization strategies that are available to the parties and parties' incentives to pursue certain strategies. In places where there is an overlap between the registration and the voting period, or where voter registration is automatic, for example, it is much less costly for parties to mobilize new voters, since they do not need to track down new registrants weeks later. Electoral administration also affects whether and when voters are likely to encounter party representatives or partisan messages on Election Day, and it seems plausible that this also affects the development of partisanship.

In the next chapter, I take a closer look at Election Day, examining some of the structures of electoral administration that most profoundly affect what popular voting looks, feels, and sounds like for citizens in modern democracies. Recently, most popular attention to issues of electoral administration have focused on how electoral administration directly affects who votes, by making voting more or less difficult. But electoral administration does not just affect the costs of voting. It also affects the social, material, and psychological benefits of voting.

70. Maloy, *Smarter Ballots.*

Individual decisions about electoral administration may not have as much impact on the number or kind of political parties as decisions about the structure of electoral contests, but the cumulative effect of electoral administration on the character of party politics and on the practice of popular voting may well be profound. Moreover, it is typically easier to change electoral administration policies than it is to change voting rules. Consequently, electoral administration has been the focus of much popular reform enthusiasm. That alone provides enough reason for democratic theorists to give it more attention.

5

Election Day!

In *The American Ballot Box in the Mid-Nineteenth Century,* Richard Bensel paints a picture of the carnival-like, often chaotic, and sometimes violent Election Day in nineteenth-century America. Crowds of men gathered at the polling place not only to cast their own ballots, but to jeer and cheer other voters[1] and to partake of the copious quantities of free liquor that parties provided to their supporters.[2] Designated "challengers" from each party stood by the voting window, prepared to challenge the eligibility of any unfamiliar or suspicious-looking voter.[3] Party agents wandered the edges of the crowd, distributing voting tickets with the party's slate of candidates and often negotiating bribes for citizens' support.[4] The accepted standard limiting disorder at the polling place was simply that "a 'man of ordinary courage' be able to make his way to the voting window."[5]

This drunken festival atmosphere contrasts starkly with the typically calm and more or less orderly atmosphere of contemporary polling places in the United States and most established democracies, where citizens wait in line to cast their votes in private booths, where the names and eligibility of voters are checked against an existing registry, where provision of goods and services for voting is typically banned, and where campaigners and

1. Bensel, *American Ballot Box*, 11–13.
2. Ibid., 57.
3. Ibid., 18–19.
4. Ibid., 30–31, 57–59.
5. Ibid., 21.

canvassers are required to maintain an ample perimeter around the polling place. Despite occasional hiccups or poll-worker confusion, the processes of mobilizing voters, winning supporters, and tallying votes remain nearly invisible in the background of most citizens' immediate experience of voting. The attention to details of election administration in the run-up to the 2020 US federal elections is the exception that proves the rule. Many citizens became suddenly aware of the minutiae of vote-processing and counting. But the politicization of voting methods and electoral administration in 2020 appears so extraordinary precisely because of how bureaucratized Election Day had become.

The transformation of Election Day over the past century and a half demonstrates how different laws and norms of electoral administration can create vastly different Election Day experiences. The experience of voting can, in turn, affect the way that citizens understand the value of voting and their own role within the electoral process. Enabling the practice of popular voting to realize its full value, therefore, requires attention to even seemingly minor aspects of election law that affect how citizens perceive and interpret elections.

In this chapter, I examine three aspects of electoral administration that profoundly affect the Election Day experience: where and when citizens cast their ballots, the locus of authority over electoral administration, and the role of political parties in electoral administration. The majority of this chapter focuses on electoral administration in the United States, where norms and laws in these areas have undergone rapid changes in the past few decades. Where appropriate, though, I discuss electoral administrative practices in other democracies, and consider how far my conclusions can be applied outside of the United States.

In the first section, I provide a framework for assessing electoral administration. This section draws on arguments from the previous chapters about popular voting's distinctive democratic purposes and also introduces some specific issues in bringing these arguments to bear on election bureaucracy. I argue that effective election administration must successfully balance a number of tensions, most notably the tension between the individual and collective aspects of voting.

In the second section, I discuss how and when people vote. In particular, I address the growing trend of "convenience voting." Convenience voting represents a break from traditional simultaneous, in-person voting, allowing citizens to vote days or weeks in advance of an election and/or to vote by mail. Some polities have also experimented with telephone or internet voting. Most US states have made some form of convenience voting available to all eligible voters, and the share of the vote cast in person on Election Day has been steadily falling for the past few decades. A substantial majority of votes in the 2020 US presidential election were cast before Election Day. Outside of the United States, a number of other countries, including Germany and Australia, have seen a smaller, but growing, share of votes cast before Election Day. Switzerland has had a robust postal voting system for decades. Convenience voting aims to make it easier for more people to vote, but the shift from same-day in-person voting does not just decrease the cost of voting. It also changes the optics of elections and how individuals experience the act of casting a ballot. I argue that public debates around convenience voting have focused too much on the material costs of voting and have not given enough attention to how the method of voting affects citizens' experience of voting and the political culture surrounding voting. A holistic assessment of convenience voting should consider its effects on the material cost of voting alongside its broader effects on the practice of popular voting.

The third and fourth sections of this chapter focus on the distribution of responsibility for electoral administration. Here I use the term "electoral administration" broadly to mean the fulfillment of any public function necessary to realize the value of popular voting in a democracy. Thus, electoral administration includes not only collecting, counting, and securing votes (and voters), but also providing for the material and cognitive accessibility of elections. Electoral administration includes ensuring that it is not too costly or difficult to vote, providing information on how to vote, and mobilizing the citizenry. The creation and application of legal rules governing electoral practice is a central aspect of electoral administration, but formal state actions do not exhaust the realm of electoral administration, and the aim of these sections is to ask what role local governments and quasi-public entities like political parties should have in administering elections.

In the third section, I discuss the division of responsibility for electoral administration between local governments and centralized election bureaucracy or national governments. The United States has historically allowed substantial autonomy to state and local governments, but there have always been calls for greater centralization of electoral administration. These calls become louder and more frequent whenever election administration becomes more politicized, as it has in recent years. Calls for centralizing election administration usually invoke concerns about unfair discrepancies in voting procedures across different localities. I argue that while fairness and formal equality are of central importance to the unique practice of voting, local control of elections may also help support the distinctive value of voting in a number of ways. This is true for two main reasons: first, citizens in the United States trust local and state officials much more than they trust federal officials; second, some aspects of local control of elections support citizens' sense of a personal connection to and ownership of the electoral process. I conclude the section with some commentary on how these considerations might bear on an important debate in US election law over the status of preclearance requirements.

In the fourth section, I address the role of political parties in electoral administration. Though the bureaucratization of elections and progressive electoral reforms have significantly diminished the role of parties on Election Day, in many established democracies, and especially in the United States, parties still play a crucial role in maintaining the material, cognitive, and symbolic accessibility of elections. Contemporary parties take on much of the work of mobilizing voters, defraying the material costs of voting, and informing citizens about how to register and how to cast a valid vote. There are genuine reasons for concern about parties' suitability to perform these public functions. But, as I argued in the previous chapter, these concerns can be allayed by employing normative standards for party systems that emphasize parties' mobilizing functions. I argue that the visibility and activity of parties on Election Day plays a vital role in maintaining the value of popular voting practices. Political parties extend to citizens a personal invitation to participate, demonstrate to citizens that their vote is valued, provide social rewards for participating, and encourage citizens to think of themselves not just as consumers or judges of politics, but as political agents in their own right.

Why the Election Day Experience Matters

A central theme that will emerge in this chapter is that if elections are to effectively fulfill their distinctive role in contemporary democracy, then electoral administration needs to successfully balance a number of tensions. Like any bureaucracy, electoral administration must manage tensions around efficiency, accountability, and neutrality if it is to be legitimate.[6] Electoral administration also needs to balance additional and related tensions that arise from voting's distinctive role in contemporary democracy. These include the tension between the formal, procedural equality of elections on

---

6. Mozaffer and Schedler, "Comparative Study of Electoral Governance," 8.

the one hand and the drama of political competition and mass participation on the other; and the tension between the essential collective aspect of voting on the one hand, and the dignity and indispensability of individual votes on the other hand.

Voting's distinctiveness rests, in part, on its ability to encapsulate the intersection of these various democratic values in a singular political moment. But tensions still arise because, in practice, it is difficult to create an Election Day experience that reveals multiple aspects of voting. When electoral administration falls short, it is often because it fails to appropriately balance these tensions, placing too much weight on one aspect of voting at the expense of another. Reforms to electoral administration over the past century have tended to emphasize proceduralism at the expense of political drama, and individual votes at the expense of collective agency.

Richard Bensel's description of voting in 19th-century America reveals how the design of the polling place manifested the dual aspect of voting's formal proceduralism and competitive drama: "the voting window, set in the outside wall of a building, separated election officials from voters. Inside the polling place, the election process was usually quiet and orderly, with officials and ballot boxes efficiently arranged within an enclosed room. The public space outside the window, on the other hand, was chaotic with only minimal attempts at law enforcement."[7] In Bensel's portrait of 19th-century voting, the voter remained outside the polling place window, amid the debating and bargaining, cheering and jeering of party agents and party supporters. The voter himself was part of the competitive fray, even while his vote, once cast, was secured and treated with formal and equal dignity.

Of course, the chaotic atmosphere of Election Day in the 19th century allowed party agents to engage in many questionable electioneering practices, and Bensel describes numerous breaches in the procedural integrity of elections: from bribed or drunken officials[8] to coordinated efforts to overwhelm the ability of election clerks to record all votes in an orderly fashion, and thereby to sneak in extra, illicit votes.[9]

A concern that the competitive aspect of elections will always taint the procedural aspect has led to more radical separation of these two aspects of voting in many contemporary electoral practices. In most developed democracies, not only the counting of votes, but the act of voting itself

7. Bensel, *American Ballot Box*, 13.
8. Ibid., 51.
9. Ibid., 40–41.

is quiet and orderly, with campaigning, mobilization, and competition for votes relegated to some separate sphere outside the legal protective perimeter that surrounds polling places. Convenience voting often makes this separation even starker, with citizens' voting in private settings that are not construed as political.

The achievement of an orderly polling place has undoubtedly improved the integrity of individual votes and vote-counting, but it has also isolated voters themselves from the competitive aspect of elections. The creative component of political competition seems to belong exclusively to a class of political elites; voters are only supposed to witness this competition, not to take part in it. The optics of the sanitized act of voting have led scholars to use metaphors of spectatorship to describe the experience of voting. The idealized version of this spectatorship portrays voters as neutral judges of the political competition. When they cast a vote, they are simply assessing which party or candidate won the competition. To the extent that voters fail to act as neutral judges (as they do more often than not), and vote instead based on pre-existing political preferences, scholars suggest that voting is analogous to expressing support for a favored "team," or endorsing the "brand" whose "products" they like best.[10] As spectators, voters may be the material or the judges of political competition, but voters are not competitors themselves.

Contemporary electoral administration emphasizes the procedural integrity of elections at the cost of obscuring the political agency of voters. Sanitizing the Election Day experience of the drama (and chaos) of political competition may better secure and express the formal equality of voters, but it leaves us with the question: equality of what? The hallmark of democracy is not just that members of the community are treated as equals, but that they are equal *as political agents.* The optics of the contemporary voting experience encourage metaphors of spectatorship that neglect the political agency involved in the act of voting. Voters do not just issue a judgment on political competition; they take sides in the competition, and collectively, they shape the character of political life. Voting is distinctive not just because it instantiates and expresses the equality of all citizens, but because it instantiates and expresses the equality of all citizens as political agents, as the "makers" of democracy.

Focus on the material accessibility and formal proceduralism of voting can also sometimes come at the expense of the symbolic accessibility of

10. See, e.g., Aldrich, *Why Parties? A Second Look*, 19.

voting. For elections to fulfill their distinctively valuable role in democracy, it is not enough that all citizens have the opportunity to vote. Citizens also need to understand that they are expected to vote. They need to believe that voting is *for* them. In modern representative democracy most political decision-making takes place at a far remove from most citizens. It is, therefore, important that the Election Day experience allows citizens to see how political activity fits into their immediate communities and everyday lives. Citizens may also need a personal invitation to vote—a reminder that their voice is valued, and that their participation is essential to democracy. Bureaucratizing the electoral process and shielding voters from the drama of party competition may come at the expense of this symbolic accessibility.

The tendency of electoral administration to protect voters from the competitive aspect of elections and therefore to obscure the political agency involved in voting has accompanied a tendency to emphasize the importance of individual votes at the expense of the distinctive, collective experience of voting. In this chapter, I argue that seemingly progressive electoral reforms that aim to lower the costs of voting for individuals, or to protect the independence of voters, can have perverse effects because they fail to appreciate voting's distinctive value as a moment of mass participation. As I argued in chapter 1, one of the most distinctive aspects of popular voting's value is that it helps citizens locate their individual agency within the shared agency of the citizenry. To do this, the experience of voting should make the collective nature of democracy salient to citizens. Voting is not just an individual act undertaken separately by many individuals; voting is something we do together. Citizens come to the polls not just to express a personal opinion, but to make a shared decision.

Balancing these tensions in electoral administration is not just a matter of trading off conflicting values. When the competitive or collective aspects of voting are obscured, then it becomes unclear why accessibility and formal equality are so particularly important in elections. The procedural equality of elections is different from, say, procedural equality in law enforcement; the equal counting of votes expresses citizens' equality as political agents. Formal voting equality is distinctively valuable precisely because voting is an exercise of political agency. Likewise, the accessibility of voting is particularly important because of voting's uniqueness as a form of mass participation. Individual votes are indispensable to elections, precisely because *everyone* is expected to vote.

A Defense of Election Day

Since the early 1980s, and particularly since 2000, the United States has seen a rapid shift toward early, absentee, and postal voting—what Paul Gronke calls "convenience voting." Even prior to the emergency expansion of early and mail-in voting in response to the 2020 coronavirus pandemic, most US states allowed some period of early in-person voting before Election Day, no-excuse absentee voting, or both. Utah and Hawaii have recently joined Oregon, Washington, and Colorado in conducting elections entirely by postal mail. California is moving in that direction as well. In the 2004 US presidential election, approximately 20 percent of ballots were cast outside of traditional precinct polling places.[11] By 2016, that proportion had risen to 40 percent, and in 2020, it leaped to more than 60 percent.[12] This trend is not unique to the US; as mentioned, Swiss elections have been conducted primarily by post for decades. Since 2000 several regions in the UK have begun allowing "on-demand" postal voting, and a few localities have seen pilot programs for "multi-channel" elections, allowing citizens to vote via telephone, computer, or mobile device.[13]

Proponents of convenience voting claim that increased voter convenience makes elections more accessible and consequently should increase turnout, especially among those who face the most difficulty getting to the polls on Election Day. Individuals who take advantage of early and mail-in voting do report that they are more convenient, and across the country there has been substantial popular support for moving toward more flexibility in voting.[14] Furthermore, non-voters consistently report being "too busy" as a major reason for not voting,[15] so it seems natural to expect that expanded opportunities to vote could make a difference in many individuals' decision whether or not to vote. Most importantly, it is commonly asserted that convenience voting most benefits disadvantaged groups that have historically voted in smaller numbers. The flexibility offered by early and absentee voting should make voting easier for those who lack control over their work

11. Fortier, *Absentee and Early Voting*, 45–46.
12. Precise figures on the usage of convenience voting are hard to come by due to the decentralized character of US election administration, but various estimates tell a consistent story about recent trends (Gronke and Miller, "Early Voting in America," 384–88).
13. Wilks-Heeg, "Treating Voters as an Afterthought?," 105.
14. Gronke and Miller, "Early Voting in America," 383.
15. Fortier, *Absentee and Early Voting*, 48.

schedule, those who have to care for young children or family members, those who have health problems, and those who find it difficult to arrange transportation to the polls.

The chief drawback of convenience voting is that it may have a detrimental effect on the Election Day experience, and thus on the perceived value of voting. Proponents of convenience voting might be inclined to dismiss this as a trivial concern. Viewed through traditional models of rationality, the idea that changing where and when voters cast their ballot might significantly affect political attitudes may seem implausible. Moreover, proponents of convenience voting argue that any loss to the festival atmosphere of Election Day is outweighed by the value of making voting more accessible to poor and to young voters, and of expanding the electorate.

Empirical evidence on the turnout effects of convenience voting, combined with a clear understanding of voting's distinctive purposes, should lead us to reconsider these arguments, though. Studies of early and postal voting have yielded conflicting accounts of the effect that convenience voting has on voter turnout. The effects of convenience voting provisions differ across contexts and depend on the specifics of the policies and their implementation, but a few patterns can be identified. First, early and absentee voting provide a modest boost to turnout at best.[16] Second, for most forms of convenience voting, the increase in turnout appears to be greatest immediately after the new voting methods are introduced and declines as the novelty of voting early or by mail wears off.[17] Third and finally, convenience voting provisions have mostly failed to deliver on their promise of bringing new populations into the electorate; the people most likely to take advantage of convenience voting are older[18] and more politically engaged—people who are likely to vote no matter what.[19] There are, of course, exceptions to these general patterns, but as I will explain later in this section, examining

16. Gronke et al., "Convenience Voting," 442; Leighly and Nagler, "Effects of Non-Precinct Voting Reforms." Studies of postal voting in Switzerland and of experiments with on-demand postal and e-voting in the UK have similarly found similarly modest effects (Wilks-Heeg, "Treating Voters as an Afterthought?," 103–5; Luechinger, Rosinger, and Stutzer, "Impact of Postal Voting on Participation").

17. Giammo and Brox, "Reducing the Costs of Participation," 298–99; Gronke and Miller, "Voting by Mail and Turnout in Oregon."

18. Berinsky, "Perverse Conquences," esp. 478–80; Leighly and Nagler, "Effects of Non-Precinct Voting Reforms." Early studies of convenience voting also found that early and absentee voters tended to be wealthier and more educated, but these patterns are not evident in more recent studies. Gronke et al., "Convenience Voting," 443.

19. Gronke et al., "Convenience Voting," 444.

those exceptions further underscores the limitations of a focus on voting's convenience.

Understanding the distinctive value of voting in contemporary democracy may help to explain these counter-intuitive results. Voting plays a unique role in contemporary democratic practice as a form of participation in which *all* citizens are expected to participate. Both the maintenance of this expectation over time and its value are tied to the optics and the general experience of elections as special moments of mass participation. Mass electoral participation makes manifest the equal political agency of all citizens in a democracy. The phenomenon of mass participation in popular elections emphasizes two important aspects of that equal political agency. First, democracy is a collective undertaking. Even though citizens may have different political preferences or policy goals, decision-making in a democracy is something that we are committed to doing together. Witnessing so many people taking part in elections makes the collective nature of democracy impossible to ignore. Second, *each* citizen is an equal agent in democratic self-rule. The expectation of universal participation in elections makes clear that the community regards the input of every individual citizen as important.

Proponents of convenience voting have been too quick to dismiss the significance of the Election Day experience in supporting the value of popular voting. As Dennis Thompson observes: "When citizens go to the polls on the same day, visibly and publicly participating in the same way in a common experience of civic engagement, they demonstrate their willingness to contribute on equal terms to the democratic process."[20] The experience of standing in line with others to cast a vote, or seeing images of people voting across the country in news coverage makes the collective nature of democratic decision-making tangible and immediate. Witnessing the incredible volunteerism and mobilization of resources needed to handle the volume of citizens turning up to take part in political decision-making drives home the message that it is important that all citizens have a part in democratic self-rule. And when I go to the polls on Election Day, I don't just observe this message, I participate in expressing it.

As I argued in chapter 1, this spectacle of elections forms part of a constellation of core features of popular voting that together realize distinct and important facets of democratic values. Historically, the Election Day experience has played a central role in this constellation, and it remains unknown

---

20. Thompson, *Just Elections*, 34.

how shifts in how we vote will affect citizens' perceptions of voting's collective dimensions. The widespread shift toward convenience voting alters the optics of elections in two ways. First, it changes the context for the act of voting. We are sensitive to our environment, and especially to our social environment. When voting takes place at home, or at the same service counter where we apply for a vehicle registration, then voting will be experienced more as a solitary activity than as something that is, at its heart, done with others. Second, widespread convenience voting also changes what we *witness* on Election Day, regardless of which method of voting we use ourselves. Even if I hear reports of large numbers of early and absentee voters, these numbers lack the immediacy and concreteness of actually seeing crowds of people voting at the same time.

Much of the value of popular voting as a practice derives from the connection between the concrete act of voting and the abstract value of democracy. The Election Day atmosphere does not just convey the "specialness" of voting, it reveals *why* voting is special. By participating in a moment of massively shared decision-making, citizens contribute to a collective project of democratic self-rule. The experience of voting should be different than the experience of filling out a credit card application or a customer satisfaction survey. The experience of voting should give voters a sense of themselves as *political* actors, as participants in an undertaking with many, many other different people.

It might seem that these concerns are easily outweighed by the value of the increased accessibility that convenience voting affords. After all, if voting is to manifest the equal political authority of all citizens, then all citizens actually need to be able to vote. If elections are not widely accessible, then their expressive effects will be distorted, signaling that it is acceptable to exclude some citizens from voting. But convenience voting tries to increase the accessibility of elections without sufficient attention to why accessibility is so important for *voting* in particular. Moreover, convenience voting often fails to achieve its own aim because it focuses on a narrow set of the material costs of voting while neglecting or even increasing other symbolic barriers to voting.

If popular voting is to effectively fulfill its role in modern democratic systems, then voting needs to be materially, cognitively, and symbolically accessible. Convenience voting eliminates only some of the barriers to material accessibility while neglecting other, more intransigent cognitive and symbolic hurdles. Actually casting a ballot represents a only a portion of the cost of voting. Citizens must incur prior costs to acquire information about how to vote and to plan accordingly.[21] Convenience voting policies that simply increase the number of voting methods available to citizens increase the cognitive burden of this sort of planning. This cost may not be felt deeply by citizens who have experience navigating complex bureaucracies and know where to find the information they need, but for others it may be more burdensome. The costs of becoming informed about and planning to take advantage of convenient voting methods may explain why early voting tends to attract people who would vote anyway.[22] These high-propensity voters tend to be more attuned to sources of political information, to have a higher sense of personal political efficacy, and to have experience successfully navigating government bureaucracies. Convenience voting policies are unlikely to attract habitual non-voters to the polls without substantial efforts to assist new voters in taking advantage of them.[23] They may even perversely deter potential voters by making the voting process appear more complex and daunting.[24]

Exceptional cases in which early voting has expanded the electorate illuminate the limitations of a focus on voting's convenience. In 2008 large numbers of Black citizens in North Carolina—many of whom were not habitual voters—took advantage of their state's early voting provisions to cast a ballot in the federal election. This reversal of the demographic bias in convenience voting resulted from the Obama campaign's massive mobilization efforts to assist these new voters to register and vote early.[25] Researchers have also noted absentee voting has a more substantial positive effect on turnout when coupled with effective party mobilization to encourage and assist voters in casting absentee ballots.[26]

Coordinated party efforts to increase the use of convenience voting are more successful at expanding the electorate because they do not simply reduce material barriers to voting. They also reduce symbolic barriers by *reaching out* to citizens and providing them with a reason to vote. Studies of mobilization efforts have shown that asking someone to vote, especially in person, is one of the most effective ways of mobilizing new voters.[27] When

---

21. Dyck, Gaines, and Shaw, "Effect of Local Political Context," 1092.
22. Berinsky, Burns, and Traugott, "Who Votes by Mail?," 190; Stein, "Early Voting," 68.
23. See Oliver, "Effects of Eligibility Restrictions and Party Activity," 504.
24. Gronke et al., "Convenience Voting," 444–46.
25. McDonald, "Return of the Voter."
26. Oliver, "Effects of Eligibility Restrictions and Party Activity."
27. Gerber and Green, *Get Out the Vote!*, 36. Gerber and Green argue that "face to face interaction makes politics come to life and helps voters to establish a personal connection with the electoral process" (41).

party members reach out to mobilize new voters—whether they encourage them to vote in traditional or non-traditional ways—they increase the symbolic accessibility of elections. They communicate to citizens that voting is *for* them, that their vote is valued and expected. These sorts of contacts create a sense of personal connection to the democratic process, while also assuring citizens that they are up to the task of political participation.

I will discuss the value of party mobilization later in this chapter. Here I just want to note how this sheds light on the limitations of convenience voting as a mechanism for increasing voter turnout. Convenience voting focuses exclusively on lowering the cost of voting without attending to the reasons that citizens have for voting. Voting will always involve some cost, however small, so those who cast a ballot must value voting enough to offset this cost. Convenience will only make a difference for people who already place some positive value on voting. Those who have a low sense of political efficacy, who feel disconnected from the political process, or who fail to see the connection between their individual vote and the collective project of democracy are unlikely to place much value on voting. Lowering the cost of voting by offering a wider range of times and places that an individual can vote will not make much of a difference in the turnout decision of these citizens.

The material barriers to voting are real and do need to be addressed, but not without considering the reasons that people have for voting in the first place. In the remainder of this section I discuss a set of approaches to increasing the accessibility of voting that also support the experience of elections as momentous occasions, and of voting as a massively shared collective activity.

AUTOMATIC AND SAME-DAY VOTER REGISTRATION

For citizens to vote in most contemporary democracies, they must first become registered to vote. In many countries, voter registries are compiled automatically. India, for example, creates its voter registries using census data. Where registration is not automatic, citizens must actively take steps to demonstrate their eligibility and get on the voter rolls. In many places, citizens are required by law to register to vote. In others, including the United States, voters may choose to register, but are not required to.

Registration is typically more costly than voting itself, but how costly it is, and how likely citizens are to bear those costs, depends not only on what citizens must to do to register, but also *when* they must do it. Most US states require voters to register several days or weeks before they can vote in an election. However, many states have begun allowing same-day voter registration. In fact, since 2010, the number of states with same-day voter registration has doubled. The District of Columbia and 21 states now have some form of same-day registration.[28]

Allowing same-day registration boosts turnout at least as much, and probably more than convenience voting provisions (average estimates put the effect of same-day registration at about 5 percentage points).[29] Same-day registration boosts voting's accessibility through three main mechanisms. First, it reduces the overall burden of voting by enabling voters to bundle the material and cognitive costs of registering with casting a ballot. Second, and consequently, same-day registration makes mobilizing new voters a more viable and cost-effective electoral strategy since campaigns need to expend fewer resources to bring new voters into the electorate.[30] Third, same-day voter registration allows voters to join the electorate when interest in voting is highest.

Unlike convenience voting provisions, the mechanisms by which same-day registration increases voter turnout reinforce the experience of Election Day that contributes to voting's distinctive value. Same-day registration acknowledges that elections create unique democratic *moments* when citizens' political agency is particularly salient. Same-day registration enables citizens who are swept up in the election moment to participate. It thus boosts the important socialization function of popular voting occasions. And because same-day registration targets the material costs of the first and most demanding step in voting, it is more likely to introduce new groups of voters into the electorate.

AN ELECTION DAY HOLIDAY

Another approach to making voting more accessible is to make Election Day a national holiday. Holding elections on a weekend or national holiday is standard practice in most democracies. Estimates of the turnout gains

---

28. "Same Day Voter Registration."

29. Brians and Grofman, "Election Day Registration's Effect on U.S. Voter Turnout"; James, "Electoral Administration and Voter Turnout," 378.

30. Part of what enabled the 2008 Obama campaign to successfully use early voting to mobilize new voters in North Carolina was the fact that the early voting period overlapped with the registration period. Volunteers did not have to worry about following up with newly registered voters weeks after their first meeting.

from making Election Day a holiday are hard to come by,[31] but some studies suggest a potential turnout boost between 3 and 6 percentage points.[32] An Election Day holiday supports the distinctive role of popular voting in two ways. First, an Election Day holiday lowers the material costs of voting for some workers. Of course, the material benefits from making Election Day a holiday will vary across employment sectors, and will depend on the legal protections and cultural norms around operating businesses on a holiday. An Election Day holiday will most effectively and equitably reduce barriers to voting alongside special attention to the position of service-sector workers who are typically expected to work on holidays.

The main benefit of an Election Day holiday is not its effect on the material cost of voting, though. Establishing an Election Day holiday also signals the centrality of voting to a democratic polity, marking elections as special occasions to be celebrated and honored. An Election Day holiday creates more favorable conditions for communities and organizations to hold celebrations and festivals that emphasize the shared, collective aspect of democracy and provide social rewards to voting. An Election Day holiday would also enable many more citizens to volunteer for campaigns or as poll workers, increasing the opportunities for citizens to experience valuable personal contacts and reminding them that political agency is for everyone.

MANDATORY VOTING

By far the most effective thing a polity can do to boost voter turnout is to make voting mandatory. Unlike most other turnout-boosting measures, mandatory voting focuses on giving voters a reason to vote, rather than on reducing the cost of voting. I have argued for the value of mandatory voting in other work,[33] so I will not dwell on it here. But given its effectiveness at increasing turnout and its consonance with voting's distinctive purposes, I would be remiss not to at least briefly mention it. Where they are effectively enforced, mandatory voting policies are thought to be responsible for an estimated 10 to 15 percentage point increase in voter turnout,[34] and their effects are greatest where baseline turnout is lowest.

---

31. Blais, "What Affects Voter Turnout?," 115.

32. James, "Electoral Administration and Voter Turnout," 381.

33. Chapman, "The Distinctive Value of Elections and the Case for Compulsory Voting."

34. Blais, "What Affects Voter Turnout?," 112–13; Birch, *Full Participation*, 96–97; James, "Electoral Administration and Voter Turnout," 381.

Mandatory voting's effectiveness does not seem to depend exclusively on material incentives. Penalties for non-voting in most mandatory voting regimes are modest (involving, for example, fines in the neighborhood of 20–50 US dollars), and non-voters can often have those fines waived if they offer an acceptable excuse (such as illness, travel, or caregiving obligations). The key to the effectiveness of mandatory voting is that it combines these material incentives with the expressive force of the law. Mandatory voting uses the community's most powerful means of public communication—the law—to establish the expectation of universal electoral participation. Mandatory voting sends the message that citizens' contributions are not just allowed. Each and every citizen's contribution is, in fact, essential to the project of democracy.

CONVENIENCE VOTING BEST PRACTICES

Providing voters with a greater variety of convenient ways to cast their ballot is a popular way to increase the material accessibility of elections. These policies will not draw new voters into the electorate unless citizens perceive a positive reason to vote. Convenience voting on its own does not provide this positive motivation to vote. In fact, as I have argued, convenience voting may erode citizens' perception of the distinctive value of voting, because it distances the actual act of voting from the spectacle of collective political action.

It may well be too late to reverse the trend away from traditional polling place voting, at least in the United States, but even if that is true, the concerns that I have raised in this section can still provide relevant guidance on some ways to maximize the benefit and minimize the harms of convenience voting. I want to briefly note two ways this is true. First, this discussion should lead us to consider what might be lost in a shift toward convenience voting and to look for ways to mitigate that loss. In particular, we should look for ways to make the drama of mass participation salient to citizens whenever and wherever they vote.

Second, and perhaps counter-intuitively, consideration of the experience of voting and optics of Election Day may give us reason to favor universal vote-by-mail systems over the currently more common practice of offering voters many options for how to vote. This may seem surprising, since regimes that only offer early and mail-in voting as options will still enable at least some citizens to experience traditional in-person voting. However, the meaning of that experience changes as fewer people take part in it. Meanwhile, regimes that offer many different options for how to vote have significant downsides.

First, they introduce additional complexity into voting decisions, and make it less likely that citizens will receive a consistent and clear message about when and how to vote.

Perhaps more seriously, complex convenience voting regimes diminish the commonality of the voting experience. Despite the fact that all votes contribute to a common decision-making procedure, early voting, mail-in voting, and Election Day voting can come to be seen as different sorts of political acts. Worse still, they can be treated with varying degrees of legitimacy. As the 2020 US election revealed, this is particularly trouble-some when voting methods become politicized and choices about how to vote align with partisanship. It is easy to overrate the problems and underrate the validity of methods of voting that you have not used yourself, especially if no one else you know used them either. It is easy to write off mail-in voting as mostly fraudulent if everyone you know voted in person.

Even though universal vote-by-mail systems deprive citizens of the experience of voting in the physical presence of others, they nevertheless at least offer voters a common experience. Combined with other efforts to remind voters of this commonality and to make the *collective* aspect of voting salient during the election moment, universal vote-by-mail systems may be better able to preserve the value of the traditional Election Day experience than systems with multiple "convenient" voting options. There is much we still don't know about the long-term effects of different forms of convenience voting, and I believe there remain good reasons to be concerned about these effects. But if a widespread return to traditional Election Day voting is not in the cards, universal vote-by-mail seems likely to be the next best thing.

Local Control of Elections

The trend in state-by-state adoption of convenience voting illustrates the substantial decentralization of electoral administration in the United States. The US has very little in the way of centralized election bureaucracy. Even federal elections in the US are characterized by an exceptional amount of local control. Decisions regarding the location of polling places, the kind of voting technology that will be used, the design of ballots, even who will appear on the ballots are made at the state or local level. Constitutional amendments and Congressional legislation provide a handful of require-ments and restrictions, but states and localities still retain a great deal of freedom in conducting elections, and they usually oversee them exclusively. Literacy tests and poll taxes are no longer permitted, but states may still set residency requirements, require that voters register in advance of elections, and demand photo identification in polling places. States (and often localities) also have substantial discretion in how they maintain and update their records of registered voters. And, of course, states also retain the right to disenfranchise convicted felons.

Some of the most fundamental features of American elections—like the secret ballot—are established in state, not federal, law.[35] Federal law determines the date on which federal elections are to be held, but states may allow early voting, absentee voting, or they may identify the date of a federal election as the deadline to vote by mail. Even when the federal government does legislate regulations on the conduct of elections, as, for example in the Voting Rights Act, or the National Voter Registration Act, oversight and enforcement of these laws is handled by the courts, rather than a federal election bureaucracy.

The extent of local control of elections in the United States has long been controversial, with some reform advocates (primarily progressives) pressing for greater centralization of election bureaucracy more akin to that of many European democracies. Two important pieces of legislation from the past few decades have moved some degree toward greater centralization of electoral administration. The National Voter Registration Act (NVRA) established requirements for how states maintain their voter registries. It also required that states expand opportunities for citizens to register to vote. The NVRA requires that citizens be able to register at a number of offices providing public services, most notably, those providing services primarily to people with disabilities, and those issuing driver's licenses (because of this provision, the legislation became known as the "Motor-Voter Act").

The Help America Vote Act (HAVA) of 2002 expanded some of the registry maintenance requirements of the NVRA, but also went much further toward a centralization of electoral administration. Enacted in response to the 2000 presidential election controversies, the HAVA provided federal funds for states to replace outdated voting equipment and to make other improvements to their voting systems. It also established some minimum requirements for voting systems, and perhaps most significantly, established the Election Assistance Commission, charged with, among other things, assisting states in HAVA compliance and administering a voting system certification program.

---

35. Some federal laws—including the Help America Vote Act—do assume that voters should be provided privacy in the act of marking the ballot, but they do not ensure that voter's choices remain secret after they have been cast.

The NVRA and HAVA reflect concerns with the inconsistency and potential inequality arising from local control of elections, but these acts still leave substantial autonomy to states and local governments. As I write this, a yet more sweeping bill—known as H.R. 1 or the For the People Act—passed by the US House of Representatives in 2021 has become the focal point of recent efforts to more closely regulate states' administration of elections, particularly in the wake of controversial Supreme Court decisions on the Voting Rights Act, campaign finance, and legislative redistricting. The For the People Act of 2021 would, among other things, require states to enable automatic and same-day voter registration and to allow early voting. Even this bill, though, still leaves states and localities with some discretion regarding administration and oversight of elections. As I write this, it also appears unlikely that The For the People Act of 2021 will become law in anything like its current form.

Is this to be lamented? Would the practice of popular voting better fulfill its purposes in our democracy with more nationwide consistency and a centralized election infrastructure? Here, again, there is a tension between competing aspects of voting's value. On the one hand, as I discussed in the previous section, there is a great deal of value in establishing a common experience of voting across all jurisdictions, and especially in ensuring the equity and fairness of voting procedures. On the other hand, part of the value of voting lies in how it makes citizens' agency in and ownership of democracy apparent, in how it connects the massive collective activity of democracy to citizens' immediate lives and communities. Centralizing election bureaucracy may undermine that sense of connection to and ownership of the electoral process. In the remainder of this section, I discuss how to navigate this tension in light of the account of voting's value that I have offered in this book.

The focus of this discussion is on the fact of decentralization itself than with any particular policies that states or localities may adopt. I take it for granted here that states and localities sometimes (perhaps often) adopt wrongheaded or unjust election laws and procedures. I also take it for granted that the federal government is similarly capable of adopting bad election policies. I am interested in assessing the extent to which it is important that federal election administration be centralized and standardized.

The progressive instinct to centralize electoral administration stems in large part from a concern that local variation generates political inequality among citizens in different communities.[36] The Help America Vote Act of

---

36. At the time of this writing, there is a different, perhaps more salient, driver of progressive concerns about local control of elections: the efforts of Donald Trump's supporters to consolidate

2002 was a direct reaction to the controversy surrounding Florida's role in the 2000 presidential election that put a spotlight on some of the concerns about fairness that arise with local variation in election administration. The confusing design of the "butterfly ballot" meant that voters in Palm Beach County were more likely to cast an erroneous vote than were voters living elsewhere.[37] Different precincts used different kinds of voting technology, and these technologies also had different error rates. As it happened in Florida, poorer counties tended to have worse technologies,[38] and consequently, these counties saw more ballots invalidated. The varying availability of volunteer and paid poll workers to answer questions and the lack of a uniform system for determining when to count a questionable ballot[39] acted as more potential sources of inequality among counties and precincts. And, of course, the decentralized administration of federal elections led to major jurisdictional battles when the election results were contested.[40]

There are (at least) three reasons that we might be worried about the effect that this patchwork of electoral administration has on the ability of elections to fulfill their distinctive and valuable role in contemporary democracy. First, and most seriously, local variation in elections raises concerns about inequality. Concrete, formal equality is the hallmark of voting. All citizens are expected to participate in elections, and each person's vote counts exactly the same as any other person's. The immediacy and publicity of voting equality is essential to voting's distinctive role in democratic practice. Voting makes manifest the *equal* political authority of all citizens in a democracy. But voting equality for all citizens has not been easily won or maintained, and in the past century of US history, local control of elections has presented some of the biggest obstacles to the ideal of equal franchise. The Voting Rights Act of 1965 and subsequent court decisions like *Harper v. Virginia* and *Thornburg v. Gingles* purportedly put an end to the literacy

---

control of local and state processes that control election administration. While this effort is troubling and deserves attention, it is important not to overlearn from it. Those wishing to consolidate power will direct their efforts wherever the power lies. It is not an inherent flaw of local control that bad actors try to exploit it. The question to ask is how different administrative systems compare in terms of their vulnerability to such efforts. It is far from obvious that a centralized election bureaucracy would be more resistant to capture by anti-democratic movements.

37. Wand et al., "Butterfly Ballot Did It."

38. It's worth pointing out, though, that money doesn't always buy more votes. Some of the more expensive voting machines don't necessarily have significantly better error rates than other, less expensive technologies (Streb, *Rethinking American Electoral Democracy*, 90–96).

39. Epstein, "'In Such Manner,'" 14–15.

40. Sunstein, "Introduction: Of Law and Politics," 3–4.

tests, poll taxes, racial gerrymandering, and other measures that states and local communities used to suppress or dilute the Black vote. But more recent election law jurisprudence has weakened some of these protections. Moreover, many aspects of electoral administration that are neutral on the face of it can be exploited for partisan advantage. In designating the location and hours of polling places, defining registration, residency, and ID requirements for voting, state and local governments affect the costs of voting and may, in turn, affect the extent and distribution of turnout.

Concerns about voter equality can arise even where eligibility or turnout are not at issue. Voting equality should mean that all individuals have an equal chance of casting a valid ballot, which requires equality both in the casting and the counting of ballots. But differences in how communities recruit and train poll workers may affect the likelihood that voters will be properly instructed in how to complete and cast their ballots. Such differences may also affect the length of lines at polling places. Different ballot designs, voting technologies, and ballot processing and counting procedures have different ballot rejection rates. Because of these differences citizens from one county may have a greater chance of casting a valid ballot than citizens from the next county over. This is particularly problematic if greater burdens tend to fall on already disadvantaged communities. But it may also be worrisome insofar as state and jurisdictional boundaries track salient political divisions.

Even in the absence of objectionable inequalities, the effect of patchwork administration on public perceptions of elections may be an additional cause for concern. When local variation in electoral administration draws attention, especially in a close or contested election, it may undermine public faith in the integrity of the electoral process. When voting administration is so different from one locality to the next, election procedures may seem arbitrary and subject to manipulation. The absence of clear and consistent standards for electoral administration can lead to public distrust of the process. Whether or not such fears are justified, public perceptions of the fairness of the electoral process can significantly affect how well voting fulfills its distinctive role in democracy. If local control of elections prevents the promulgation of clear and public standards for election administration, then it may pose a barrier to fostering public trust in the democratic value of elections.

Finally, local control of elections might also seem to diminish the collective experience that makes voting so distinctively valuable. The physical and social context of voting can affect the way that people think about the act of voting and about the decision they face. Citizens from different places may have different levels of interaction with poll workers. Some citizens will face long lines at the polls while others will face no line at all. Some citizens will vote only in public buildings like fire stations and public schools; others may vote in hotels, churches, or the YMCA. Some will vote in designated precinct polling stations; others may vote at any of a number of vote centers. This collection of small differences can add up to significant differences in the way that citizens from different places experience the act of voting. Voting's distinctive value arises largely from its uniqueness as a form of mass participation in which all citizens are expected to contribute to the exercise of political authority on manifestly equal terms. But local differences in the way elections are administered could erode this value if they obscure citizens' sense that they are engaged in a shared activity with *all* of their fellow citizens.

Each of these worries about local control addresses an important aim of electoral administration. Elections should be administered in a way that is actually fair and consistent with voting equality. Electoral administration should be concerned not only with the objective quality of election procedures, though, but also with public perceptions of the efficacy of voting. Electoral administration should both foster public faith in the integrity of elections and cultivate an experience of voting that is consistent with its distinctive and valuable role in a democracy.

On the other hand, there are also good reasons for valuing local administration of elections that in some cases outweigh or diminish the force of these concerns with local control. Much like the Election Day experience I defended in the previous section, local administration of elections is valuable in large part because it contributes to a sense of a *personal* connection to the political process. Local variation in voting procedures might seem to undermine citizens' sense that their actions are connected to those of others in distant parts of the country. But the sense of democracy as a massively shared activity is not just vulnerable to the possibility that I might not see what it has to with others, but also to the possibility that I might not see what it has to do with *me*.

In a political system in which most decision-making belongs to the realm of professional legislatures and complex bureaucracies so far removed from the universe of the ordinary citizen, the sight of volunteers (sometimes neighbors or acquaintances) sitting at tables in the local school or fire station is a refreshing and reassuring reminder that the final check on governmental power really remains in the hands of the people in a concrete, recognizable way. Voting in a familiar setting, like a library, school, or local business, that has been temporarily adapted to serve as a polling station, establishes a clear connection between political participation and the day-to-day lives of citizens. When poll workers are drawn from the local communities—ordinary citizens taking a break from their routines to work the polls—it is easier to see how democracy is a thing made up by the actions of everyday ordinary citizens (like me!), and not just the prerogative of a special, political class.

The value of a personal connection to the political process has been well documented in empirical studies of "get out the vote" efforts. Door-to-door canvassing is one of the most effective methods of generating turnout,[41] not, it seems, because canvassers offer good reasons to vote—in fact, the message canvassers use doesn't seem to matter much at all.[42] Canvassing brings otherwise reluctant voters into the electorate by offering them a personal invitation to vote, a reminder that elections have something to do with them. The value of this personal connection is further highlighted by two aspects of canvassing that do seem to make a difference: the duration and "chattiness" of the conversation between canvassers and potential voters, and whether the canvassers "match" the ethnic profile of the neighborhood they are canvassing.[43] The personal attention of the canvasser signals that she is interested in more than a generic, faceless vote, but cares that I, personally, am the one to cast that vote. And the ethnic match signals that elections are important to "people like me." Given this impact of even a fleeting personal connection to an election, it makes sense, then, that seeing members of their community and not anonymous bureaucrats in charge of the administration of elections would help to draw people into the process and give them a heightened sense of efficacy.

In their discussion of the efficacy of door-to-door canvassing, Green and Gerber point out that the canvasser may be doing more than just emphasizing a personal connection to the democratic process. These volunteers also exhibit "willingness to devote time and energy" that "signals the importance of participation in the electoral process."[44] This is even more apparent in local administration of elections. As Alec Ewald points out, "localism multiplies the number of citizens who actually do the work of running elections."[45] The scale of the volunteer effort required to run the hundreds of thousands of precinct polling places in the US is staggering. This gives a huge number of citizens a direct role in the oversight and control of the democratic process, but it also means that many more citizens will know a close friend, family member or neighbor who views elections as sufficiently important that it is worth spending a day directly administering and overseeing the process.

41. Gerber and Green, *Get Out the Vote!*, 34.
42. Ibid., 36.
43. Ibid.
44. Ibid., 41.
45. Ewald, *The Way We Vote*, 110.

Volunteer poll workers also reinforce the "civic" value of voting that exists independent of the value of the outcomes voted for. Citizens do not volunteer to be poll workers so that they can influence policy. Their activity aims rather at preserving the structure of democracy and ensuring that citizens can effectively exercise their right to vote. The willingness of so many citizens to volunteer a significant amount of time to the administration of elections helps to disseminate and reinforce the popular understanding of voting's centrality to democratic citizenship. Local control of elections may also help to enforce the norm that there is a duty to vote, since citizens who are likely to see someone they know working at their precinct polling place may seek social affirmation by voting.[46]

Citizens' sense that elections are embedded in their own community context and connected to their day-to-day experience of government can also contribute to public trust in the electoral process. Centralizing and professionalizing electoral administration might allow for the promulgation of clear and consistent guidelines for running elections, but it does so at the expense of other factors that affect public trust and belief in the legitimacy of the political process. One of the advantages of decentralized electoral administration is that citizens may feel better able to hold local public officials to account for their decisions. Moreover, citizens in the United States tend to trust state and local governments to a much greater degree than they trust the federal government.[47]

Additionally, while a centralized election bureaucracy might be able to make clear standards of electoral administration transparent, this would not necessarily increase the actual publicity of the electoral process. Even if common guidelines for running elections and information about administrative decisions are made publicly available, they lack the immediacy of the experience of seeing people I know conducting the business of elections, or even taking part in it myself. People tend to trust what is familiar and close to them. The legitimacy of bureaucratic neutrality may not offer a complete substitute for this powerful inclination. Perhaps this partly explains why independent electoral commissions are negatively correlated with citizens' assessment of election quality.[48]

46. For evidence for the effectiveness of social pressure in enforcing the norm of voting, see Gerber, Green, and Larimer, "Social Pressure and Voter Turnout."

47. Hart, "Local and State Elected Officials."

48. Birch, "Electoral Institutions and Popular Confidence," 313. Birch suggests that the apparent negative effect of independent electoral commissions on popular confidence in elections may result from endogeneity—that is, she suggests independent electoral commissions may be more

Of course, citizens' subjective assessment of the quality of elections does not always reflect the objective quality of elections, and there remains a worry that local control might promote public trust in election procedures at the expense of actual voting equality. In assessing this concern, it is important to note that some inequalities are more problematic than others. For example, communities often have unequal rates of invalidated ballots. Where these inequalities arise from simple cultural differences among communities—like a preference for older forms of voting technology (or for unproven cutting-edge technology)—they may not be seriously problematic. On the other hand, inequalities that arise from differences in communities' financial resources, that target the members of certain social groups, or that reinforce existing problematic social inequalities should receive more serious attention.

Because of the history of local- and state-level elections laws aimed at suppressing Black turnout, high-profile cases of poorly administered elections in already disadvantaged neighborhoods,[49] and recent controversial polling place closures,[50] voter-roll purges,[51] and strict voter ID laws, it might seem that local control of elections will always be a source of problematic inequalities. But centralized election administration can produce bad policies just as well as decentralized administration can. In many cases, local control of elections has allowed for the introduction of progressive practices that might have been politically infeasible at the federal level. The secret ballot, for example, was adopted on a state-by-state basis, and many states extended the franchise to women before the passage of the 19th amendment.[52] Measures that seem at the limits of federal electoral reform aspirations—including most of the provisions in H.R. 1—are already being used in some states. Many commentators have observed that local control of elections provides

likely to be created when there is already low confidence in elections due to corruption. Stuart Wilks-Heeg suggests independent electoral commissions might negatively affect citizens' perceptions of electoral integrity because an independent electoral commission is likely to have public conflicts with the government, drawing attention to the political nature of electoral administration (Wilks-Heeg, "Treating Voters as an Afterthought?," 108).

49. See, for example, the controversy surrounding the 2004 election in Ohio, in which long lines and voting machine problems raised suspicion about surprising vote tallies across Ohio, and especially in a number of inner-city precincts.

50. Sullivan, "Southern U.S. States Have Closed"; Fowler, "Why Do Nonwhite Georgia Voters Have To Wait In Line For Hours?"

51. Smith, "Use It or Lose It."

52. Ewald, *The Way We Vote*, 132. Ewald also argues that for much of US history, local election practices were more inclusive of the poor and of immigrants than federal or state law.

a barrier to "systemic corruption" of high-stakes federal elections. But local control also offers the benefit of allowing for innovation and experimentation in new voting technologies and institutions, which may act as an important hedge against systemic bias.[53]

The preceding discussion demonstrates that while local control of elections may have its problems, increased centralization and bureaucratization of election administration is not an unequivocally good thing. But control of electoral administration is not all or nothing, and this examination of the benefits and drawbacks of local control can provide insight into which aspects of election administration can or should be centralized, and which are best left to the discretion of local communities. There are countless aspects of electoral administration that can be evaluated in this way. Here I want to briefly discuss a few to illustrate the tensions between federal and local claims for control and how they can be addressed.

The most significant benefit of local control of elections is its ability to reinforce citizens' sense of personal connection to the electoral process. The strongest case for local control, then, can be made for those decisions that have the most visible effect on the way that elections fit into the day-to-day life of the community, like the selection of polling places, and the recruitment and training of poll workers. Allowing local control over these aspects of electoral administration can give citizens the sense that electoral administration is more responsive to them. More importantly, local control reinforces the symbolic accessibility of elections: it establishes a connection between citizens and the electoral process by helping to ensure that elections are well integrated into the life of the community.

A one-size-fits-all approach to electoral administration fails to appreciate the variety of the rhythms, routines, and relationships that characterize different communities. In many communities, citizens tend to gather in certain businesses or public spaces that are associated with the common life of the community, and it makes sense to locate polling stations in these places. In commuter towns, though, it may make more sense to conveniently locate large voting centers along major commuting routes. In some cities, identifiable and self-contained neighborhoods feature dense networks of relationships and largely circumscribe the lives of the cities' residents. In other cities, neighborhood boundaries are more porous and abstract. These features affect the appropriate approach to drawing precinct boundaries. Local governments are in the best position to understand the social geography of

53. Ibid., 108.

their communities, and to determine how the physical location of polling places can best be integrated into that social geography.

Communities may likewise differ in terms of the best way of recruiting poll workers, and the kinds of interactions these workers should be trained to have with voters. As I argued earlier, volunteer poll workers from the local community can help to establish a personal connection between citizens and the electoral process, and this sense of connection can be strengthened by informal, "chatty" interactions. On the other hand, in communities where citizens do not have a great deal of trust in their neighbors or local officials, more formal interactions with professional administrators may be necessary to reinforce citizens' faith in the neutrality of election procedures and enable citizens feel secure in their right to vote. Decentralized control over the recruitment and training of poll workers allows different communities to take different approaches as needed.

The most serious concern about local control of elections is the possibility that it might compromise the formal equality that is the hallmark of elections, either because powerful groups can manipulate local election procedures to exclude or burden less powerful groups, or because communities with fewer resources may be further disadvantaged by lower-quality elections. The HAVA has begun to address the second of these concerns by providing some federal funding for voting system reform. But subsequent election controversies have demonstrated the need for more stable funding for electoral administration to ensure that communities are able to afford reliable voting technology and are able to pay a sufficient number of poll workers to monitor the integrity of balloting, assist voters, and minimize lines.

The concern about discriminatory manipulation of electoral administration is more difficult to address without substantially circumscribing local control of elections.[54] In the United States, much of the federal government's existing role in election administration involves prosecuting cases of discrimination, fraud, or other violations of election law. This role seems appropriate. However, it may not be sufficient, because such litigation can often take years to remedy discriminatory practices.

One way of supplementing this role is to impose a *preclearance* requirement on at least some jurisdictions or for some kinds of policies, requiring that changes to election law or policy obtain federal approval before going

54. For example, one of the areas where I have suggested local control is most valuable—the selection of polling places—has also been a source of major controversy in recent years. Voting rights activists charge that some election officials—most notably in Georgia—have strategically closed polling places to suppress turnout among certain groups.

into effect. The Voting Rights Act of 1965 imposed just such a requirement on jurisdictions with a history of discriminatory election practices. However, in 2013, the US Supreme Court determined in *Shelby County v. Holder* that the coverage formula that had been used to determine which jurisdictions would be subject to the preclearance requirement could no longer be considered constitutional. Since the US Congress has not yet managed to pass an updated coverage formula, the preclearance tool is not currently in use.

Implementing a new preclearance coverage formula presents something of a trilemma. An effective formula must have three properties: it must accurately identify jurisdictions most likely to implement discriminatory policies; it must be able to garner sufficient support in Congress; and it must be able to survive constitutional challenges. In the current political environment, it is very difficult to envisage a formula that can meet all three of these requirements. The most recent effort as of this writing, the John Lewis Voting Rights Advancement Act of 2021, appeared to have support of majorities in both houses of Congress, but in November 2021, it was blocked by a Senate filibuster. This act would have introduced a new coverage formula based on a state's recent history of voting rights violations. It also would have introduced a new practice-based preclearance requirement, requiring any jurisdiction with a substantial minority population to obtain pre-approval for certain kinds of changes to election law or administrative policy.[55]

Reviving the preclearance requirement of the Voting Rights Act has been a central focus of recent reform discourse around combating discriminatory election policies because of its proven track record. However, given the hurdles to reviving preclearance, it is worth devoting more attention to other possible ways to supplement the current legal system for remedying discriminatory election law. One important place to look is in the structure of electoral administration and oversight at the state and local level. As with other aspects of election law, there is a great deal of variety across states in the structure of election bureaucracies and oversight, from elected officials to bipartisan election commissions. It stands to reason that different institutional structures may do a better job of ensuring fair electoral procedures. Researchers and reformers would do well to devote more attention to evaluating different structures of electoral oversight and promoting those that function best.

55. "H.R.4—117th Congress (2021–2022)."

The Role of Parties in Electoral Administration

In his account of American elections in the 19th century, Richard Bensel emphasizes the dominance of parties on the Election Day scene. Party agents did not just canvass and campaign on Election Day; they did most of the administrative work of elections. Party agents printed and distributed the "tickets" that voters would cast as their official ballots,[56] and party agents assisted voters in altering their tickets if they did not want to vote the entire party list for every office. Pairs of opposing party agents often served in official roles as "judges of election" in charge of determining the eligibility of voters.[57] The major parties were typically also consulted in the appointment of election clerks and inspectors, who were charged with monitoring the casting and counting of ballots.[58] Party agents reminded citizens of the election, and incentivized them to vote with free alcohol[59] and even the promise of payment in cash or kind.[60] Party agents sometimes assisted voters in paying the poll tax or provided transportation to the polls.[61]

Parties do not have the same presence on Election Day anymore. Indeed, depoliticizing electoral administration and weakening the influence of the party machine—most famously through the introduction of the secret ballot—is often lauded as one of the greatest successes of the progressive movement. Most US states even prohibit campaigning within a certain perimeter around the polling place.[62]

Though the adversarial aspect of Election Day has been quieted, parties still play an important role in electoral administration—that is, they play an important role in making sure that elections effectively serve their democratic purposes. At least in the United States, political parties are still instrumental in ensuring the accessibility of elections. Party agents and volunteers are often the ones registering voters. Though public officials do this task as well, they typically do not reach out to citizens, and lack the capacity to assist all would-be voters. Just as party agents once paid the poll tax for paupers and assisted illiterate voters in selecting or marking a ticket, contemporary parties take up the task of informing citizens about voter registration requirements and

56. Bensel, *American Ballot Box*, 14.
57. Ibid., 18.
58. Ibid., 38.
59. Ibid., 57.
60. Ibid., 59.
61. Ibid., 42, 79–83.
62. "State Laws Prohibiting Electioneering."

guiding them through the process. And parties remain active on Election Day, disseminating information about where and how to vote, canvassing door-to-door to mobilize citizens, and providing transportation to the polls. Parties, in short, still bear much of the responsibility for ensuring that elections are not just formally open to all, but that elections are in fact materially, cognitively, and symbolically accessible to all citizens. And, through their mobilization efforts, parties are largely responsible for realizing the mass participation that is crucial to voting's distinctive value.

The extent of parties' responsibility for electoral administration may seem worrisome because parties do not fulfill these public functions in a neutral way. Party agents in the 19th century did not just encourage citizens to vote; they typically bribed and occasionally threatened them to vote for their preferred party. Contemporary parties, of course, act from similar partisan motivations when they mobilize and assist voters. Party agents do not typically try to mobilize citizens unless they expect that those citizens will cast a favorable vote.

Political parties should be expected to act strategically as they compete to win elections, but this strategic behavior might raise concerns about the continuing role of parties in electoral administration. Prima facie, it seems that any organizations we rely on to fulfill public functions—in this case, mobilizing, informing, and assisting voters—should be subject to equal treatment norms in how they fulfill this role. But parties do not treat all voters equally; they give preferential treatment to their own supporters. Parties' role in electoral administration is one of their tools of competition.

Allowing non-neutral parties to play an important role in electoral administration also presents more specific problems for the democratic value of elections. First, parties' strategic focus on the turnout battle as an arena of electoral competition risks undermining the publicly shared understanding of elections as moments of mass participation and the expressive value of formal equality in elections. In chapter 1, I argued that voting's value derives from its uniqueness as a form of mass participation in which all citizens are expected to take part. By participating in the same way, with exactly the same level of influence as millions of their fellow citizens, citizens express and perform their willingness to contribute to the democratic project on radically, manifestly equal terms. But partisan efforts to selectively mobilize only likely supporters, or even to demobilize opponents, may distort this message of equality.

Parties' role in electoral administration may also present a second threat to the democratic value of elections: parties' public role may give them undue influence over voters' decisions. As I argued in previous chapters, the ideal of perfectly independent citizens choosing one party over another based on its merits is neither realistic, nor particularly democratic. But democratic norms undoubtedly require that citizens experience *some* degree of independence from party elites in forming their political judgments. In particular, democratic norms should deny bribery, physical intimidation, and deception as legitimate bases for partisan loyalty. We might also be concerned about the sort of influence party agents might gain if their providing voters with material assistance makes voters feel indebted to the party. Moreover, canvassers who bring new voters to the polls might wrongly draw support from citizens' emotional or affective response to the canvasser, rather than from citizens' political judgment.

Despite these concerns, we should be wary of depoliticizing elections too much. Limiting the role of parties in electoral administration might increase the formal equality of elections, but formal equality is only one aspect of voting's distinctive value. Elections balance formal, procedural equality with the drama of political competition. Insulating ordinary citizens from competition among the candidates and parties relegates citizens to the role of spectators—at best, neutral judges of the competition among political elites. One of the virtues of parties' performing the public function of mobilization is that they encourage citizens to take a side in the fray—to see themselves as political actors in their own right. Parties play an important role in the cognitive and emotional mobilization of the citizenry; they stir up excitement and enthusiasm in their efforts to win supporters. And as I argued in chapter 4, partisan mobilization at its best helps citizens to see themselves as political agents and to form durable political identities.

Voting's distinctive value derives from the fact that it identifies all citizens as political agents. Parties' presence on Election Day helps to reinforce this value of voting to the extent that parties make voting recognizable as a *political* act. But if a greater role for parties on Election Day means diminished formal equality and voter independence, is this trade-off worth it? After all, what distinguishes democracy from oligarchy is that all citizens have equal political power in a democracy. Parties' role in electoral administration encourages many voters to see themselves as political agents, but if parties do not treat voters equally or exercise undue influence over voters, then we may wonder how much that feeling of agency is really worth.

This dilemma of parties' role in electoral administration is more tractable if we shift the focus of evaluation from the behavior of individual parties to the party *system*. Strategic parties may not treat all potential voters equally and may sometimes exercise what seems like inappropriate influence over individual decisions. But in assessing the value of parties' role on Election Day, it is more appropriate to examine the characteristics and cumulative effects of the party system as a whole.

In chapter 4, I outlined a normative standard for party systems based on a model of parties-as-mobilizers. Party systems comply with this standard when—at least over the long term—they encourage parties to adopt mobilization strategies; that is, when they incentivize or otherwise encourage parties to activate new voters and to reach out to neglected supporters of an opposing party. Parties may have a short-term incentive to focus only on mobilizing their existing supporters, or on attracting the most organized and politically active groups, but while individual parties may thus not treat all citizens equally, those individuals who are neglected by one party will be ideal targets for another. A political party cannot rely on the low-hanging fruit of the already organized. Samuel Beer describes the political party instead as a desperate hunter: "keenly on the scent of votes and pressed sharply by its rival in the chase, it probes every neglected thicket in the political landscape for its quarry."[63] Democratic party systems incentivize and encourage political parties to find and reach out to neglected groups, to draw them into the political arena and thereby to increase the number of their supporters.

This attempt to change the balance of political competition by bringing new citizens into the arena is one of the hallmarks of the modern political party, and as a result political parties have often been responsible for the political mobilization of newly enfranchised groups. Describing 19th-century elections in America, Richard Bensel observes: "illiterate and ignorant men, steeped in poverty and lacking any other claim to social respectability, were not only permitted to cast their tickets, they were enticed, cajoled, treated, and blessed as they did so."[64] Because of their efforts to expand their base of supporters, parties have played a significant role in the historical development of voting's value as a form of *mass* participation.

In their mobilization efforts, party agents may not regard all voters equally, instead giving special attention to their likeliest supporters. But the party *system* creates incentives for parties to cast a broader net. The competitive party system drives parties to draw more and more citizens into the political arena. Though party agents may not abide by norms of equal treatment in fulfilling their public functions in electoral administration, the system that relies on parties as primary mobilizers nevertheless promotes

63. Beer, *Modern British Politics*, 349.
64. Bensel, *American Ballot Box*, 85.

practical political equality while also treating citizens as political agents in their own right.

Concerns about assigning parties a significant role in electoral administration reflect the tension between the formal, procedural element of elections and its competitive, political element. Critics of party influence imagine citizens to be outside the fray—independent judges of the party competition. But this is both an unrealistic and an undesirable view of political life, in that it leaves all of the creative power to party elites. The fantasy of independence perversely deprives citizens of political power. Mobilization and party influence, on the other hand, draw citizens into the fray—they are no longer spectators or judges, but political actors in their own right. Partisan mobilization is effective precisely because it creates a personal invitation for citizens. It encourages us to see that the political fight is *our* fight.

Conclusion—Bring Back the Whiskey Barrels?

A century and a half of progressive electoral reform has won privacy and security for individual voters on Election Day, protecting the integrity of their votes from the deception, bribery, and extortion of local party machines. But these same reforms have also increasingly sanitized the voting experience, pushing evidence of political competition and collective struggle into the background. Current frontiers of electoral reform—the push to centralize and standardize electoral administration and to provide more "convenience voting"—promise to further promote the formal equality of votes, but also risk further diminishing the experience of voting as a *collective activity* and an exercise of political agency.

In this chapter, I have argued that the Election Day experience should emphasize both the formal, procedural equality of elections and the collective, competitive political agency of voting. This is not an argument for a return to public voting or machine politics. The privacy of the polling booth goes a long way toward protecting the most vulnerable citizens from intimidation and exploitation and limiting the translation of social and economic power into political power. Democracy is probably not well served by political operatives selling a glass of whiskey for a party vote. But whiskey barrels on Election Day do not just serve such a quid pro quo. They also symbolize a communal, celebratory Election Day atmosphere that encourages voters to see elections as a crucial part of the life of their community and to see themselves as participants in political competition. The push toward centralization, the rapid increase in convenience voting provisions, and the ongoing efforts to render partisanship invisible on Election Day all cultivate an atmosphere in which voters relate to electoral competition as subjects and spectators rather than as political agents in their own right.

Elections serve as the most tangible experiences of popular sovereignty in modern democracies. They should be remarkable moments in the life of a democratic community. If elections are to effectively fulfill their unique and valuable role in contemporary democracies, then the experience of voting should give citizens a sense of ownership of the political process. It should communicate to voters that they are equal political agents, and that their voices are not only welcomed, but required for a fully functional democracy.

Voting will never be perfect. But thoughtful, intentional reform can enable our practice of popular voting to better realize its democratic value. Still, given the many flaws of contemporary voting practices, and the inherent challenges to improving them, skeptics may wonder why we should continue to bother with voting. Democratic theorists have offered radically different models of democracy that do not revolve around a practice of popular voting anything like the one we have now. Practices of popular voting with the core features I laid out in chapter 1 are a central component of all large, modern democracies. But this fact may well be historically contingent. It is certainly possible to imagine other ways of doing democracy, and it is also possible to imagine an alternative trajectory of democratic development in which voting practices look different and serve a different set of values. If our current voting practices are the product of historical accident, shouldn't that affect how we assess their value and the normative claims they make on us?

I take up this question in the next chapter. In response to potential radical criticisms, I argue that there are reasons internal to the idea of democracy itself to value our existing democratic practices, even imperfect ones, and to give them weight in our practical deliberations. I argue further that appreciating the requirements of democracy as an equally shared collective activity can help us understand how to do that.

6

Valuing Democracy in Practice
(A RESPONSE TO RADICAL CRITICS)

In October of 2019, a group of 150 French citizens gathered for the first of seven meetings to discuss the future of French climate policy. The group was charged with recommending measures that would enable France to meet its ambitious greenhouse gas emission target in a way that was consistent with a spirit of social justice. What was extraordinary about this meeting was that its participants were not elected, nor were they appointed because of their special expertise, skill, or social position. Instead, they were chosen by a more-or-less random process designed to select a representative cross-section of French citizens. By all accounts, these chosen participants took their mission seriously. During their seven meetings over the next several months, the selected citizens interviewed experts, reviewed research and public commentary, formulated ideas in working groups and deliberated over them extensively. By the close of the convention in June 2020, the group had recommended 149 proposals to the French parliament.[1]

In this book, I have argued that the practice of popular voting instantiates unique values and performs essential functions in modern democratic systems. But the democratic systems with which we are familiar, and the paradigm of electoral democracy that they reflect, may not be the only way to realize the values of democracy. Experiments like the French Citizen

---

1. For an extended description of this event, see Giraudet et al., "Deliberating on Climate Action."

Climate Convention have inspired some democratic theorists to imagine a future for democracy radically different from its present. And in this alternative vision for democracy, voting would occupy a very different role. In fact, there might be no popular voting at all.

In the introduction and at a few other points in this book, I have referred to recent radical criticisms of voting. Some of these criticisms are anti-democratic. But not all. Some critics of voting are thoroughly committed to the ideal of democracy and its associated values. They argue, though, that the practice of popular voting is only contingently and loosely related to them. According to this view, our attachment to the practice of popular voting can get in the way of efforts to radically change how we conceptualize and institutionalize democracy—efforts that could lead to a more complete realization of democracy's value. The aims of radical reform projects vary. 20th-century political theorists envisioned a "participatory society" characterized by democratically governed workplaces and associations.[2] More recently, democratic theory has turned its attention to the idea of "lottocracy." In a lottocracy, we would use random selection, rather than election or appointment, to fill public offices. The Citizen Climate Convention used a lottery to select the members of a special one-time-only deliberative body. But why not have more such bodies? Why not use lotteries even to fill seats in regular legislatures?[3] To proponents of lottocracy or similar radical visions of democracy, the arguments in this book may seem at best irrelevant, and at worst counter-productive, to the project of improving democracy.

In this chapter, I address this line of criticism head on. I do not disagree with the claim that democracy's value *might* be realized just as well—perhaps even better—in a radically different kind of political system. However, I do disagree with voting's critics about what this possibility means for the ethics of democracy. I argue that even imperfect existing practices of democracy—including and especially popular voting—carry substantial normative weight in our decisions about how to preserve, promote, and *do* democracy.

This chapter, then, defends the kind of democratic theory that I have deployed in this book—a democratic theory that begins where we are, examining and interpreting the political practices that are widely thought to have democratic value in regimes that are widely considered to be democratic. This method stands in contrast to another kind of democratic theory that begins with definitions, conceptual analyses, and etymologies of democracy

2. Pateman, *Participation and Democratic Theory*.
3. Guerrero, "Against Elections."

and attempts to describe institutions and practices that might best realize these practices. Both varieties of democratic theory can help us better understand the nature and value of democracy. However, only the former—the kind I have done in this book—can serve as a reliable guide for citizens as to what democracy requires of us here and now.

I offer two arguments in defense of this claim. The first is that, given the uncertain prospects of radical change, we should hesitate to put at risk the values that we do find in existing democratic systems. And when there are trade-offs between pursuing radical change or pursuing incremental improvements with a high probability of success, we often ought to choose the latter.

This approach to democratic ethics and reform can be justified by reference to certain facts about democracy: first, democracy requires coordinating collective activity; but beyond that, its requirements are second, underspecified and third, contested. If we add to these three facts a fourth—that the complex and multi-faceted ideal of democracy can only be realized within complex and multi-faceted systems—it should be clear that beneficial forms of democratic coordination are difficult to achieve and likely fragile. We should not be too quick to trade hard-fought, if incomplete, democratic gains for the slim chance of something that might or might not be better.

These four facts about democracy also point to a deeper and often overlooked reason for devoting our energies to improving existing practices of democracy. This reason derives from the value of democracy as equally shared political agency. Treating citizens as equal agents in a shared democratic project should include giving weight to citizens' existing beliefs about and attitudes toward political practices and institutions. Though the ideal of democracy is underspecified, it nevertheless provides reason to value the ways of doing democracy that we have worked out together over time. A certain respect for widely shared beliefs about what democracy looks like should, therefore, play an important role in practical reasoning about the ethics of citizenship and democratic reform.

The value of existing democratic practices does not make them immune to criticism or reform, any more than other products of democratic politics. But efforts to change political systems pose a dilemma for democratic ethics. On the one hand, we all can recognize that our practices of democracy fall short of our ideals. Insofar as we think our existing practices of democracy are flawed, it might seem that we should not feel constrained by them but should instead look directly to democratic principles for guidance. On the other hand, though, interpretations of democracy's requirements are themselves subject to deep and serious disagreement. How can we make improvements to our democracy in a way that is itself compatible with the spirit of democracy?

In the second half of this chapter, I offer an account of democracy as shared agency that can shed light on the murky ethics of democratic reform politics. I suggest that existing democratic institutions and practices can be thought of as shared plans for a collective activity. Thinking of democratic structures in this way does not magically resolve the dilemma of democratic reform, but it does render it in more familiar terms, and reveals that citizens may have more practical experience navigating analogous ethical problems than we realize. This account of democracy as shared agency also shows that we have good reason to honor our existing democratic practices. Flawed though they might be, they enable a form of collective empowerment that would not otherwise be possible.

This model of democracy as shared agency, and of democratic practices as shared plans, also illuminates the role that normative political theory can play in deliberation about the ethics of citizenship. Plans require interpretation that tacks between the aims those plans are meant to serve—the principles and desired outcomes of democratic governance—and facts about existing rules, prevalent beliefs and norms, and how they function together. Engaging in this kind of interpretation is one of way of doing democratic democratic theory. This approach to political theory animates the account of voting I have offered in this book.

The Radical Critique of Elections

According to some critics, the centrality of voting in popular conceptions of democracy—which I have defended in this book—is bound up with a fatally flawed paradigm of electoral democracy. These critics would argue that the normative guidance I offer in this book is misdirected. Rather than working to realize the most valuable version of popular voting practices we can, radical critics of electoral democracy argue that we should direct reform energy and creativity toward remaking democracy from the ground up, with an entirely different set of institutions, practices, and norms.

Radical criticisms of this sort are not new, and there are far too many versions to respond directly to all of them. Therefore, in this section, I will focus on an account that has recently gained prominence in both academic and popular audiences: Hélène Landemore's argument for shifting from a paradigm of electoral democracy to a new paradigm that she calls "open democracy."

Landemore's criticisms of voting overlap substantially with other radical democratic theory, but her recent book *Open Democracy* offers one of the most thorough attempts to date at describing a plausible alternative.

Landemore's critique of electoral democracy has three components. First, Landemore attributes rising dissatisfaction with political institutions to the flawed paradigm of electoral democracy.[4] This attribution frequently appears in other calls to radically rethink democratic institutions.[5] It is, of course, undeniable that existing institutions of electoral democracy have not enabled us to avoid dissatisfaction, distrust, or any of our other contemporary dysfunctions. But, in arguing that dissatisfaction is *attributable* to the paradigm of electoral democracy, Landemore suggests that democratic institutions animated by a different paradigm (such as her own open democracy) would avoid these problems. There is, of course, no way to directly test this hypothesis. So far there is also no convincing indirect evidence for the hypothesis that our paradigm of democracy is responsible for our present discontents. And there are numerous plausible explanations for rising dissatisfaction that do not primarily implicate our paradigm of democracy.

The second and third components of Landemore's argument merit more attention. She claims that elections are inherently elitist and exclusionary and that there exists an alternative paradigm of democracy—open democracy—which, when institutionalized, will better realize the suite of values associated with democracy.

Elections, without a doubt, have an elitist pedigree. They emerged before widespread, let alone universal, suffrage. This pedigree, of course, does not determine the character or function of elections today. Institutions often have effects and take on social meanings that are unintended, unanticipated, and even unwelcome by those who created them. The development of the modern party system, innovations in voting and nomination rules, and the extension of the franchise have radically changed the meaning and function of modern elections. Landemore claims, however, that the paradigm of electoral democracy is "tainted" by its historical associations.[6] And, much more importantly, she argues, even on the best normative reconstruction, inequality and exclusion are baked into electoral democracy. This is because electing our representatives necessarily creates a distinction between a ruling elite and everyone else.[7]

4. Landemore, *Open Democracy*, 28–29.
5. E.g., Van Reybrouck, *Against Elections*.
6. Landemore, *Open Democracy*, 51.
7. Ibid., 33–40, 80.

The most serious flaw of electoral democracy, according to Landemore, is that it enables the "enclosure of power."[8] Some people have direct access to political power and other people don't. Her proposal for an alternative paradigm, appropriately named "open democracy," is focused on avoiding this problem. The core difference between open democracy and electoral democracy is the conception of representation at the heart of each paradigm. In electoral democracy, democratic representation is built on three principles: authorization, responsiveness, and accountability. But, Landemore argues, these principles are not intrinsically democratic. We do not value them for their own sake. Rather, we value these principles of democratic representation because we think they help realize equality, popular sovereignty, and other conditions that are intrinsically democratic and intrinsically valuable.[9] Landemore asserts, furthermore, that a democratic model of representation should be built on intrinsically democratic principles. From these claims, she concludes that we should view political representation as democratic insofar as it embodies the core democratic principles of inclusion and equality.[10]

Like electoral democracy, Landemore's alternative paradigm of open democracy is a form of representative democracy in which some citizens regularly exercise power on behalf of others. But the similarities end there. In an electoral democracy, rule by the people is secured by binding these empowered representatives to their constituents. In an open democracy, rule by the people is secured by enabling citizens to move freely into and out of the role of representative. Landemore sees potential models for her vision of open democracy in experimental institutional innovations like the Citizen Climate Convention I described at the outset of this chapter, or the Icelandic constitutional reform process that she details in *Open Democracy*.[11] The key features of these experiments that she hails are that they deployed lottocratic or self-selection mechanisms to select representatives and that they adopted an open posture in their proceedings, inviting commentary from the public and taking the input they received seriously.

Though the arguments I have offered in this book operate within the paradigm of electoral democracy that Landemore criticizes, there is, nevertheless, a way of reading them as compatible political projects. Landemore maintains that she does not intend to offer a blueprint for institutional reform

8. Ibid., 3–5.
9. Ibid., 88.
10. Ibid., 81–82.
11. Ibid., 12.

and observes that her "instincts as a reformer are more conservative than [her] instincts as a political theorist."[12] She consistently caveats her claims about the performance of open democracy with the phrase "in theory,"[13] acknowledging that many of her claims are speculative and subject to empirical falsification. Thus, her primary recommendation throughout her book is more (cautious) experimentation with institutions of open democracy.[14] For electoral democracies, where transition costs and risks of destabilizing decent democratic systems are high, she notes that immediate radical change is not advisable, but experimentation should be incremental and complementary to existing institutions.[15]

Despite all these caveats, Landemore at times asserts a more substantial and immediate role for her theory in the ethics of democracy. She suggests that the institutional principles of open democracy can "orient and guide political reform,"[16] and that the paradigm of open democracy can serve as a model for how citizens should understand their role in a democracy.[17] She also criticizes "seemingly conservative" efforts to "shore up" existing institutions under threat.[18]

This apparent inconsistency in how Landemore describes the guidance offered by her theory demonstrates that, even if her radical democratic theory and my democratic democratic theory are compatible, we will nevertheless see tensions and trade-offs if we try to put both into practice. Because we care about democracy at the level of political systems, differing paradigms or models of democracies may not easily co-exist. This is true for two reasons. First, of course, there will be trade-offs in how we allocate resources for reform—to institutional innovation and experimentation with open democracy, or to incremental improvements in electoral democracy such as efforts to increase turnout. Second, and more seriously, models of citizenship or political institutions that might function perfectly well within a broader paradigm of open democracy could have perverse effects within our own more familiar systems. The status of popular voting is a prime example. According to Landemore, moments of mass participation are not essential to open democracy. Rather, the paradigm of open democracy suggests a

12. Ibid., 219.
13. E.g., ibid., 11, 83, 95, 100, 203, 220.
14. Ibid., 32, 121, 200.
15. Ibid., 207.
16. Ibid., 20.
17. Ibid., 219.
18. Ibid., 199.

model of citizenship that is more fluid—perhaps like the strictly pluralist model of participation I sketched in chapter 1. It would be a mistake for citizens to treat the open democracy model of citizenship as a guide for us here and now, though. Whatever their status in hypothetical open democracies, moments of mass participation do play an essential role in *our* democracies. Our ethic of citizenship should reflect this.

However nice it may sound in theory, then, any reconciliation or division of labor between radical democratic theories like Landemore's, and more familiar, interpretive theories like my own will not be clean or easy. At least not when it comes to an ethic of citizenship or democratic reform. We may sometimes have to choose between pursuing Landemore's radical vision for open democracy and pursuing improvements to electoral democracy. In the rest of this section, I will make the case that, when faced with trade-offs between these alternate reform paths, we should usually resolve these trade-offs in favor of more incremental reforms that strengthen our existing systems of electoral democracy. In the next section, I will argue that the concept of democracy itself provides reasons for us to be attentive to and to value existing democratic practices, even when they are imperfectly or contingently related to democratic ideals.

The first reason to generally favor incremental reforms to electoral democracy over more radical proposals is grounded in an attentiveness to risk or loss. In what follows, I am going to assume that, when considering consequential institutional or social reforms, we ought to be clear-eyed about what is at stake in a decision. We should appreciate what we stand to lose if things don't go our way.

The account of voting's value that I have offered in this book shows us exactly what we stand to lose in the pursuit of non-electoral visions of democracy. Popular voting creates moments of authority that can be truly shared by the whole citizenry. It reconciles the massive collective project that is democracy with the dignity of individual contributions. And it concretely and transparently manifests political equality through universal suffrage, inclusive mobilization, and the equal weighting of votes. Popular voting—especially in regular elections—also breaks habits of disengagement, socializes citizens into participation on equal terms, incentivizes broad-based and inclusive political organization, provides a spur to political innovation, and reminds public officials that they serve at the behest of *the entire citizenry*. This is all in addition to the vital minimalist achievements of electoral democracy—encouraging the peaceful transfer of power, discouraging ill-advised wars, and coordinating resistance to tyranny. Existing voting systems do not do these things perfectly, of course, but all regimes that we commonly consider democratic do them to some extent, and many can be made to perform even better with incremental improvements guided by the principles I have described in this book.

There is much to lose, then, if we neglect efforts to fortify popular voting practices in the pursuit of some alternative model of democracy. There is probably also less to gain than radical democrats imagine. Here, I will focus on a set of risks that theorists of political realism have identified as especially salient in political life. These are risks that arise from how we create, distribute, and (mis)manage power;[19] from moral corruption or even ordinary vices among leaders and citizens;[20] and from excessive moralism joined with the state's tremendous capacity for violence.[21]

All three of these sources of risk loom large in the prospects of radical democratic reform. Radical democratic theories, including Landemore's open democracy, treat the distribution of power as a central concern. But they approach the problem of power in the wrong way. Open democracy's appeal stems from the idea that we can eliminate or at least greatly reduce inequalities in social and political power through the right institutional design. Realists are skeptical of this ambition. Checking the concentration of power or preventing its abuses is a constant battle on shifting terrain.

Realist political theory invites us to look at where power accumulates and who wields it. From this standpoint, the paradigm of electoral democracy has two major virtues. First, it explicitly faces up to the power hierarchies it creates (between representatives and ordinary citizens), and it treats the control of those in power as its chief concern. Second, electoral democracy creates countervailing sources of power capable of checking social and political elites.[22] Elections, whatever else they might do, enable citizens to pool their collective power so that they can say "no" to the most powerful people in their midst. Open democracy, despite its attractions, has not yet proven that it can do the one thing democracies must be able to do: counteract social power. The most celebrated radical democratic experiments—including Iceland's crowd-sourced constitutional reform process, the French Citizen Climate Convention, or the earlier British Columbia Citizens Assembly—have failed to change policy in the way their participants intended. Defenders attribute these failures to the stranglehold of elites over the institutions

19. Shapiro, *Politics Against Domination.*
20. Galston, "Realism in Political Theory."
21. Rossi and Sleat, "Realism in Normative Political Theory."
22. Bagg, "Power of the Multitude."

of government.[23] But this response misses the key lesson we should take away from these failures—the power created by these institutional innovations has not yet proven sufficient to counteract the power of these social elites. Perhaps one day we will hit on some radical institutional innovation that can produce a potent countervailing force. But in the meantime, we should not neglect the tools that electoral democracy gives us for managing elite power.[24]

In addition to managing power in a democracy, we also need tools for managing ordinary human weaknesses, among citizens and leaders alike. A successful democratic system will have institutions, norms, and practices that help align citizens' attitudes and behaviors with the requirements of democratic citizenship. I have argued throughout this book that the practice of popular voting performs important functions in this respect. Another source of risk in radical reforms, then, arises from the difficulty of predicting how untested institutional arrangements will interact with human psychology to shape citizens' habits and dispositions.

Finally, perhaps the chief concern of contemporary political realists is excessive moralism in public life. I do not share the belief of some contemporary realists that morality and politics are entirely separate domains. However, I do share the realists' attentiveness to the risks that accompany moralism in public life, and I believe that these risks are particularly pronounced in radical reform projects. The risk of excessive moralism in public life is that we focus too much on the value we are trying to promote and underweight the value(s) we sacrifice to get there. Sacrifice is unavoidable in politics (as in life). But sacrifices should be recognized for what they are. The risk of excessive moralism is that it prevents us from identifying the value in things that are imperfect or from appreciating the legitimate grounds on which others might disagree with us. Realists worry about the cruelty that moralism can unleash because of these blind spots. This risk can

---

23. Landemore, *Open Democracy*, 180.

24. It is worth noting that several democratic theorists, who might be described as radical realists, have called for new lottocratic, plebeian institutions that could provide an additional way for the masses of ordinary citizens to check the power of elites. But despite their explicit focus on the power hierarchies between elites and masses that electoral institutions reinforce, these new plebeians do not call for fully replacing elections with lottocracy. This is because they are generally skeptical that we can ever be rid of elites. If elite power will always be with us, elections are powerful tools for containing it, especially when combined with other tools that create additional and separate countervailing power (Arlen and Rossi, "Must Realists Be Pessimists About Democracy"; McCormick, "Contain the Wealthy and Patrol the Magistrates"; McCormick, *Machiavellian Democracy*).

be overstated, of course. As I argued in response to minimalist democratic theorists in chapter 2, the mere fact that ideals and normative concepts can be abused to license bad behavior is not a good reason to stop believing in them or using them. I believe moral progress is possible and desirable. But I also believe that we should be particularly wary of radical reform projects, like open democracy, precisely when they tell us that we are mistaken for cherishing our existing ways of doing democracy and fighting to make them the best they can be. We should be skeptical of claims that the best way to obtain a truly valuable democracy is to turn our backs on the democracy we already have, especially when they promise that we won't miss it in the end, anyway.

Plans, Practices, and Democracy as Shared Agency

Attentiveness to the risks associated with radical democratic reform and to what we stand to lose in the pursuit of them provides reason enough to focus on preserving and improving our existing democratic practices. But there is another deeper, and I think, more important reason that stems from the character of democracy as a collective activity undertaken on equal terms. Appreciating this aspect of democracy helps us to understand why and how we should value democratic institutions and practices *even when we can imagine a better democracy without them.*

Every plausible justification for democracy also justifies giving weight to existing norms and institutions in our practical deliberations about how to promote democracy and the values it serves. For example, some theorists argue that democracy is justified because it ensures citizens have opportunities to participate in the intrinsically valuable and uniquely human exercise of political agency. These theorists typically recognize that the design and endorsement or contestation of democratic institutions and principles is itself a particularly valuable form of political agency. Those who argue that democracy is valuable because it demonstrates equal respect for citizens' moral capacities likewise acknowledge that among the capacities we should respect are "capacities to think reflectively about procedures."[25] Perhaps democracy is valuable because it allows citizens to live freely under rules of our own making, but then surely this extends to the rules for adjudicating political disagreement and distributing political power. Even if democracy is only justified insofar as it tends to produce better outcomes than feasible alternatives, this still gives us reason to take seriously the beliefs, attitudes,

25. Waldron, "The Constitutional Conception of Democracy," 64.

and practices that motivate citizens to abide by democratic procedures. These different theories of democracy's value sometimes point to different sets of ideal institutional arrangements, but they also all provide reasons for valuing and attending to the actual practices that democratic communities work out for arranging our collective projects of self-rule.

So, whatever reasons we have for valuing democracy also give us reason to care about many existing democratic institutions and practices, even when they are non-ideal. When determining how we can best contribute to and promote the realization of democratic values, we should give some weight to the conception of democracy that is operative in our community. But what does this look like in practice? There must be some bounds on the political arrangements that can be considered democratic and that we have reason to value. Moreover, none of the reasons for valuing or respecting existing democratic practices that I have discussed above rule out actively working for more radical reforms. How should we balance an appreciation for existing democratic practices with an appropriate critical perspective? Furthermore, conflicts and contradictions will arise among different pieces of our democratic systems. How should we navigate these conflicts in determining what democratic citizenship requires of us?

In the remainder of this chapter, I sketch an account of democracy as a jointly intended collective activity enabled by a set of interlocking and shared plans. I believe this account of democracy as shared agency offers a helpful way of approaching these questions. Philosophical accounts of planning agency can be highly technical and may seem opaque to non-specialists. But what they describe is something that should be familiar to anyone who has ever tried to do anything with a group of people. Viewing democracy as shared agency—and viewing democratic practices as part of a shared plan for democracy—does not make the ethics of democracy simple, easy, or formulaic. But I hope that it renders it less mysterious. The ethical dilemmas of democracy are not so unique as they might seem.

MODELING DEMOCRACY AS SHARED AGENCY

Political theorists have offered many definitions and accounts of democracy, but we can reasonably characterize most accounts of democracy as involving two key ideas: political equality, and collective empowerment. We can see that these ideas are essential to the concept of democracy by looking at uncontroversial cases of what democracy is *not*. Democracy denotes a form of political organization distinguished from monarchy and oligarchy.

Any plausible conception of democracy should be able to account for these central exclusions. The distinction between democracy and oligarchy is best understood as being about the distribution of political power. Democracies distribute political power more equally than oligarchies and monarchies. Democracy may be compatible with some forms of political hierarchy, but a conception of democracy that requires less hierarchy is more plausible than a conception that requires more, all else being equal.[26]

Democracy is not just the absence of monarchy and oligarchy, though. The concept of democracy also excludes mere anarchy by specifying that the people *do something*, that is, rule together.[27] By "mere anarchy," I mean the common sense (if imaginary) notion of a total state of nature, lacking in beneficial forms of political agency. When democracy refers to a form of political rule it must include content that excludes mere anarchy.[28] Thus, the basic concept of democracy as a form of political rule suggests that any plausible conception of democracy must provide for some kind of collective empowerment. Conceptions of democracy that entail more empowerment for the polity will generally be more plausible than those that entail less, all else equal.

Understanding that democracy is fundamentally concerned with political equality and collective empowerment suggests that we can usefully think of democracy as a form of *shared agency*. In what follows, I offer what I think is a plausible and attractive conception of democracy as a kind of collective activity involving what Michael Bratman has called "joint" or "shared" intentions.[29] Bratman's framework of shared intentions describes a kind of

26. Arguments for elitist conceptions of democracy always rely on the claim that all else is not equal. Defenders of such conceptions claim that the best possible approximation of an ideal of non-hierarchical political rule can only be achieved by accepting (and even protecting) some forms of political hierarchy, like centralized elite organization for political parties. In characterizing these forms of political rule as "democratic," their defenders never claim that they are more plausible interpretations of what the ideal of democracy requires than other equally workable and less hierarchical conceptions. Rather, they claim that attempts to further diminish political hierarchy are ultimately self-undermining, insofar as they lead to more insidious forms of hierarchy, or erode the conditions for collective agency (Schattschneider, *Party Government*; Schattschneider, *Semisovereign People*; Rosenbluth and Shapiro, *Responsible Parties*).

27. Ober, "The Original Meaning of 'Democracy.'"

28. I use the term "mere anarchy" here to distinguish between two ways of using the term anarchy. Some contemporary philosophers use the term anarchy to refer to the absence of a coercive state, while still allowing for non-coercive forms of political organization. The basic concept of democracy as I describe it here would not necessarily be incompatible with anarchy understood in this broader sense. (I'm grateful to Piki Ish-Shalom for helping me to see this.)

29. See Bratman, *Faces of Intention*; Bratman, "Shared Valuing"; Bratman, *Shared Agency*.

collective activity that is characterized by the ongoing intention of individual members of a group to participate in the activity with other members of the group and by a continual process in which the members of the group adjust and respond to each other as co-agents in their shared activity.[30]

The model of democracy as a jointly intentional collective activity has been defended by other democratic theorists interested in the ethics of citizenship.[31] These theorists argue that Bratman's account of shared intentions captures an important sense of what it means to attribute the activity of political rule to an entire political community in the absence of hierarchical organization. On the shared intentions model, when individuals contribute to a collective activity, they are acting from an intention that refers not only to their own activity, but to the activity of the whole group. But while the content of a shared intention refers to the activity of the whole group, the intention itself need not be attributed to the group as a whole. Shared intentions are composed entirely of the mental states of the *individuals* within the group. What distinguishes shared intentions from typical cases of individual intentions is their content: they refer to the activity of the whole group, not just the individual's contributions, and they "interlock" in a particular way.[32] Otherwise, they decompose into mental states that function in the same way as individual intentions. This makes joint intention different from other modes of collective activity that require the formation of a group agent with the ability to form intentions separate from those of the individuals that make it up.[33]

---

30. I want to make a couple of points about the scope of this discussion. First, this is not meant to be a complete, fully specified, conception of democracy, but is better thought of as a module that might fit into a variety of democratic theories. Its attractiveness is much clearer from theories that include a non-instrumental account of the value of democracy, but I do think even those who regard democracy's value as purely instrumental might find this account of democracy's collective activity useful. Second, in defending the shared intentions conception of democracy, I invoke the characteristics of large, diverse communities with more or less Weberian states because these are communities that concern many—if not most—normative political theorists (including myself). This is also the application that is perhaps the most salient to ordinary users of the word democracy, and I think it is likely that the tension between the normative claims of democratic reforms and the democratic value of existing practices is most significant in these communities. I do not intend to argue here that a statist conception of democracy is necessarily a better or more correct specification of the concept of democracy than a conception geared toward smaller-scale communities.

31. Stilz, *Liberal Loyalty*, 178–82; Beerbohm, *In Our Name*, 44–49.

32. Bratman, *Shared Agency*, 50–52.

33. The classic example of a group agent is a corporation. We can attribute an action—say: purchasing another company—to the corporation as an entity in spite of the fact that many of the individuals who contributed to the corporation's actions—lawyers, accountants, filing clerks—may not have intended the ultimate result. And while some executives in the corporation probably do

Bratman identifies three conditions necessary to describe an activity as jointly intended. First, the participants must each intend that the group will do the activity together. Second, the participants must intend to do the activity together "in accordance with and because of" each of their intentions "and their meshing sub-plans." Third, the satisfaction of the first two conditions is common knowledge.[34] It can be helpful to consider an example: suppose you and I decide to play a game of basketball together. We can be said to share an intention to play basketball together if: 1) I intend that we play basketball and you also intend that we play basketball; 2) we each intend that we play basketball in part because the other also intends it, and it is also part of our intention that we form and execute a set of plans that will enable us to play basketball together; and 3) we both know that we both have these kinds of intentions. Unpacking this example further allows us to see how individual intentions and shared intentions fit together. For us to jointly intend to do an activity together, we need not jointly intend everything about how the activity will go. This is particularly clear when it comes to competitive activities. You and I can share an intention to play basketball together without also sharing an intention that I win. Similarly, we need not jointly intend every detail of our plans to play basketball together. Some things, like when and where we will meet, who will bring the basketball, whether or how we call fouls, we will need to settle on together. Others, such as the mode of transportation we will each use to get to the court, we can leave to the individual participants to decide. What is crucial is that we each form our own sub-plans in a way that "meshes" or "interlocks" with the plans that we share and we each expect the other to do the same.

We can scale up this model to characterize democratic activities like the election of a representative as cases of joint intention. Citizens share an intention to elect a representative insofar as 1) each intends that we elect a representative together; 2) we intend to elect a representative in accordance with our fellow citizens' intention to elect a representative and our shared and meshing sub-plans; and 3) all of this is common knowledge. Elections, like basketball games, are competitive. We can share an intention to elect

---

intend the result, we do not just attribute the intention to them qua individuals. We can attribute the intention (and subsequent action) to the corporation as a unit because of the decision-making authority assigned to those executives within the corporation's decision-making structure. Thus, we can say that Facebook, not Mark Zuckerberg, bought Instagram.

34. This set of conditions is taken from Bratman's essay "Shared Valuing," 9. In subsequent work, Bratman has delineated the conditions somewhat differently, but the substance of them remains the same.

a representative even though we do not also share an intention to elect a particular candidate. We can also share an intention to elect a representative even if we have many different motivations for doing so, just as you and I can play basketball together even if we do so for different reasons. What matters is that citizens have enough of a shared conception of what the activity of election requires of us, and that we expect each other to plan so that our individual actions taken together will result in the election of a representative.

Moving up a level of generality, we can also characterize democracy, that is, rule by the people, as a jointly intended collective activity. If democracy is understood as a form of joint or shared intention, this means that: 1) each member of the political community intends that the people rule; 2) each intends that we rule by way of the agency of each citizen, and according to a set of shared or meshing plans for ruling; and 3) the satisfaction of the first two conditions is common knowledge.

Bratman's is only one among many philosophical accounts of shared agency, but its relatively weak conditions make it attractive for illuminating the ethical implications of a conception of democracy as a collective activity. Unlike other models, the shared intentions model of collective agency does not involve built-in obligations, and it does not require the agents involved to think of themselves as a group in any way apart from the activity they are undertaking together.[35] Shared intentions do not even require consent: a person can still be said to intend to participate in a collective activity, even if that person has no opportunity to reflect on the alternatives. The joint intentions framework can thus characterize the collective agency of people who are born into their citizenship.[36] Bratman's framework also allows that individuals may have different motivations for contributing to a shared activity. This makes joint intentions a plausible framework for conceptualizing democracy in a diverse society.

35. John Searle and Margaret Gilbert have presented alternative models of basic collective action, but both of their models are more demanding in their understanding of the conditions required for even modest sociality. Searle posits the need for a distinctive kind of "we-intention" that is different in kind, not only in content, from ordinary individual intentions (Searle, *The Construction of Social Reality*). Gilbert argues that group action requires a kind of "plural subject," and that involvement in this kind of plural subject necessarily entails certain forms of commitment and moral obligation. Because acting together entails moral obligation on Gilbert's account, she identifies much stricter conditions of consent (or voluntary commitment) to participate in the shared activity (Gilbert, *Living Together*, esp. 179–85).

36. Some forms of deception and coercion certainly undermine the conditions for jointly intentional action (Bratman, *Shared Agency*, 37–38), but there remain many conditions, especially those that characterize individuals' relationship to modern forms of social and political organizations, that fall between direct coercion and consent.

Despite the relative weakness of the conditions for shared intention, this framework still captures democracy's essential features of political equality and collective empowerment. It is the intentions of participants that distinguish the collective action of democracy from situations in which individual actions collectively produce an accidental result—like a stampede or a riot.[37] Attributing intention to all of the members of the group, and including the condition that the members intend to accomplish their intention "by way of the agency of each" also distinguishes democracy from hierarchical forms of collective action in which the collective activity is intended only by some members of the group who may regard others not as co-agents in the collective project, but as mere means.

Some philosophers have objected that Bratman's joint intentions model of shared agency does not characterize *large-scale* collective activity like democracy.[38] They would argue that a requirement that interlocking intentions to practice democracy be held by individual citizens is too demanding for a complex society. Most political decision-making in modern societies is delegated to representatives, and political divisions are often characterized by deep enmity.

This objection overlooks distinctive features of democracy, though. Intentions can be attributed to individuals even if they are not always—or even usually—salient. And based on survey evidence and popular discourse, it is reasonable to think that in most established democracies, most citizens do intend their democracy. More generally, it just seems right that democracy is attenuated to the extent that citizens don't share the intention to have democracy, regardless of how institutions are structured. Democracy without such a shared intention is almost certainly more fragile. But more importantly, the idea that citizens might be empowered *in spite of themselves* is both counter-intuitive and unsettling. The joint intentions model of shared agency is undoubtedly demanding. But an account of democracy—one of our highest political ideals—should be demanding.[39] No political community has ever fully met the conditions for a jointly intended democracy. There are always some citizens who actively resist democracy in favor of an authoritarian or oligarchic regime. There are many more who are simply

---

37. More controversially, the focus on intentions also distinguishes democratic decision-making from opinion polling (see Applbaum, "Forcing a People to Be Free," 363, 375).

38. See, e.g., Kutz, "Acting Together"; Shapiro, "Massively Shared Agency."

39. For a more thorough defense of the joint intentions model of democracy against "minimalist" models of massively shared agency and against an alternative model of "group agency" see Chapman, "Shared Agency and the Ethics of Democracy."

indifferent to the form of their political regime. But all this tells us is that democratic governance remains an aspiration.

SHARED INTENTIONS AND THE IMPORTANCE OF PLANS

Understanding democracy as a jointly intentional collective activity offers an attractive model of what collective empowerment might look like in a pluralist society because it does not require participants to share motivations or a group identity beyond that of co-agents in a collective activity of democracy. At the same time, though, the requirement that each citizen intends the collective activity, and that each intends that they accomplish it "by way of the agency of each" builds in an element of political equality essential to any conception of democracy.

The conditions of the shared intentions model of collective activity are sufficiently minimal to be compatible with a range of views about the institutional or cultural requirements of democracy. Even so, these conditions can still provide some guidance for normative theorizing about democracy. In the remainder of this chapter, I will discuss in greater detail one aspect of the shared intentions model as applied to democracy: the role of shared plans. I argue that attending to the need for widely recognized plans to enable collective projects like democracy sheds light on the ethics of democratic citizenship and democratic reform. I also argue that one important task for democratic theory is to *interpret* existing plans for democracy, to show how they can be maximally effective and a guide to action.

In the joint intentions model, citizens intend that their own acts of participation fit together (in Bratman's terms, "mesh") with those of others to generate democracy. When I intend that my fellow citizens and I rule democratically, I will only succeed in carrying out my intention if the group succeeds in carrying out the shared goal. Acting purposefully in pursuit of a shared intention, then, requires conditions that allow me to form a reasonable expectation that my individual actions will fit together with the actions of other individuals to achieve our shared goal. We need a shared *plan* for how we will accomplish our shared intention.

When I decide how I will pursue an ordinary individual intention, I form a plan based on what I think is the best way for me to accomplish that intention (consistent with all my other plans for pursuing my other intentions), and then I carry out that plan. But when I am acting on a shared intention, I cannot simply decide what I think would be the best way for the group to accomplish our goal, and then act according to my own plan. The members of the group may have different ideas of the best plan, after all, and they may not be consistent. Thus, Michael Bratman argues that joint intentions must be pursued through a web of "meshing sub-plans."[40] If I intend to participate in a collective activity, I must do so in a way that is responsive to the participation of other agents and their own approaches to fulfilling that intention.

Shared plans are crucial to the success of any non-hierarchical collective enterprise, including democracy. Even if I and every other citizen of my political community all wish to play our part in governing democratically, and all know of this universally shared desire, we have no way of acting purposefully on these wishes unless we have some way of identifying what parts we will each perform to collectively produce democracy.

Building on Bratman's account of joint intention, Scott Shapiro characterizes the importance of planning for joint activity. He asserts that "shared agency, that is acting together, is distinguished from individual agency, that is, acting alone, by virtue of the plans of the agents."[41] This is not to say that individuals do not need to have plans, but rather that planning takes on a different form and a greater significance for groups of agents. Individuals can change plans as needed to account for new circumstances or intentions, and easily adjust to achieve consistency among their various plans. Such adaptation is more difficult for group activity in which individuals rely on the predictability of others' actions, and a shared understanding of how their individual actions will together accomplish a goal, in order to act purposefully in the world. Stable shared plans exist to enable this kind of predictability and control. They settle the matter about *what* is to be done and *how* we will do it.[42] Shared plans thus enable citizens to hold and act on a shared intention for democratic self-rule.

SHARED PLANS AND NORMATIVE REASONS

I want to highlight two features of plans that have emerged from the preceding discussion. These two features illuminate why existing practices should be given special weight in an ethics of democracy. First, shared plans create reasons through specification. Most collective activities could be carried out in any number of ways. Given the range of plausible descriptions of democracy that political theorists have offered, it seems likely that democracy fits

---

40. Bratman, "Shared Valuing," 9.
41. Shapiro, *Legality*, 137.
42. Ibid., 129.

into this category. On the face of it, the fact that I have a reason to contribute to democracy in my community does not seem to imply that I must do so in any particular way. Plans are what transmit the reasons I have for forming and acting on an intention into reasons to take specific steps to realize that intention.[43] This is especially true for shared goals like democracy that cannot be achieved without the coordinated actions of many individuals. If I want to contribute to democracy, I cannot simply do whatever I happen to think would be the most democratic thing for citizens to do, without regard for how my action fits with the actions of my fellow citizens, and for how they will interpret and respond to it. To meaningfully participate in democracy, I need to act according to an understanding—shared with my fellow citizens—of how my individual actions will be interpreted as participation and of how they will fit together with those of my fellow citizens to produce democratic self-rule. Claims about how citizens should participate in, promote, or support democracy cannot, therefore, be derived directly from abstract ideals of democracy, but must also be attentive to the particular set of shared plans for democracy in *their* community.

Second, the authority of a plan does not depend on its being the best plan. Yes, part of the business of democratic theory is to identify the best conception of democracy, to articulate the set of institutions, social practices, and attitudes that best instantiates rule by the people (given the reasons we have for valuing rule by the people). And yes, this exercise might reveal how a community's existing plan for democracy deviates from that of some ideal democracy. That does not mean that citizens should cease to follow their existing plan. Shared plans are necessary in part because people disagree about which is the best way to pursue their collective goal.[44] The point of a plan is to establish a practical settlement of this disagreement. If the ability of a plan to transmit reasons for pursuing a goal into reasons for pursuing it in a particular way depended on its being the *best* plan, it would not be able to serve this coordinating function. Treating a given plan as authoritative does not necessarily mean endorsing the plan or regarding it as the best possible way of accomplishing a goal. Treating my community's plan for democracy as authoritative simply means accepting it as a guide for action—recognizing that it provides the best guide for how I should act to contribute to democracy, given how I expect my fellow citizens to act. It means voting

---

43. See Bratman, "Reflections." See also Richardson, *Practical Reasoning about Final Ends*, esp. 69–77.

44. Shapiro, *Legality*, 132–33.

in elections, even if I think our democracy could be improved by replacing elections with random selection to office.

Of course, there are limits on the authority of plans and the reasons of specification that they create. Any reasons that a citizen has for following her community's plan for democracy derive from the reasons that she has for engaging in the shared activity of democracy in the first place. For a plan to effectively transmit reasons to contribute to democracy into reasons to contribute in particular ways, a community's shared plan needs to be at least minimally effective in achieving a plausible instantiation of democracy that is consistent with the value of democracy. Limits on the kind of duties that can be derived from a community's particular plan for democracy and the strength of those duties will, therefore, depend in part on the reasons we have for valuing democracy. Some of these reasons will allow for a greater variety of plans than others. At the same time, though, if democracy is to be a useful concept in pluralist societies, it should allow for at least some flexibility and compromise as communities work out a widely accepted plan for how they will carry out their shared intention that they rule democratically.

DEMOCRACY, PLANS, AND THE INTERPRETIVE TASK OF POLITICAL THEORY

Normative democratic theory has an obvious role to play in articulating the value of democracy and identifying the minimal requirements for institutions and practices to warrant deference in an ethics of democracy. Democratic theory also has a role to play in the refinement and revision of shared plans for democracy that may realize some of the value of democracy, but that are nevertheless still far from ideal. Recognizing the significance and authority of existing shared plans for democracy does not require us to give up on the project of democratic reform. Rather, it ought to provide guidance for *how* we pursue democratic reform: how we frame and address normative claims about democracy, and how we translate democratic ideals into an ethics of citizenship.

Democratic theorists who hope to offer an ethic of democracy for citizens, leaders, and activists in the world we have now should take up the tasks of understanding contemporary communities' existing plans for democracy, articulating the normative requirements of those plans, and identifying how democratic arrangements can and should be reformed in ways that preserve the integrity of citizens' shared understandings for how they will go about the collective project of democracy.

One way to understand this sort of project in democratic theory is as a form of constructive interpretation. The term "constructive interpretation" has been used to describe various normative projects that might be characterized as internal critique of existing practices.[45] The understanding of constructive interpretation I am drawing on here is that articulated by Ronald Dworkin in *Law's Empire*.[46] Dworkin described constructive interpretation as "imposing purpose on an object or practice in order to make of it the best possible example of the form or genre to which it is taken to belong."[47] When democratic theorists apply the method of constructive interpretation to existing democratic practices, they are not simply looking for *any* explanation that might make sense of them. Rather, a constructive interpretation imposes on democratic practices the purposes that make the most sense of them *as a plan for democracy.*

Constructive interpretation involves both an empirical and a normative component. It is empirical because an interpretation must "fit" the practice it explains. The interpretation must make sense given the actual features—what Dworkin calls the "raw data"—of the practice. The raw data of democratic practice includes not only formal institutions or rights and responsibilities of citizens and officials, but also norms and habits of participation and discourse, as well as citizens' attitudes toward these features of their practice, and expectations about how they function together.

The normative component of constructive interpretation arises in the definition of the "form or genre" to which the object being interpreted belongs. This enables the interpreter to make a value judgment about the purpose that, when ascribed to the object, shows it "in its best light."[48] The joint intentions conception of democracy I have discussed in this section suggests that when constructively interpreting democratic practices, normative democratic theorists might regard them as belonging to the genre of "shared plans for democracy." This means that the value judgments that theorists make in ascribing purpose to a democratic practice (like popular voting) will be informed by an understanding of both democratic principles and the nature and functions of shared plans.

---

45. Aaron James suggests that John Rawls can be thought of as engaging in a kind of constructive interpretation (James, "Constructing Justice for Existing Practice"), and James himself applies this method to look at the practices of international trade (James, *Fairness in Practice*).

46. I want to emphasize that I am drawing on Dworkin's stated definition of constructive interpretation, and not on his own application of it.

47. Dworkin, *Law's Empire*, 52.

48. Ibid., 53.

Constructive interpretation is a tool for both evaluating and improving the objects of interpretation. Once the interpreter has identified the interpretation that best fits a practice, she can explain how the practice should be revised to best serve the purpose she ascribes to it. Constructive interpretation thus provides critical purchase for the reform of existing norms and democratic practices to make them more coherent and consistent with the best interpretation of the existing plan for democracy.

This book has been an exercise in constructive interpretation. I have endeavored to illuminate the value and purposes of our existing practice of popular voting. One goal of this constructive interpretation has been to show how much there is to honor and celebrate in this practice. But another goal has been to figure out how we can make it still better. Practices of popular voting can be made to better fulfill the purposes they are supposed to serve. Our plan for electoral democracy can be made more coherent and effective with reforms that reinforce the key value-making features of popular voting: universal participation, aggregative equality, and momentousness.

SCALING UP SHARED INTENTIONS: CAN THERE REALLY BE A SHARED PLAN FOR DEMOCRACY?

Speaking about "interpreting" a plan may raise the following concern: if a plan needs to be interpreted, is it really a plan? If the point of a shared plan is to coordinate how a group of people will enact their shared intention, then it may seem that the plan should be apparent—it should not require interpretation. It may be hard to see how a shared plan can sufficiently be a guide to action—how it can really "settle the matter" of what is to be done—if it is open to interpretation.

This might seem to point to a problem with "scaling up" a shared intentions account of collective activity. The philosophy of shared intentions that I have drawn on here usually focuses on small-scale examples of joint action: painting a house or writing a novel together. Modern democracy is a far cry from these face-to-face interactions. Given the size (and pluralism) of contemporary political communities, and the complexity of the task of governing, it may seem that disagreement, conflict, and communication difficulties will render any kind of shared plan (and therefore any shared intention) impossible.

Disagreement and conflict about shared plans are not unique to large-scale cases of collective activity, though. Even in fairly intimate cases of shared intention, conflict, disagreement, and uncertainty about what the plan requires will almost inevitably arise. Consider the example of a couple who decide to paint a house together. Whatever initial plan they might settle on, it is likely that there will be miscommunications or misunderstandings that lead to disagreement about what their plan actually requires (perhaps they agreed to work only on weekday evenings, but did not settle whether this included Friday evenings). They may also find that they have failed to recognize some inconsistencies in their plan, or they may find that their plan is underspecified; they have not yet resolved some aspect of potential conflict (perhaps one of the rooms in the house has wood paneling on the wall, but they have not decided whether they will paint it along with the drywall). And, of course, they may encounter unforeseen circumstances that prevent them from acting on their plan as they have understood it (perhaps their chosen paint color is out of stock and ordering it will disrupt their timeline for finishing the house).

When faced with these situations in which the requirements of a shared plan are not straightforward, the participants in a shared activity need not act as if they have no plan at all. It is hard to imagine any kind of shared activity that could get off the ground if the participants had to start from scratch in creating a new plan every time they encountered one of these difficulties. Instead, in resolving conflict and deciding how to act, the participants can look to the shared plan as a whole and try to decide which course of action will fit best within the general approach they have already agreed upon. This will often be a matter of *interpreting* the shared plan; for example, to deal with the out-of-stock paint color, the house-painting couple will need to assess whether their timeline or their preferred paint color is more central to their shared plan to paint the house. Can one be more easily revised to fit with the other aspects of their plan? Of course, not all conflict can be resolved by appealing to and interpreting an existing plan in this way, but if it were not often possible, collective action, even on the smallest scale, would be much too fragile.

The potential for disagreement and conflict over a community's shared plan for democracy and over the shared plans of more intimate cases of shared intention is a difference of degree, not of kind. It is undoubtedly more challenging to develop, maintain, and revise shared plans on such a massive scale. As a massively shared intention, democracy will likely require more conscious effort to maintain a broadly recognized plan. It will certainly require formal institutions that stabilize and ensure compliance with participation norms. But the role of plans in resolving disagreement and conflict in small-scale cases of jointly intentional activity can still serve as a model for reforming democratic institutions and practices.[49] The language of shared plans also provides citizens with a familiar framework for wrestling with the ethics of our role as citizens contributing to a collective project of democracy.

Though formal institutions play an important role in maintaining the stability of a massively collective activity like democracy, formal rules alone are not a sufficient guide for citizens and democratic leaders who want to act to support democracy. Institutions that may have been designed to coordinate individual actions toward a shared purpose can sometimes be self-undermining. Different democratic institutions may work at cross-purposes and many commonly held guiding beliefs may, on reflection, be inconsistent with each other. Unforeseen changes in technology or the political context can introduce dysfunction into a set of democratic arrangements that have been well designed for a different context. The institutions and formal rules that facilitate coordinated collective activity do not provide sufficient guidance for how to resolve inconsistencies within the rules or to reform dysfunctional institutions.

Just as in the house-painting example, dealing with conflict and uncertainty in how best to contribute to the collective project of self-rule does not require redesigning a political system from scratch. Instead, figuring out how to reform democratic institutions and practices calls for an act of interpretation that identifies which elements of the various institutions, norms, guiding beliefs, and practices that characterize the community's collective project of democracy are most central to the community's shared plan. Then we can recognize those that are more peripheral or even deviant, and might be revised without compromising either the ultimate aim of the collective activity— democratic self-rule—or the ability of citizens to coordinate their contributions toward that shared aim. That is what this book has endeavored to do.

Conclusion

The practice of popular voting—with all its attendant spectacle—is the cornerstone of the shared plan for democracy in contemporary democracies. The nature and role of this practice has evolved over time. The way we vote today, and what it means to us, is a product of centuries of political activity. Our contemporary practice of popular voting owes as much or more to the actions and rhetoric of activists who have fought for suffrage expansions and real opportunity to vote than it does to the legislators who have codified their

49. I am very grateful to Michael Bratman for helpful conversation on this issue.

demands into law and policy. The practice of popular voting is as much about the norms and expectations that citizens actively circulate in our communities, and about the mobilization strategies adopted by electoral campaigns and other political organizations, and about the discursive tropes and images deployed in media coverage of elections, as it is about formal institutions or official administrative policies. Any reason we have for valuing democracy also gives us reason to value voting as itself a product of citizens' collective, democratic agency. We do not need to believe that our practice of popular voting is the undeniable result of pure reasoning about democracy's requirements in order to value it. We can value our practice of voting, love it, and work hard to improve it, because it is *ours*.

This does not mean that we shouldn't strive to reform and improve our voting practices. As I have argued throughout this book, there are many ways that norms, institutions, and administrative policies can be made to better serve the purposes of popular voting. But as I have also argued, we must examine the practice comprehensively and with a view to its place within a democratic system if we are to understand those purposes. Earnest electoral reformers and radical critics alike have often failed to do this.

We cannot reason about what democracy requires from us or from our institutions just by contemplating democratic principles. Democracy is, fundamentally, a kind of collective activity. Normative claims about the ethics of participation or democratic reform, therefore, need to be sensitive to the practical demands of collective action. I have suggested that what this means for the ethics of democracy and the role of political theory can be usefully illuminated with the philosophical framework of joint intentions. This framework highlights how shared agency depends on mutually recognized and authoritative shared *plans*. A collective activity in which the participants can be seen as equal agents—especially one on the scale of modern democracy—requires that participants develop shared plans that will guide their contributions to the collective project, ensuring that the various individual contributions fit together to produce the intended result. Because of the need for shared plans to coordinate individual participation in a collective activity, the ethics of democratic participation and reform cannot be derived directly from an ideal conception of democracy. They also depend in large measure on the actual practices and shared understandings of democracy that exist in a particular community. Only when we understand the role of existing practices, institutions, and norms within our community's shared plan for democracy can we provide an adequate guide for how citizens and political leaders should act to best promote and support *our* democracies.

Conclusion

Popular voting is *the* central practice of modern democracies. I have offered a vindication of voting and its outsized role in our civic lives. Popular voting, including the spectacle that surrounds it, brings to life unique aspects of democratic values and performs essential functions in a healthy democratic system. Popular voting combines an expectation of approximately universal participation, an application of aggregative equality, and a rhythm of decisive participatory moments into a practice that interrupts the ordinary business of government with periodic reminders that democracy depends on all of us. I have provided ample empirical research—along with many anecdotes—that supports this account of voting's value. But sometimes it is easiest to appreciate the value of something we take for granted by imagining our lives without it. Let me conclude, then, by offering a thought experiment to illuminate voting's purposes as well as its limits.

The Future of Voting: A Thought Experiment

Maybe it is just because I live and work in Silicon Valley, but often I meet people who believe we are on the cusp of—or already experiencing—a dramatic technological revolution. This new technology has the potential to alter many aspects of our lives. And it could, if we let it, prompt us to take a hard look at why and how we vote.

I am not talking about internet voting. Internet and mobile phone voting are already viewed as the next frontier of convenience voting reforms.

Numerous polities have begun to experiment with internet voting. Currently, concerns about security remain the biggest barrier to its widespread adoption, but these concerns will likely recede in the coming decades. Either we will manage to address them, finding ways to make internet voting, if not perfectly secure, then at least as secure as mail-in voting, or we will simply learn to live with the security risks as we have in so many other aspects of our lives. If internet voting becomes common, it will probably roll out much like early and mail-in voting have: with some excitement and some trepidation, and not much reflection.

No, the technology I am talking about is artificial intelligence. It is easy to imagine a not-so-distant future in which artificial intelligence is better than we are at knowing what we want in most domains. We may already be living in that world. In the future, though, we may even admit it. And then we may allow AI to make our lives go better by filling our grocery carts, choosing our clothing, our route to work, our doctors, our schools, our homes, our college courses. We might even let AI choose our romantic partners or career paths. To make a satisfactory choice in any of these domains requires us to have some information about the options in front of us, and about how those options serve our interests and reflect our values. We all know that sometimes we make bad choices, choices we regret. Usually this is because we lack some relevant information or because we aren't in a state of mind to process this information appropriately. But sometimes we also misunderstand our own values or interests. We can be remarkably self-deceptive. To think that it is worth letting AI make some choices for us, we don't need to believe that AI will always make the best choice, only that it will choose better than we will for ourselves.

This—for now, imaginary—future offers a useful thought experiment. Could we replace voting with a sufficiently powerful and well-trained artificial intelligence? There are many ways we could construct such a scenario, but let's imagine the strongest and simplest version.[1] In this thought experiment, a single program would build a profile of each and every citizen, observing our choices in other domains and using them to predict our preferences over the available candidates for office. The program would then aggregate these preferences according to a decision rule designed with an eye to aggregative

1. A much more plausible future than the one I describe here might see people relying on a personal AI app, which would match them with candidates, but not commit them to voting that way. This version of an election AI, while less objectionable than the one I focus on would also have fewer benefits. It would, for example, not eliminate distortions introduced by abstention, and it would probably have to be more limited in its scope.

equality. In short, it would use data about our preferences to give us the electoral outcomes we most want. And we wouldn't have to lift a finger.

Imagine: a democracy without election campaigns. No negative advertising, no simpering and dissembling politicians. If the AI election ever did gain popular support, it would be on the strength of that proposition. But the real benefit of the AI election would come from its potential to track citizens' preferences much more accurately than the voting-based elections we use now.

Many people think that politics is an area in which we are particularly bad at making choices. We may find it especially difficult to identify and interpret information that is relevant to political decisions. We may also be especially self-deceptive when it comes to our political values and preferences. Political scientists have offered many theories for why, when it comes to politics, and especially to voting, we might not be very good at making satisfactory choices.[2]

You may not find such theories all that compelling. I don't either, for reasons discussed in chapter 2. But I also don't think our political judgments are typically *better* than our judgments in other domains. So, if we find ourselves willing to let AI choose a home or a school or a course of medical treatment for us, why not let it vote for us? It is easy to imagine AI forming a profile of me by tracking my purchases, or movements, or phone use, or engagement on social networks, by seeing what I read and watch, and by analyzing what I write in my emails and text messages and then using this profile to infer how I would vote, were I maximally informed and reflective. Given all we know about cognitive biases and the limits of human abilities to process information, it does not seem implausible to me that a computer, given an adequate chance to learn about me, could choose political candidates that would make me happier or that would align better with my most deeply held values than those I would choose for myself. AI could improve our voting choices by diminishing various human biases and imperfections in decision-making. And it would be efficient, saving us the time it takes to become a conscientious and informed voter.

What reasons might we have for rejecting a proposal for an AI election? Such an AI would undoubtedly make mistakes, but would they be more frequent or more serious than the mistakes individuals make for ourselves? Perhaps, but I doubt it. Likewise, even the best AI would probably be biased in some ways. But would its biases be more severe than the biases that we take for granted in our electoral systems? Probably not. Security is no doubt

2. See chapter 2 for an overview of some of these theories.

the biggest remaining obstacle, but since this is a thought experiment, let us posit that we can reduce security risks so that they are no greater than those of the typical electoral system. For this thought experiment, we are faced with a choice, then, between voting for our representatives much as we do now, or using an artificial intelligence to select them—an artificial intelligence that could report citizens' preferences with greater accuracy and less bias than the best electoral system.

If you are like me, though, you would still reject the AI election. Something very serious and important would be lost if we replaced voting with a powerful algorithm to give us the government we seem to want. And that tells us something important about why we vote.

If the point of voting is just to collect comprehensive and accurate information about citizens' preferences, I don't think we can rule out the AI. The reason we should reject the AI is because we know that voting is *not* just about collecting and aggregating information about individuals. Popular voting is a practice of citizens' exercising our agency and doing so together. Voting creates democratic moments whose value is not reducible to the value of the information contained in the ballots.

The idea of citizens' surrendering the most powerful tool of popular sovereignty to an artificial intelligence no doubt seems creepy and far-fetched. Before such a notion could gain any traction with the public, we would first need to get used to relying on AI in other domains, and we would also need to reconcile ourselves to the extent of surveillance and data collection needed to make artificial intelligence, well, intelligent. That world may not be as far off as we might like to think, but it is not here yet.

But even if the AI election is not a live option, the thought experiment is a useful one. Reflecting on what it is that we do when we vote, and why it is important that we do it ourselves, can help us evaluate the reform proposals that are salient here and now, including and perhaps especially internet and mobile phone voting. The AI thought experiment invites us to consider not just whether there will be voting in the distant future, but also what the immediate future of voting will look like.

Throughout this book, I have argued that we need to expand the current paradigm of electoral reform debates, which focus primarily on opportunity, convenience, and security. The AI thought experiment helps us see why. It matters that electoral decisions incorporate not just citizens' preferences but their active, reflective choices. It also matters that when citizens make these choices, they are conscious of their role in *collective* decision-making. And finally, it matters that citizens regularly come together to contribute to collective decision-making. Our agency as individuals and as a collective must be connected to electoral outcomes; it is not enough that an accurate report of our preferences is what determines the outcome. Popular voting socializes citizens into their role as political agents and shapes a democratic political environment. If we want popular voting to do these things, then we must be thoughtful about how we construct the experience of voting for all citizens. Exactly what election moments look like will undoubtedly change along with our technology and culture. But, guided by a clear understanding of voting's purposes, we can direct those changes in ways that preserve and even enhance the value of our central democratic practice.

Democratic Systems and the Limits of Voting

The AI election thought experiment also brings some of the limitations of voting into sharp relief. In addition to potentially generating more accurate information about citizens' political preferences, an AI would have the advantage of being able to gain more precise and fine-grained information. We often think and talk about elections as opportunities for voters to voice their opinions about what the government ought to do. But voting is a blunt instrument for influencing government. The preferences that citizens can express during elections are, at best, summaries of our preferences over many different issues, or perhaps general policy "moods."[3] The narratives that emerge to characterize electoral choices overlay an immense number of political decisions that citizens might wish to influence. Of course, we sometimes vote directly on specific issue in referenda, but expanding the number of questions on the ballot quickly produces decision fatigue and increasing abstention. Popular voting, then, on its own, is only good at aggregating preferences for a limited set of decisions about how we govern ourselves—primarily about who is authorized to wield public power.

This should not be viewed as a problem with voting, though. Rather, it marks the boundaries of voting's role within a democratic system. Contemporary democracies are sustained by a host of other activities that enable citizens to influence government in more fine-grained ways. Healthy democratic systems foster practices in which citizens disseminate ideas, proposals, and representative claims, and deliberate over the merits of these. Democratic systems foster practices in which citizens organize groups for collective action, and in which these groups petition the government (through lobbying

3. Stimson, *Public Opinion in America*.

or constituent contact, for example) on issues of special concern to them. Democratic systems foster practices in which citizens consult and collaborate to solve public problems. They also foster practices in which citizens monitor and publicize the activities of the government. And democratic systems foster practices in which citizens organize to resist or prophesy when laws are unconscionable and the path to changing them is unclear.

Popular voting is not more important than these practices or the institutions that structure and facilitate them. All these activities jointly compose a complex democratic ecology. They are mutually supporting and interact to create a thriving political community. Voting warrants special attention, though, precisely because its effects on our attention are among its chief contributions to democracy. Periodically assembling the body of the people to participate on manifestly and concretely equal terms in making a decision of great consequence creates arresting moments that infuse politics with energy, excitement, and purpose. These moments can provide an opportunity to marvel at and celebrate the miracle of what modern democracies have accomplished. They can also remind us how fragile and incomplete this accomplishment is and how much work we have yet to do. Most importantly, they remind us that we cannot complete this work of democracy unless we do so together.

ACKNOWLEDGMENTS

If we count from the time I told my advisor, Philip Pettit, that I'd like to write my dissertation on voting, this book has been more than 10 years in the making. During that time, so many people have helped this book come into being in its current form that it is hard to know where to even begin expressing my gratitude.

In 2019, I had the good fortune to host a manuscript workshop. I am tremendously grateful to the participants in that workshop: Melissa Schwartzberg, Joshua Cohen, Russell Muirhead, Eric Beerbohm, and David Plunkett along with my colleagues Rob Reich, Josh Ober, Alison McQueen, Andy Hall, Mike Tomz, and Michael Bratman. Discussions in that workshop helped me clarify the core ideas in the book and prompted me to reorganize the chapters and some of the arguments in ways that have made the book so much better. I am humbled and grateful that they were willing to give my manuscript, rough though it was, so much time and attention. I am also grateful to my department chair at the time, Judy Goldstein, for supporting and funding the workshop, to Eliana Vasquez for handling the logistics, and to Brett Parker for taking notes.

Mary Shiraef, José Luis Sabau, and Lisa Wang provided invaluable research assistance.

I have presented chapters or ideas from this work at many conferences and workshops over the years, including the American Political Science Association Annual Meeting, the MANCEPT workshops in Political Theory, the Western Political Science Association Conference, the Midwest Political Science Association Conference, the University of Pittsburgh Political Science Department, the Philosophy, Politics, and Economics Society Conference, the Georgetown Institute for the Study of Markets and Ethics Symposium on the Ethics of Democracy, the University of California, the San Diego Political Theory Workshop, the University of Notre Dame Political Theory Workshop, the NYU Political Theory Workshop, the University of Illinois Urbana-Champaign Political Science Workshop, the UC Berkeley Workshop in Law, Philosophy, and Political Theory, the REDEM project workshop, Stanford's Center for Democracy Development and the Rule of Law, and the Stanford Political Theory Workshop. I am grateful to the participants in all of these workshops for their time and thoughtful engagement and for innumerable insights and challenges.

For comments on pieces of the book and helpful conversations about these ideas, I am very grateful to Andy Sabl, Nan Keohane, Dinsha Mistree, Ned Foley, Lisa Disch, Rune Slothuus, Jacob Levy, Kevin Elliott, Samuel Bagg, Prithvi Datta, David Estlund, Seana Shiffrin, Benjamin Miller, Melissa Schwartzberg, Joshua Cohen, Russell Muirhead, Eric Beerbohm, David Plunkett, Rob Reich, Josh Ober, Alison McQueen, Andy Hall, Mike Tomz, Michael Bratman, John Ferejohn, Paul Sniderman, Justin Grimmer, Avi Acharya, Vicky Fouka, Juliana Bidadanure, Daniel Weinstock, Sean Ingham, Itai Sher, Hun Chung, Yuna Blajer de la Garza, Jonathan Rodden, Justin Grimmer, Minh Ly, Pam Karlan, Jim Fearon, David Laitin, Nenad Stojanović, Wendy Salkin, Brookes Brown, and two anonymous reviewers.

This book grew out of my Ph.D. dissertation. I am indebted to my advisors on that project—Philip Pettit, Stephen Macedo, Annie Stilz—and to Christopher Achen for invaluable advice, feedback, and support. This book also benefitted from the many participants in the Princeton Graduate Political Theory Workshop and University Center for Human Values Graduate Fellow Workshop who endured multiple presentations of this work and shaped its early development. I am also deeply grateful to my fellow graduate students and friends, especially Brookes Brown, Trevor Latimer, and Amy Hondo for their companionship, encouragement, and many, many insights.

Since coming to Stanford, I have also benefitted greatly from the support of my colleagues. Many I have already mentioned have contributed insights and feedback in the making of this book. Others have offered encouragement, enthusiasm, friendship, and grace. It is impossible to enumerate all the sources of support for which I am grateful. I want to acknowledge two of my colleagues, in particular, without whom I cannot imagine having finished this book. Alison McQueen has read more drafts of chapters or sections of this book than I can keep track of. Her comments are unfailingly insightful and constructive. I have also benefitted greatly from her practical advice on book writing and all matters academic. I am beyond lucky to have her as a mentor and friend. Wendy Salkin has been my writing buddy for the past two years. Thanks to her companionship and encouragement, writing has become something I look forward to. I can't imagine how I would have managed to keep making progress on this book amidst the ups and downs of these pandemic years without her.

My parents taught me that curiosity is a gift and nurtured my love for learning. They sacrificed for my education. They also taught me that formal education was a waste if it led me to ignore or dismiss what others had to say. If people are going to share their wisdom with you, you have to let them know that you value it and then you have to listen. And the most important things there are to learn are best learned in the context of deep and respectful relationships. Of all the things my parents taught me, that is the one I am perhaps most grateful for.

I got married the same year I began working on the dissertation that became this book. I am very grateful to my husband, Ricky, for his material and emotional support (and forbearance) these past 10-plus years. Without him, I never would have begun writing this book, much less finished it. Ricky was the one who handed me a copy of William Riker's *Liberalism Against Populism*, which first sparked my interest in the theory of electoral democracy. He was also the one who finally convinced me of the value of imposing routine and structure on my research and writing practices. That, along with his affirmation and willingness to do far more than his fair share of the dishes when I have a deadline approaching, has enabled me to persevere through the long process of writing a book. Everyone should be so lucky to have such a partner.

Finally, my son PJ has made an invaluable contribution to this book by having nothing to do with it. Okay, yes, he helps me to look at concepts anew as I try to find ways to explain them to a preschooler, and yes, he inspires me as I think about the world he will inherent. But mostly he keeps me grounded and sane and gives me an excuse to take a break and play with Lego.

BIBLIOGRAPHY

International Institute for Democracy and Electoral Assistance. "About | The Global State of Democracy Indices." Accessed December 12, 2019. https://www.idea.int/gsod-indices/about.

Abramowitz, Alan I., and Steven W. Webster. "Negative Partisanship: Why Americans Dislike Parties But Behave Like Rabid Partisans." *Advances in Political Psychology* 39, no. Suppl. 1 (2018): 119–35.

Achen, Christopher, and Larry Bartels. *Democracy for Realists: Why Elections Do Not Produce Responsive Government.* Princeton, NJ: Princeton University Press, 2016.

Achen, Christopher, and Aram Hur. "Civic Duty and Turnout in Japan and South Korea." *Korean Election Studies* 1 (2011): 45–68.

Adler, Katya. "Turnout Sharply down in French Election." *BBC News,* May 7, 2017, sec. Europe. https://www.bbc.com/news/world-europe-39833831.

Ajala, Olayinka. "What to Expect as 84 Million Nigerians Go to the Polls." *The Conversation,* February 14, 2019. http://theconversation.com/what-to-expect-as-84-million-nigerians-go-to-the -polls-111457.

Aldrich, John. *Why Parties? A Second Look.* Chicago, IL: University of Chicago Press, 2011.

Alex Graves. "Game On." *The West Wing.* NBC, October 30, 2002.

Allen, Danielle S. *Talking to Strangers: Anxieties of Citizenship since Brown v. Board of Education.* Chicago, IL: University of Chicago Press, 2006.

Almond, Gabriel A., and Sidney Verba. *The Civic Culture: Political Attitudes and Democracy in Five Nations.* Newbury Park, CA: Sage Publications, 1989.

Alt, James, Ethan Bueno de Mesquita, and Shanna Rose. "Disentangling Accountability and Competence in Elections: Evidence from U.S. Term Limits." *The Journal of Politics* 73, no. 1 (2011): 171–86.

Anderson, Christopher J., Andre Blais, Shaun Bowler, Todd Donovan, and Ola Listhaug. *Loser's Consent: Elections and Democratic Legitimacy.* Oxford, UK: Oxford University Press, 2005.

Ansolabehere, Stephen, Jonathan Rodden, and James M. Snyder Jr. "The Strength of Issues: Using Multiple Measures to Gauge Preference Stability, Ideological Constraint, and Issue Voting." *American Political Science Review* 102, no. 2 (May 2008): 215–32.

Applbaum, Arthur. "Forcing a People to Be Free." *Philosophy and Public Affairs* 35, no. 4 (Fall 2007): 359–400.

Arlen, Gordon, and Enzo Rossi. "Must Realists Be Pessimists About Democracy? Responding to Epistemic and Oligarchic Challenges." *Moral Philosophy and Politics* 8, no. 1 (2021): 27–49.

Arrow, Kenneth J. *Social Choice and Individual Values.* 3rd edition. New Haven CT and London: Yale University Press, 2012.

Ashworth, Scott. "Electoral Accountability: Recent Theoretical and Empirical Work." *Annual Review of Political Science* 15, no. 1 (2012): 183–201. https://doi.org/10.1146/annurev-polisci -031710-103823.

Austen-Smith, David, and Jeffrey S. Banks. *Positive Political Theory I: Collective Preference*. Ann Arbor, MI: The University of Michigan Press, 2000.

Auter, Zac. "Number of Americans Closely Following Politics Spikes." Gallup.com, September 22, 2016. https://news.gallup.com/poll/195749/number-americans-closely-following-politics-spikes.aspx.

Bagg, Samuel. "The Power of the Multitude: Answering Epistemic Challenges to Democracy." *American Political Science Review* 112, no. 4 (2018): 891–904.

Banducci, Susan, Jeffrey Karp, Michael Thrasher, and Colin Rallings. "Ballot Photographs as Cues in Low-Information Elections." *Political Psychology* 29 (2008): 903–17.

Bawn, Kathleen, Martin Cohen, David Karol, Seth Masket, Hans Noel, and John Zaller. "A Theory of Political Parties: Groups, Policy Demands and Nominations in American Politics." *Perspectives on Politics* 10, no. 3 (September 2012): 571–97.

Beer, Samuel H. *Modern British Politics: Parties and Pressure Groups in the Collectivist Age*. New York: Norton, 1982.

Beerbohm, Eric. *In Our Name: The Ethics of Democracy*. Princeton, NJ: Princeton University Press, 2012.

Bensel, Richard. *The American Ballot Box in the Mid-Nineteenth Century*. Cambridge, UK: Cambridge University Press, 2004.

Berinsky, Adam. "The Perverse Consequences of Electoral Reform in the United States." *American Politics Research* 33, no. 4 (2005): 471–91.

Berinsky, Adam, Nancy Burns, and Michael W. Traugott. "Who Votes by Mail? A Dynamic Model of the Individual-Level Consequences of Voting-by-Mail Systems." *The Public Opinion Quarterly* 65, no. 1 (Summer 2001): 178–97.

Birch, Sarah. "Electoral Institutions and Popular Confidence in Electoral Processes: A Cross-National Analysis." *Electoral Studies* 27 (2008): 305–20.

———. *Full Participation: A Comparative Study of Compulsory Voting*. New York: United Nations University Press, 2009.

Black, Duncan. *The Theory of Committees and Elections*. Cambridge, UK: Cambridge University Press, 1958.

Blais, André. *To Vote or Not to Vote?: The Merits and Limits of Rational Choice Theory*. Pittsburgh, PA: Pittsburgh University Press, 2000.

———. "What Affects Voter Turnout?" *Annual Review of Political Science* 9 (2006): 111–25.

Blais, André, and Christopher H. Achen. "Civic Duty and Voter Turnout." *Political Behavior* 41, no. 2 (June 2019): 473–97. https://doi.org/10.1007/s11109-018-9459-3.

Bonotti, Matteo. *Partisanship and Political Liberalism in Diverse Societies*. Oxford, UK: Oxford University Press, 2017.

Bowler, Shaun, and Todd Donovan. *Demanding Choices: Opinion, Voting, and Direct Democracy*. Ann Arbor, MI: University of Michigan Press, 1998.

Bratman, Michael. *Faces of Intention: Selected Essays on Agency and Intention*. Cambridge, UK: Cambridge University Press, 1999.

———. "Reflections on Law, Normativity, and Plans." In *New Essays on the Normativity of Law*, edited by Stefano Bertea and George Pavlakos, 73–85. Portland, OR: Hart Publishing, 2011.

———. *Shared Agency: A Planning Theory of Acting Together*. New York: Oxford University Press, 2014.

———. "Shared Valuing and Frameworks for Practical Reasoning." In *Structures of Agency: Essays*, 293–310. Oxford, UK: Oxford University Press, 2007.

Brennan, Geoffrey, and Loren Lomasky. *Democracy and Decision: The Pure Theory of Electoral Preference*. Cambridge, UK: Cambridge University Press, 1993.

Brennan, Geoffrey, and Philip Pettit. "Unveiling the Vote." *British Journal of Political Science* 20, no. 3 (1990): 311–33.

Brennan, Jason. *Against Democracy*. Princeton, NJ: Princeton University Press, 2016.

———. "Medicine Worse Than the Disease? Against Compulsory Voting." In *Compulsory Voting: For and Against*, by Jason Brennan and Lisa Hill, 1–107. New York: Cambridge University Press, 2014.

———. *The Ethics of Voting*. Princeton, NJ: Princeton University Press, 2011.

Brettschneider, Corey. *Democratic Rights: The Substance of Self-Government*. Princeton, NJ: Princeton University Press, 2007.

Brians, Craig Leonard, and Bernard Grofman. "Election Day Registration's Effect on U.S. Voter Turnout." *Social Science Quarterly* 82, no. 1 (March 2001): 170–83. https://doi.org/10.1111 /0038-4941.00015.

Broadwater, Luke. "Schurick Guilty of Election Fraud in Robocall Case." *Baltimore Sun*, December 6, 2011. https://web.archive.org/web/20140111092927/http://www.baltimoresun.com /news/breaking/bs-md-schurick-robocalls-verdict-20111206,0,6200720,full.story.

Broder, David S. *Democracy Derailed: Initiative Campaigns and the Power of Money*. New York: Harcourt, 2001.

Bruter, Michael, and Sarah Harrison. *Inside the Mind of a Voter*. Princeton, NJ: Princeton University Press, 2020.

———. "Understanding the Emotional Act of Voting." *Nature Human Behaviour* 1, no. 1 (January 10, 2017): 1–3. https://doi.org/10.1038/s41562-016-0024.

Burnett, Craig M., and Vladimir Kogan. "Ballot (and Voter) 'exhaustion' under Instant Runoff Voting: An Examination of Four Ranked-Choice Elections." *Electoral Studies* 37 (2015): 41–49.

Cain, Bruce. *Democracy More or Less: America's Political Reform Quandary*. Cambridge, UK: Cambridge University Press, 2014.

Campbell, Angus, Gerald Gurin, and Warren Miller. *The Voter Decides*. Evanston, IL: Row, Peterson, and Company, 1954.

Campbell, David. "Social Networks and Political Participation." *Annual Review of Political Science* 16 (2013): 33–48.

———. *Why We Vote: How Schools and Communities Shape Our Civic Life*. Princeton, NJ: Princeton University Press, 2006.

Canes-Wrone, Brandice, David W. Brady, and John F. Cogan. "Out of Step, Out of Office: Electoral Accountability and House Members' Voting." *The American Political Science Review* 96, no. 1 (2002): 127–40.

Caplan, Bryan. *The Myth of the Rational Voter: Why Democracies Choose Bad Policies*. Princeton, NJ: Princeton University Press, 2007.

Carlsson, Fredrik, and Olof Johansson-Stenman. "Why Do You Vote and Vote as You Do?" *KYKLOS* 63, no. 4 (November 2010): 495–516.

Chalmers, Douglas A. *Reforming Democracies: Six Facts about Politics That Demand a New Agenda*. New York, NY: Columbia University Press, 2013.

Chambers, Simone. "Democracy and Constitutional Reform: Deliberative versus Populist Constitutionalism." *Philosophy and Social Criticism* 45, no. 9–10 (2019): 1116–31.

Chapman, Emilee Booth. "New Challenges for a Normative Theory of Parties and Partisanship." *Representation* 57, no. 3 (March 15, 2020): 385–400. https://doi.org/10.1080/00344893.2020 .1738539.

———. "Reconsidering the Ideal of Non-Factionalism in Party Politics." Unpublished Manuscript, 2019. On File with the Author.

———. "Shared Agency and the Ethics of Democracy." *Georgetown Journal of Law and Public Policy* 18, no. 2 (2020): 705–32.

———. "The Distinctive Value of Elections and the Case for Compulsory Voting." *American Journal of Political Science* 63, no. 1 (2019): 101–12. https://doi.org/10.1111/ajps.12393.

———. "There Is a Duty to Vote: Grounds for the Folk Theory of Voting Ethics." Unpublished Manuscript, 2020. On File with the Author.

Chong, Dennis, and James N. Druckman. "Framing Theory." *Annual Review of Political Science* 10 (2007): 103–26.

Christiano, Thomas. *The Rule of the Many: Fundamental Issues in Democratic Theory*. Boulder, CO: Westview Press, 1996.

"Civic Engagement." OECD Better Life Index. Accessed August 16, 2021. https://www.oecdbetterlifeindex.org/topics/civic-engagement/.

Cobb, Rachael V., D. James Greiner, and Kevin M. Quinn. "Can Voter ID Laws Be Administered in a Race-Neutral Manner? Evidence from the City of Boston in 2008." *Quarterly Journal of Political Science* 7, no. 1 (March 21, 2012): 1–33. https://doi.org/10.1561/100.00010098.

Cohen, Joshua. "Deliberation and Democratic Legitimacy." In *The Good Polity: Normative Analysis of the State*, edited by Alan Hamlin and Phillip Petit, 17–34. New York: Blackwell, 1989.

———. "Money, Politics, and Political Equality." In *Philosophy, Politics, Democracy: Selected Essays*, 268–302. Cambridge, MA: Harvard University Press, 2009.

———. "Procedure and Substance in Deliberative Democracy." In *Philosophy, Politics, Democracy: Selected Essays*, 154–80. Cambridge, MA: Harvard University Press, 2009.

———. "Reflections on Deliberative Democracy." In *Philosophy, Politics, Democracy: Selected Essays*, 326–47. Cambridge, MA: Harvard University Press, 2009.

Conconi, Paola, Nicolas Sahuguet, and Maurizio Zanardi. "Democratic Peace and Electoral Accountability." *Journal of the European Economic Association* 12, no. 4 (2014): 997–1028.

Cooney, Jr., Robert P. J. *Winning the Vote: The Triumph of the American Women Suffrage Movement*. Santa Cruz, CA: American Graphic Press, 2005.

"Cost and Participation—Statewide Elections." Office of the Secretary of State, State of Oregon, Elections Division. Accessed December 9, 2019. https://sos.oregon.gov/elections/Documents/Historic_Cost_Participation.pdf.

Cox, Gary W. "Electoral Rules, Mobilization, and Turnout." *Annual Review of Political Science* 18 (2015): 49–68.

Dahl, Robert A. *A Preface to Democratic Theory*. Expanded edition. Chicago, IL: University of Chicago Press, 2006.

Dalton, Russel J. "Citizenship Norms and the Expansion of Political Participation." *Political Studies* 56, no. 1 (2008): 76–98.

Dasgupta, Partha, and Eric Maskin. "On the Robustness of Majority Rule." *Journal of the European Economic Association* 6 (2008): 949–73.

De Mesquita, Bruce, Michael T. Koch, and Randolph M. Siverson. "Testing Competing Institutional Explanations of the Democratic Peace: The Case of Dispute Duration." *Conflict Management and Peace Science* 21, no. 4 (2004): 255–67.

Dermont, Clau. "Taking Turns at the Ballot Box: Selective Participation as a New Perspective on Low Turnout." *Swiss Political Science Review* 22, no. 2 (2016): 213–31.

Disch, Lisa. "Democratic Representation and the Constituency Paradox." *Perspectives on Politics* 10, no. 3 (September 2012): 599–616.

———. "Toward a Mobilization Conception of Representation." *American Political Science Review* 105, no. 1 (February 2011): 100–114.

Donovan, Todd, Caroline Tolbert, and Kellen Gracey. "Campaign Civility under Preferential and Plurality Voting." *Electoral Studies* 42 (June 1, 2016): 157–63. https://doi.org/10.1016/j.electstud.2016.02.009.

———. "Self-Reported Understanding of Ranked-Choice Voting." *Social Science Quarterly* 100, no. 5 (August 2019): 1769–76.

Downs, Anthony. *An Economic Theory of Democracy.* New York: Harper and Row, 1957.

Drutman, Lee. *Breaking the Two-Party Doom Loop: The Case for Multiparty Democracy in America.* New York: Oxford University Press, 2020.

Dworkin, Ronald. *Law's Empire.* Cambridge, MA: Harvard University Press (Belknap Press), 1986.

Dyck, Joshua J., Brian J. Gaines, and Daron R. Shaw. "The Effect of Local Political Context on How Americans Vote." *American Politics Research* 37, no. 6 (November 1, 2009): 1088–1115.

Epstein, Richard A. "'In Such Manner as the Legislative Thereof Shall Direct': The Outcome in Bush v Gore Defended." In *The Vote: Bush, Gore, and the Supreme Court,* edited by Richard A. Epstein and Cass R. Sunstein, 13–37. Chicago, IL: University of Chicago Press, 2001.

Ewald, Alec C. *The Way We Vote: The Local Dimension of American Suffrage.* Nashville, TN: Vanderbilt University Press, 2009.

Ferraz, Claudio, and Frederico Finan. "Electoral Accountability and Corruption: Evidence from the Audits of Local Governments." *American Economic Review* 101, no. 4 (June 2011): 1274–1311. https://doi.org/10.1257/aer.101.4.1274.

Fishkin, James. *Democracy and Deliberation: New Directions for Democratic Reform.* New Haven, CT: Yale University Press, 1993.

Fishkin, James, Thad Kousser, Robert C. Luskin, and Alice Siu. "Deliberative Agenda Setting: Piloting Reform of Direct Democracy in California." *Perspectives on Politics* 13, no. 4 (December 2015): 1030–42.

Floridia, Antonio. "The Origins of the Deliberative Turn." In *The Oxford Handbook of Deliberative Democracy,* edited by Andre Bächtiger, John S. Dryzek, Jane Mansbridge, and Mark Warren, 35–54. Oxford, UK: Oxford University Press, 2018.

Fortier, John C. *Absentee and Early Voting: Trends, Promises, and Perils.* Washington DC: American Enterprise Institute Press, 2006.

Fowler, Anthony. "Electoral and Policy Consequences of Voter Turnout: Evidence from Compulsory Voting in Australia." *Quarterly Journal of Political Science* 8 (2013): 159–82.

Fowler, Anthony, and Andrew B. Hall. "Do Shark Attacks Influence Presidential Elections? Reassessing a Prominent Finding on Voter Competence." *The Journal of Politics* 80, no. 4 (August 6, 2018): 1423–37. https://doi.org/10.1086/699244.

Fowler, Stephen. "Why Do Nonwhite Georgia Voters Have To Wait In Line For Hours?" October 17, 2020. https://www.npr.org/2020/10/17/924527679/why-do-nonwhite-georgia-voters-have-to-wait-in-line-for-hours-too-few-polling-pl?t=1647287486579.

Fraga, Bernard, and Michael Miller. "Who Does Voter ID Keep from Voting." *The Journal of Politics* 84, no. 2 (April 2022).

Freedom House. "Methodology 2019." Freedom in the World 2019, January 15, 2019. https://freedomhouse.org/report/methodology-freedom-world-2019.

Furlong, Andy, and Fred Cartmel. "Social Change and Political Engagement Among Young People: Generation and the 2009/2010 British Election Survey." *Parliamentary Affairs* 65 (2012): 13–28.

Galston, William. "Realism in Political Theory." *European Journal of Political Theory* 9, no. 4 (2010): 385–411.

Gastil, John, and Erik Olin Wright, eds. *Legislature by Lot: Transformative Designs for Deliberative Governance.* The Real Utopias Project. London, UK: Verso Books, 2019.

Gerber, Alan S., and Donald P. Green. *Get Out the Vote! How to Increase Voter Turnout.* Washington, DC: Brookings Institutions Press, 2008.

Gerber, Alan S., Donald P. Green, and Christopher W. Larimer. "Social Pressure and Voter Turnout: Evidence from a Large-Scale Field Experiment." *American Political Science Review* 102, no. 1 (February 2008): 33–48.

Giammo, Joseph D., and Brian J. Brox. "Reducing the Costs of Participation: Are States Getting a Return on Early Voting?" *Political Research Quarterly* 63, no. 2 (June 2010).

Gibbard, Allan. "Manipulation of Voting Schemes: A General Result." *Econometrica* 41, no. 4 (July 1, 1973): 587–601. https://doi.org/10.2307/1914083.

Gilbert, Margaret. *Living Together*. Lanham, ML: Rowman & Littlefield Publishers, 1996.

Giraudet, Louis-Gaëtan, Bénédicte Apouey, Hazem Arab, Simon Baeckelandt, Philippe Begout, Nicolas Berghmans, Nathalie Blanc, et al. "Deliberating on Climate Action: Insights from the French Citizens' Convention for Climate," January 26, 2021. Hal-03119539. https://hal-enpc .archives-ouvertes.fr/hal-03119539/document.

Goerres, Achim. "Why Are Older People More Likely to Vote? The Impact of Ageing on Electoral Turnout in Europe." *British Journal of Political Science* 9, no. 1 (2007): 90–201.

Goldman, Alvin. "Why Citizens Should Vote: A Causal Responsibility Approach." *Social Philosophy and Policy Foundation* 16, no. 2 (1999): 201–17.

Google Trends Ngram. "'Politics' (Searches in the United States, 2004–Present)," 2018. https:// trends.google.com/trends/explore?date=all&geo=US&q=politics.

Griffin, John D., and Brian Newman. "Are Voters Better Represented?" *The Journal of Politics* 67, no. 04 (2005): 1206–27.

Grimmer, Justin, Eitan Hersh, Marc Meredith, Jonathan Mummolo, and Clayton Nall. "Obstacles to Estimating Voter ID Laws' Effect on Turnout." *The Journal of Politics* 80, no. 3 (July 2018): 1045–51. https://doi.org/10.1086/696618.

Grimmer, Justin, and Jesse Yoder. "The Durable Differential Deterrent Effects of Strict Photo Identification Laws." *Political Science Research and Methods*, first view online (2021): 1–17. https://doi.org/10.1017/psrm.2020.57.

Grinspan, Jon. *The Virgin Vote: How Young Americans Made Democracy Social, Politics Personal, and Voting Popular in the Nineteenth Century*. Chapel Hill, NC: The University of North Carolina Press, 2016.

Gronke, Paul, Eva Galanes-Rosenbaum, Peter A. Miller, and Daniel Toffey. "Convenience Voting." *Annual Review of Political Science* 11 (2008): 437–55.

Gronke, Paul, and Peter Miller. "Early Voting in America: Public Usage and Public Support." In *America Votes! A Guide to Modern Election Law and Voting Rights*, edited by Ben Griffith, 101–22. 4th edition. Cleveland, OH: Lachina Publishing, 2019.

———. "Voting by Mail and Turnout in Oregon: Revisiting Southwell and Burchett." *American Politics Research* 40, no. 6 (November 1, 2012): 976–97. https://doi.org/10.1177/1532673X12457809.

Guerrero, Alex. "The Paradox of Voting and the Ethics of Political Representation." *Philosophy and Public Affairs* 38, no. 3 (2010): 272–306.

Guerrero, Alexander A. "Against Elections: The Lottocratic Alternative." *Philosophy and Public Affairs* 42, no. 2 (2014): 135–78.

Guinier, Lani. *The Tyranny of the Majority: Fundamental Unfairness in Representative Democracy*. New York: Free Press, 1994.

Gunther, Richard, and Larry Diamond. "Species of Political Parties: A New Typology." *Party Politics* 9, no. 2 (2003): 167–99.

Gutmann, Amy, and Dennis Thompson. *Democracy and Disagreement*. Cambridge, MA: Harvard University Press (Belknap Press), 1996.

Hall, Andrew B. "What Happens When Extremists Win Primaries?" *American Political Science Review* 109, no. 1 (February 2015): 18–42. https://doi.org/10.1017/S0003055414000641.

Hart, Kim. "Local and State Elected Officials Are Far More Trusted than Members of Congress." *Axios*, October 2, 2019. https://www.axios.com/local-state-government-trust-congress -b820f103-7952-429d-bfea-adf7fc7beaa4.html.

Healy, Andrew, and Gabriel S. Lenz. "Substituting the End for the Whole: Why Voters Respond Primarily to the Election-Year Economy." *American Journal of Political Science* 158, no. 1 (January 2014): 31–47.

Herman, Lise Esther. "Democratic Partisanship: From Theoretical Ideal to Empirical Standard." *American Political Science Review* 111, no. 4 (2017): 738–54.

Ho, Daniel E., and Kosuke Imai. "Estimating Casual Effects of Ballot Order from a Randomized Natural Experiment: California Alphabet Lottery, 1978–2002." *Public Opinion Quarterly* 72, no. 2 (2008): 216–40.

Congress.gov. "H.R.4—117th Congress (2021–2022): John R. Lewis Voting Rights Advancement Act of 2021." Legislation, September 14, 2021. 2021/2022. https://www.congress.gov/bill /117th-congress/house-bill/4.

Huber, Gregory A., Seth J. Hill, and Gabriel S. Lenz. "Sources of Bias in Retrospective Decision-Making: Experimental Evidence on Voters' Limitations in Controlling Incumbents." *American Political Science Review* 106, no. 4 (November 2012): 720–41.

Huddy, Leonie, and Alexa Bankert. "Political Partisanship as a Social Identity." *Oxford Research Encyclopedia of Politics*, May 24, 2017. https://doi.org/10.1093/acrefore/9780190228637.013.250.

Huddy, Leonie, Lilliana Mason, and Lene Aarøe. "Expressive Partisanship: Campaign Involvement, Political Emotion, and Partisan Identity." *American Political Science Review* 109, no. 1 (February 2015): 1–17.

Ingham, Sean. *Rule by Multiple Majorities: A New Theory of Popular Control.* Political Economy of Institutions and Decisions. Cambridge, UK: Cambridge University Press, 2019. https://doi .org/10.1017/9781108683821.

ISSP Research Group. "International Social Survey Program: ISSP 2004—Citizenship I Variable Report." Gesis Data Archive for the Social Sciences, 2012. http://www.gesis.org/en/issp -modules-profiles/citizenship/.

———. "International Social Survey Programme: ISSP 2014—Citizenship II Variable Report." Gesis—Leibniz Institute for the Social Sciences, October 7, 2016. https://www.gesis.org/issp /modules/issp-modules-by-topic/citizenship/2014.

Jain, Bharti. "Lok Sabha Elections: At 67.1%, 2019 Turnout's a Record, Election Commission Says." *Times of India*, May 21, 2019. https://timesofindia.indiatimes.com/india/at-67-1-2019 -turnouts-a-record-election-commission/articleshow/69419715.cms.

James, Aaron. "Constructing Justice for Existing Practice: Rawls and the Status Quo." *Philosophy and Public Affairs* 33, no. 3 (2005).

———. *Fairness in Practice: A Social Contract for a Global Economy.* New York: Oxford University Press, 2012.

James, Toby. "Electoral Administration and Voter Turnout: Towards an International Public Policy Continuum." *Representation* 46, no. 4 (2010): 369–89.

Jones, Bradley. "Many Americans Unaware of Their States' Voter ID Laws." *Pew Research Center*, October 24, 2016. https://www.pewresearch.org/fact-tank/2016/10/24/many-americans -unaware-of-their-states-voter-id-laws/.

Kam, Cindy D., and Elizabeth J. Zechmeister. "Name Recognition and Candidate Support." *American Journal of Political Science* 57, no. 4 (2013): 971–86. https://doi.org/10.1111/ajps.12034.

Katz, Richard S., and Peter Mair. *Democracy and the Cartelization of Political Parties.* Oxford, UK: Oxford University Press, 2018.

———. "The Cartel Party Thesis: A Restatement." *Perspectives on Politics* 7, no. 4 (December 2009): 753–66.

Kaufmann, Bruno, and Joe Mathews. "Opinion | Democracy Doomsday Prophets Are Missing This Critical Shift." *Washington Post*, May 8, 2018. https://www.washingtonpost.com/news /theworldpost/wp/2018/05/08/direct-democracy-is-thriving/.

King, Robert. *Judge Robert Rosenberg of Broward County Canvassing Board Uses a Magnifying Glass to View a Dimpled Chad on a Punch-Hole Ballot November 24, 2000 during a Recount of Votes in Fort Lauderdale, Florida.* 2000. Photograph. Getty Images News. https://www.gettyimages

.com/detail/news-photo/judge-robert-rosenberg-of-broward-county-canvassing-board
-news-photo/1512770.

Kousser, Thad, and Megan Mullin. "Does Voting by Mail Increase Participation? Using Matching to Analyze a Natural Experiment." *Political Analysis* 15, no. 4 (2007): 428–45. https://doi.org/10.1093/pan/mpm014.

Kutz, Christopher. "Acting Together." *Philosophy and Phenomenological Research* 61, no. 1 (July 2000): 1–31.

Landemore, Hélène. "Analysis | Can Macron Quiet the 'Yellow Vests' Protests with His 'Great Debate'? Tune in Tomorrow." *Washington Post*, April 24, 2019, sec. Analysis-Monkey Cage. https://www.washingtonpost.com/politics/2019/04/24/can-macron-quiet-yellow-vests-protests-with-his-great-debate-tune-tomorrow/.

———. *Open Democracy: Reinventing Popular Rule for the Twenty-First Century*. Princeton, NJ: Princeton University Press, 2020.

Leighly, Jan E., and Jonathan Nagler. "The Effects of Non-Precinct Voting Reforms on Turnout 1972–2008." Pew Charitable Trusts' Making Voting Work, 2010.

Lenz, Gabriel S. *Follow the Leader?: How Voters Respond to Politicians' Policies and Performance*. Chicago, IL: Chicago University Press, 2012.

Lever, Annabelle. "Compulsory Voting: A Critical Perspective." *British Journal of Political Science* 40, no. 4 (October 2010): 897–915.

———. "Liberalism, Democracy and the Ethics of Voting." *Politics* 29, no. 3 (2009): 223–27.

Lipset, Seymour Martin. *Political Man: The Social Bases of Politics*. Baltimore, MD: Johns Hopkins University Press, 1981.

List, Christian. "Social Choice Theory." In *The Stanford Encyclopedia of Philosophy*, edited by Edward N. Zalta, 2013. https://plato.stanford.edu/archives/win2013/entries/social-choice/.

List, Christian, Robert C. Luskin, James S. Fishkin, and Iain McLean. "Deliberation, Single-Peakedness, and the Possibility of Meaningful Democracy: Evidence from Deliberative Polls." *The Journal of Politics* 75, no. 01 (January 2013): 80–95.

Locke, John. *Second Treatise of Government*, edited by C.B. Macpherson. Indianapolis, IN: Hackett Publishing Company, 1980.

Lomasky, Loren, and Geoffrey Brennan. "Is There a Duty to Vote." *Social Philosophy and Policy* 17, no. 1 (2000): 62–86.

Luechinger, Simon, Myra Rosinger, and Alois Stutzer. "The Impact of Postal Voting on Participation: Evidence for Switzerland." *Swiss Political Science Review* 13, no. 2 (2007): 167–202.

Madison, James. "The Federalist Number 10," 1787.

Malkopoulou, Anthoula. "Lost Voters: Participation in EU Elections and the Case for Compulsory Voting (CEPS Working Document No. 317)." Center for European Policy Studies, July 2009. https://www.ceps.eu/ceps-publications/lost-voters-participation-eu-elections-and-case-compulsory-voting/.

Maloy, J. S. *Smarter Ballots: Electoral Realism and Reform*. New York: Palgrave Macmillan, 2019.

Mansbridge, Jane. "What Is Political Science For?" *Perspectives on Politics* 12, no. 1 (March 2014): 8–17.

Mansbridge, Jane, James Bohman, Simone Chambers, Thomas Christiano, Archon Fung, John Parkinson, Dennis Thompson, and Mark E. Warren. "A Systemic Approach to Deliberative Democracy." In *Deliberative Systems*, edited by John Parkinson and Jane Mansbridge, 1–26. New York: Cambridge University Press, 2012.

Martin, Paul S. "Voting's Rewards: Voter Turnout, Attentive Publics, and Congressional Allocation of Federal Money." *American Journal of Political Science* 47, no. 1 (January 2003): 110–27.

Maskivker, Julia. *The Duty to Vote*. New York: Oxford University Press, 2019.

May, Kenneth O. "A Set of Independent Necessary and Sufficient Conditions for Simple Majority Decision." *Econometrica* 20, no. 4 (1952): 680–84. https://doi.org/10.2307/1907651.

McAdam, Doug. *Freedom Summer*. New York: Oxford University Press, 1988.

McCormick, John P. "Contain the Wealthy and Patrol the Magistrates: Restoring Elite Accountability to Popular Government." *The American Political Science Review* 100, no. 2 (2006): 147–63.

———. *Machiavellian Democracy*. Cambridge, UK: Cambridge University Press, 2011.

McDonald, Michael P. "The Return of the Voter: Voter Turnout in the 2008 Presidential Election." *The Forum* 6, no. 4 (2008).

McKelvey, Richard D. "Intransitivities in Multidimensional Voting Models and Some Implications for Agenda Control." *Journal of Economic Theory* 12 (1976): 472–82.

McKinney, Cynthia. "Keep It Simple." In *Whose Vote Counts*, edited by Joshua Cohen and Joel Rogers, 35–39. Boston, MA: Beacon Free Press, 1999.

Mejia, Zameena. "Kenneth Cole & Rock The Vote Team Up To Get Voters On Their Feet." *Footwear News* (blog), July 29, 2016. https://footwearnews.com/2016/influencers/collaborations/kenneth-cole-rock-the-vote-collaboration-presidential-election-2016-244778/.

Michels, Robert. *Political Parties: A Sociological Study of the Oligarchical Tendencies of Modern Democracy*, translated by Eden Paul and Cedar Paul. Kitchener, Ontario: Batoche Books, 2001.

Micozzi, Juan Pablo. "Does Electoral Accountability Make a Difference? Direct Elections, Career Ambition, and Legislative Performance in the Argentine Senate." *The Journal of Politics* 75, no. 1 (2013): 137–49.

Mill, John Stuart. *Considerations on Representative Government*. Amherst, NY: Prometheus Books, 1991.

Miller, Erin. "Amplified Speech." working paper, 2020. http://cardozolawreview.com/amplified-speech/.

Miller, Gary, and Norman Schofield. "Activists and Partisan Realignment in the United States." *American Political Science Review* 97, no. 2 (May 2003): 245–60.

Miller, Warren, Arthur H. Miller, and Edward J. Schneider. *American National Election Studies Data Sourcebook 1952–1978*. Cambridge, MA: Harvard University Press, 1980.

Mohr, Zach, Martha Kropf, Mary Jo McGowan Shepherd, JoEllen Pope, and Madison Esterle. "How Much Are We Spending on Election Administration?" MIT Election Data + Science Lab, January 2019. https://electionlab.mit.edu/sites/default/files/2019-01/mohr_et_al_2017summary.pdf.

Montjoy, Robert S. "The Changing Nature and Costs of Election Administration." *Public Administration Review* 70, no. 6 (December 2010): 867–75.

Mouffe, Chantal. *The Democratic Paradox*. London; New York: Verso, 2009.

Moulin, H. "Generalized Condorcet-Winners for Single Peaked and Single-Plateau Preferences." *Social Choice and Welfare* 1, no. 2 (August 1, 1984): 127–47.

Mozaffer, Shaheen, and Andreas Schedler. "The Comparative Study of Electoral Governance—Introduction." *International Political Science Review* 23, no. 1 (2002): 5–27.

Muirhead, Russell. *The Promise of Party in a Polarized Age*. Cambridge, MA: Harvard University Press, 2014.

Ober, Josiah. "The Original Meaning of 'Democracy': Capacity to Do Things, Not Majority Rule." *Constellations* 15, no. 1 (March 1, 2008): 3–9.

Oliver, J. Eric. "The Effects of Eligibility Restrictions and Party Activity on Absentee Voting and Overall Turnout." *American Journal of Political Science* 40, no. 2 (May 1996).

Olsen, Marvin. *Participatory Pluralism: Political Participation and Influence in the United States and Sweden*. Chicago, IL: Nelson-Hall, 1982.

Neblo, Michael A., Esterling, Kevin M., Lazer, David M. J. *Politics with the People: Building a Directly Representative Democracy*. New York: Cambridge University Press, 2018.

Animal Político. "Participación del 1 de julio no rompió récord," July 2, 2018. https://www.animalpolitico.com/2018/07/participacion-ciudadana-elecciones-2018/.

Pateman, Carole. *Participation and Democratic Theory*. Cambridge, UK: Cambridge University Press, 1970.

Patty, John W., and Elizabeth Maggie Penn. *Social Choice and Legitimacy: The Possibilities Of Impossibility*. Cambridge, UK and New York: Cambridge University Press, 2014.

Pettit, Philip. *A Theory of Freedom: From the Psychology to the Politics of Agency*. Oxford, UK and New York: Oxford University Press, 2001.

"Post-Election Audits," October 25, 2019. http://www.ncsl.org/research/elections-and-campaigns/post-election-audits635926066.aspx#state%20reqs.

Prior, Markus, and Arthur Lupia. "Money, Time, and Political Knowledge: Distinguishing Quick Recall and Political Learning Skills." *American Journal of Political Science* 52, no. 1 (January 2008): 169–83.

Rahman, Omar. "Why Did Arab Voter Turnout for Israel's Election Plunge?" *Brookings* (blog), April 16, 2019. https://www.brookings.edu/blog/order-from-chaos/2019/04/16/why-did-arab-voter-turnout-for-israels-election-plunge/.

Ranney, Austin. *The Doctrine of Responsible Party Government, Its Origin and Present State*. Champaign, IL: University of Illinois Press, 1954.

Rawls, John. *A Theory of Justice*. Revised edition. Cambridge, MA: Harvard University Press (Belknap Press), 1999.

Rehfeld, Andrew. "The Child as Democratic Citizen." *The Annals of the American Academy of Political and Social Science* 633 (2011): 141–66.

Reilly, Benjamin. "Ranked Choice Voting in Australia and America: Do Voters Follow Party Cues?" *Politics and Governance* 9, no. 2 (2021): 271–79.

Relive Election Night 2016—CNN Video, 2017. https://www.cnn.com/videos/politics/2017/11/06/relive-the-stunning-2016-election-night-orig-mg.cnn.

Richardson, Henry S. "Democratic Intentions." In *Deliberative Democracy: Essays on Reason and Politics*, edited by James Bohman and William Rehg, 349–82. Cambridge, MA: The MIT Press, 1997.

———. *Practical Reasoning about Final Ends*. Cambridge, UK: Cambridge University Press, 1994.

Ries, Brian, Veronica Rocha, Meg Wagner, Sophie Tatum, Maegan Vazquez, and Jessie Yeung. "Election Night in the US." *CNN.Com*, November 7, 2018. https://www.cnn.com/politics/live-news/election-day-2018/index.html.

Riker, William. *Liberalism Against Populism*. Long Grove, IL: Waveland Press, 1982.

Rokkan, Stein, and Seymour Martin Lipset. "Cleavage Structures, Party Systems, and Voter Alignments." In *The West European Party System*, edited by Peter Mair, 91–111. Oxford, UK: Oxford University Press, 1990.

Rokkan, Stein, and Henry Valen. "The Mobilization of the Periphery: Data on Turnout, Party Membership and Candidate Recruitment in Norway." *Acta Sociologica* 6, no. 1 (1962): 11–152.

Rosenblum, Nancy. *On the Side of Angels*. Princeton, NJ: Princeton University Press, 2008.

Rosenbluth, Frances McCall, and Ian Shapiro. *Responsible Parties: Saving Democracy from Itself*. New York: Yale University Press, 2018.

Rosenstone, Steven J., and John Mark Hansen. *Mobilization, Participation, and Democracy in America*. New York: MacMillan Publishing Company, 1993.

Rossi, Enzo, and Matt Sleat. "Realism in Normative Political Theory." *Philosophy Compass* 9 (2014): 689–701.

Rutchick, Abraham M. "Deus Ex Machina: The Influence of Polling Place on Voting Behavior." *Political Psychology* 31, no. 2 (2010): 209–25. https://doi.org/10.1111/j.1467-9221.2009.00749.x.

National Conference of State Legislatures. "Same Day Voter Registration," October 6, 2020. https://www.ncsl.org/research/elections-and-campaigns/same-day-registration.aspx.

Sartori, Giovanni. *Parties and Party Systems: A Framework for Analysis*. ECPR Press Classics. ECPR Press, 2005. https://books.google.com/books?id=ywr0CcGDNHwC.

Satterthwaite, Mark Allen. "Strategy-Proofness and Arrow's Conditions: Existence and Correspondence Theorems for Voting Procedures and Social Welfare Functions." *Journal of Economic Theory* 10, no. 2 (April 1975): 187–217. https://doi.org/10.1016/0022-0531(75)90050-2.

Saunders, Ben. "Increasing Turnout: A Compelling Case?" *Politics* 30, no. 1 (2010): 70–77.

Schattschneider, E. E. *Party Government.* New York: Rinehart and Company, Inc., 1942.

———. *The Semisovereign People: A Realist's View of Democracy in America.* Hinsdale, IL: Dryden Press, 1975.

Schumpeter, Joseph A. *Capitalism, Socialism, and Democracy.* 2nd edition. Mansfield Centre, CT: Martino Publishing, 2011.

Schwartzberg, Melissa. *Counting the Many: The Origins and Limits of Supermajority Rule.* Cambridge Studies in the Theory of Democracy. New York: Cambridge University Press, 2014.

———. "Shouts, Murmurs, and Votes: Acclamation and Aggregation in Ancient Greece." *The Journal of Political Philosophy* 18, no. 4 (2010): 448–68.

Searle, John R. *The Construction of Social Reality.* New York: Free Press, 1995.

"Selma to Montgomery March." In *King Encyclopedia.* Stanford University: The Martin Luther King, Jr. Research and Education Institute, June 8, 2017. https://kinginstitute.stanford.edu/encyclopedia/selma-montgomery-march.

Shapiro, Ian. *Politics Against Domination.* Cambridge, MA: Harvard University Press (Belknap Press), 2016.

Shapiro, Scott. *Legality.* Cambridge, MA: Harvard University Press (Belknap Press), 2011.

Shapiro, Scott J. "Massively Shared Agency." In *Rational and Social Agency: The Philosophy of Michael Bratman,* edited by Manuel Vargas and Gideon Yaffe, 257–89. Oxford, UK: Oxford University Press, 2014.

Shaw v. Reno, 509 United States Reports 630 (United States Supreme Court 1993).

Shiffrin, Seana. "Speaking Amongst Ourselves: Democracy and Law." In *The Tanner Lectures on Human Values 37,* edited by Mark Matheson. Salt Lake City, UT: University of Utah Press, 2018.

Shineman, Victoria Anne. "Isolating the Effects of Costly and Incentivized Participation on Incentives to Invest in Costly Information and Informed Participation." Ph.D. dissertation, New York University, 2013.

Sivakumar, B. "Polls to Cost Country Rs 3,500 Crore This Year." The Times of India, February 18, 2014. http://timesofindia.indiatimes.com/india/Election-Commission-2014-Lok-Sabha-elections-polls-expense/articleshow/30587202.cms.

Slothuus, Rune, and Claes H. de Vreese. "Political Parties, Motivated Reasoning, and Issue Framing Effects." *The Journal of Politics* 72, no. 3 (July 2010): 630–45.

Smith, Paul. "'Use It or Lose It': The Problem of Purges from the Registration Rolls of Voters Who Don't Vote Regularly." American Bar Association, February 9, 2020. https://www.americanbar.org/groups/crsj/publications/human_rights_magazine_home/voting-rights/-use-it-or-lose-it---the-problem-of-purges-from-the-registration0/.

Southwood, Nicholas. "Democracy as a Modally Demanding Value." *Noûs* 47, no. 2 (2013): 504–21.

"State Laws Prohibiting Electioneering Activities Within a Certain Distance of the Polling Place." National Association of Secretaries of State, 2014. https://www.nass.org/sites/default/files/surveys/2020-10/state-laws-polling-place-electioneering-Oct-2020.pdf.

Election Commission of India. "Statewise Turnout for General Election—2014." September 30, 2014. https://pib.gov.in/newsite/PrintRelease.aspx?relid=105116.

Stein, Robert M. "Early Voting." *Public Opinion Quarterly* 62, no. 1 (1998).

Stilz, Anna R. *Liberal Loyalty.* Princeton, NJ: Princeton University Press, 2009.

Stimson, James A. *Public Opinion in America: Moods, Cycles, and Swings.* 2nd edition. Boulder, CO: Westview Press, 1998.

Streb, Matthew J. *Rethinking American Electoral Democracy*. 2nd edition. New York: Routledge, 2011.

Strömbäck, Jesper, and Daniela V. Dimitrova. "Political and Media Systems Matter: A Comparison of Election News Coverage in Sweden and the United States." *Press/Politics* 11, no. 4 (Fall 2006).

Sullivan, Andy. "Southern U.S. States Have Closed have closed 1,200 polling places in recent years: rights group." https://www.reuters.com/article/us-usa-election-locations-idUSKCN1VV09J.

Sunstein, Cass R. "Introduction: Of Law and Politics." In *The Vote: Bush, Gore, and the Supreme Court*, edited by Richard A. Epstein and Cass R. Sunstein, 1–12. Chicago, IL: University of Chicago Press, 2001.

Thomassen, Jacques, and Carolien van Ham. "Failing Political Representation or a Change in Kind? Models of Representation and Empirical Trends in Europe." *West European Politics* 37, no. 2 (2014): 400–419.

Thompson, Dennis. *Just Elections: Creating a Fair Electoral Process in the United States*. Chicago, IL: Chicago University Press, 2002.

Thornburg v. Gingles, 478 United States Reports 30 (United States Supreme Court 1986).

Thrasher, Michael, Galina Borisyuk, Colin Rallings, and Richard Webber. "Candidate Ethnic Origins and Voter Preferences: Examining Name Discrimination in Local Elections in Britain." *British Journal of Political Science* 47 (June 2, 2015): 1–23. https://doi.org/10.1017/S0007123415000125.

Tova, Andrea Wang. *The Politics of Voter Suppression: Defending and Expanding Americans' Right to Vote*. Ithaca, NY: Cornell University Press, 2012.

"Toward a More Responsible Two-Party System." *The American Political Science Review* (Supplement) 44, no. 3, part 2 (September 1950).

"Trends in Political Values and Core Attitudes: 1987–2007." Pew Research Center report, March 22, 2007. https://www.pewresearch.org/politics/2007/03/22/trends-in-political-values-and-core-attitudes-1987-2007/.

Tuck, Richard. *Free Riding*. Cambridge, MA: Harvard University Press, 2008.

"Universal Declaration of Human Rights," 1948. http://www.un.org/en/documents/udhr/.

Valentino, Nicholas A., and Fabian G. Neuner. "Why the Sky Didn't Fall: Mobilizing Anger in Reaction to Voter ID Laws." *Political Psychology* 38, no. 2 (2017): 331–50.

Van Aelst, Peter, Kjersti Thorbjørnsrud, and Toril Aalberg. "The Political Information Environment during Election Campaigns." In *How Media Inform Democracy: A Comparative Approach*, edited by Toril Aalberg and James Curran, 50–63. https://doi.org/10.4324/9780203803448-12.

Van Reybrouck, David. *Against Elections*, translated by Liz Waters. New York: Seven Stories Press, 2018.

Verba, Sidney, Kay Lehman Schlozman, and Henry E. Brady. *Voice and Equality: Civic Voluntarism in American Politics*. Cambridge, MA: Harvard University Press, 1995.

Vermeule, Adrian. *The System of the Constitution*. Oxford, UK: Oxford University Press, 2011.

Statista. "Voter Turnout in the UK 1918–2019." Accessed August 24, 2021. https://www.statista.com/statistics/1050929/voter-turnout-in-the-uk/.

Vyawahare, Malavika. "A Primer on India's Parliamentary Elections." NYTimes India Ink, 2014. http://india.blogs.nytimes.com/2014/04/08/a-primer-on-indias-parliamentary-elections/.

Waldron, Jeremy. "The Constitutional Conception of Democracy." In *Democracy*, edited by David Estlund. Malden, MA: Wiley-Blackwell, 2002.

Wand, Jonathon, Kenneth W. Shotts, Jasjeet S. Sekhon, Walter R. Mebane Jr., Michael C. Herron, and Henry E. Brady. "The Butterfly Ballot Did It: The Aberrant Vote for Buchanan in Palm Beach County, Florida." *American Political Science Review* 95, no. 4 (December 2001): 793–810.

Warren, Mark E. "A Problem-Based Approach to Democratic Theory." *American Political Science Review* 111, no. 1 (2017): 39–53.

PBS NewsHour. "What Does Voter Turnout Tell Us about the 2016 Election?" November 20, 2016. https://www.pbs.org/newshour/politics/voter-turnout-2016-elections.

White, Ariel R., Noah L. Nathan, and Julie K. Faller. "What Do I Need to Vote? Bureaucratic Discretion and Discrimination by Local Election Officials." *American Political Science Review* 109, no. 1 (February 2015): 129–42. https://doi.org/10.1017/S0003055414000562.

White, Jonathan, and Lea Ypi. "On Partisan Political Justification." *The American Political Science Review* 105, no. 2 (May 1, 2011): 381–96.

———. *The Meaning of Partisanship*. Oxford, UK: Oxford University Press, 2016.

Wilks-Heeg, Stuart. "Treating Voters as an Afterthought? The Legacies of a Decade of Electoral Modernisation in the United Kingdom." *The Political Quarterly* 80, no. 1 (2009): 101–10.

Wingenbach, Ed. *Institutionalizing Agonistic Democracy: Post-Foundationalism and Political Liberalism*. New York: Ashgate, 2011.

Wolin, Sheldon. "Norm and Form: The Constitutionalizing of Democracy." In *Fugitive Democracy and Other Essays*, 77–99. Princeton, NJ: Princeton University Press, 2016.

Wolkenstein, Fabio. "A Deliberative Model of Intra-Party Democracy." *The Journal of Political Philosophy* 24, no. 3 (2016): 297–320.

———. "Intra-Party Democracy beyond Aggregation." *Party Politics*, June 21, 2016. https://doi.org/10.1177/1354068816655563.

Young, Iris Marion. *Inclusion and Democracy*. Oxford, UK: Oxford University Press, 2002.

A NOTE ON THE TYPE

This book has been composed in Adobe Text and Gotham.
Adobe Text, designed by Robert Slimbach for Adobe,
bridges the gap between fifteenth- and sixteenth-century
calligraphic and eighteenth-century Modern styles.
Gotham, inspired by New York street signs, was designed
by Tobias Frere-Jones for Hoefler & Co.